Innovations in Child and Family Policy

Innovations in Child and Family Policy

Multidisciplinary Research and Perspectives on Strengthening Children and Their Families

Edited by
Emily M. Douglas

LEXINGTON BOOKS
A division of
ROWMAN & LITTLEFIELD PUBLISHERS, INC.
Lanham • Boulder • New York • Toronto • Plymouth, UK

Published by Lexington Books
A division of Rowman & Littlefield Publishers, Inc.
A wholly owned subsidiary of The Rowman & Littlefield Publishing Group, Inc.
4501 Forbes Boulevard, Suite 200, Lanham, Maryland 20706
http://www.lexingtonbooks.com

Estover Road, Plymouth PL6 7PY, United Kingdom

British Library Cataloguing in Publication Information Available

Library of Congress Cataloging-in-Publication Data

Innovations in child and family policy : multidisciplinary research and
perspectives on strengthening children and their families / [edited by] Emily
Douglas.
    p. cm.
  Includes bibliographical references and index.
  ISBN 978-0-7391-3790-1 (cloth : alk. paper) — ISBN 978-0-7391-3792-5
(electronic)
  1. Family policy—United States. 2. Families—United States. 3. Children—
Government policy—United States. 4. Child welfare—United States. I. Douglas,
Emily M., 1973–
  HQ536.I547 2010
  306.850973—dc22   2009037692

∞™ The paper used in this publication meets the minimum requirements of
American National Standard for Information Sciences—Permanence of Paper
for Printed Library Materials, ANSI/NISO Z39.48-1992.

Printed in the United States of America

For N. V. B., for your endless support
and encouragement

Contents

List of Figures   xi

List of Tables   xiii

Acknowledgments   xv

1   Introduction   1
Emily M. Douglas

EARLY CHILDHOOD AND EDUCATION

2   Hispanic Families and Family Literacy Practices: Differences by
Country of Origin   11
Patricia Hrusa Williams

3   Effects of Parental Involvement on First Graders' Approaches
to Learning   29
Esther F. S. Carvalhaes

4   Frayed Patchwork: The Need for Public Policy to Address
Short-Term Child Care Needs   49
Loretta L. C. Brady

5   The Contribution of the Helping Relationship in Promoting
Retention in a Home Visitation Program to Prevent Child
Maltreatment   63
Michelle P. Taylor and Karen McCurdy

GOVERNMENT INTERVENTION: FAMILY VIOLENCE, CHILDREN'S WELFARE, AND JUSTICE CONCERNS

6   Exploring the Effects of California's Shortened Reunification
Time Frames for Children under Three   83
Amy D'Andrade

7   The Multidisciplinary Misnomer: A West Virginia Case Study
of Multidisciplinary Treatment Teams in Child Welfare   97
Corey J. Colyer and L. Christopher Plein

8   Identifying and Responding to the Needs of Children
Residing in Domestic Violence Shelters: Results from the
North Carolina Domestic Violence Shelter Screening Project   117
*Yvonne Wasilewski, Robert A. Murphy, Leslie Starsoneck, Margaret
Samuels, Donna Potter, Audrey Foster, and Lorrie Schmid*

9   African American Caregiver Age, Social Support, and the
Well-Being of Children in Kinship Foster Care   135
Terry A. Solomon, James P. Gleeson, and Arden Handler

10   Examining "Emerging Adulthood" in the Context of the
Justice System   153
Anne Dannerbeck Janku

FAMILY SUPPORT: POLICIES AND PROGRAMS

11   The Effect of Paternal Incarceration on Early Child
Development   173
Terry-Ann L. Craigie

12   The "State" of Paid Family Leave: Insights from the 2006
and 2007 Legislative Sessions   191
Melissa Brown

13   New Parents Taking Time Off: A Look at California Paid
Family Leave   211
Stacy Ann Hawkins, Sherylle J. Tan, and Diane F. Halpern

14   The Relationship Between Non-Resident Fathers' Social
Networks and Social Capital and the Establishment of
Child Support Orders   227
Jason Castillo

15 Integrating Mothers' Views of Resources That Foster Growth
        for Children with Autism Spectrum Disorders into Policy   245
        Judy Doktor, Laura Dreuth Zeman, and Jayme Swanke

Index   261

About the Editor   265

About the Contributors   267

Figures

2.1   Average Change in Literacy Skills over First Six Months
of Intervention   21

2.2   Differences in Length of Enrollment in Months for
Hispanic Families by Language Use   22

9.1   Caregiver Age and Adverse Emotional Behavior Moderated
by Emotional Support   147

13.1   Mothers' and Fathers' Attitudes about California Paid
Family Leave   218

Tables

2.1 Differences in Risks and Social Adaptation by Country
of Origin   19

2.2 Differences in Literacy Practices, Supports, and Response
to Intervention by Country of Origin   19

3.1 Weighted Descriptive Statistics of Sample   36

3.2 Unstandardized Regression Coefficients for Spring 2000
First Graders' Approaches to Learning   39

4.1 What Are You Missing Out On?   56

5.1 Parent and Family Support Worker (FSW) Demographics   67

5.2 Linear Regression Analyses Predicting Retention   71

5.3 Exploratory Forward Regressions Predicting HRI Scores   72

6.1 Total Sample Characteristics   89

6.2 Survival Analysis of Likelihood of Reunification—
Full Sample   90

6.3 Survival Analysis of Likelihood of Adoption—
Full Sample   91

6.4 Survival Analysis of Likelihood of Reunification—Children of Substance-Abusing Parents   92

6.5 Survival Analysis of Likelihood of Reunification—African American Children   93

8.1 Number of Children Who Scored Clinically Significantly or At-Risk on Any Screening Measure and Were Referred by Shelter   122

8.2 Mean Shelter Sustainability Score with Standard Deviations by Dimension of Sustainability at Time 3   129

9.1 African American Caregiver's and Child's Socio-demographic Characteristics   140

9.2 Regression of Child Well-being (Antisocial and Adverse Emotional Behavior Indices) on Caregiver's Age, Social Support, and the Interaction of Caregiver Age and Social Support (Emotional and Instrumental Support Indices)   145

10.1 Comparison of Social Control Indicators for Emerging Adults and Other Age Groups, by Gender   162

11.1 Summary Statistics of Sample   178

11.2 Summary Statistics by Incarceration History   179

11.3 OLS and IV Estimates of the Effect of Paternal Incarceration *Ex Post* on PPVT-R Scores, Aggression, and ODD Symptoms   183

12.1 Paid Family Leave Legislation Proposed in 2006–2007   198

14.1 Factors Associated with the Establishment of Child Support Orders: Logistic Regression of Coefficients   234

Acknowledgments

Many people helped to make this book possible. First and foremost, I would like to thank the researchers who contributed to the book. The authors whose work I present in *Innovations* took a risk on a new, independent, unfunded conference: the first National Research Conference on Child and Family Programs and Policy (NRCCFPP). The conference, held at Bridgewater State College in Massachusetts in July 2008, would not have been possible without their interest, dedication, and presence. I thank them for their attendance and for their willingness to contribute to a growing specialization within academia: child and family policy.

There are a number of others, most of them at Bridgewater State College, who supported the first NRCCFPP and thus helped to make this volume a reality: Dr. Howard London, then-dean of the School of Arts and Sciences and now provost and vice president for academic affairs at Bridgewater State College, agreed to provide financial backing for the fixed costs of the conference in the event that too few participants made it impossible to run the conference. Ms. Jenna Stephenson in external affairs provided expert oversight of the conference logistics and served as my "right-hand woman." Ms. Jennifer Reid at the Institute for Regional Development donated her work-study student to assemble the beginnings of an email list for potentially interested parties. Dr. Murray Straus, codirector and professor at the Family Research Laboratory at the University of New Hampshire, my mentor and colleague, provided support and enthusiasm to pursue NRCCFPP and this book.

Once *Innovations* was under contract, the Center for the Advancement
on Research and Teaching at Bridgewater State College awarded a grant to
this project to finance the typesetting of the text contained in this volume.
My research assistant, Ms. Suzanne Corbett, helped to edit the chapters and
track the editing process. My dear friend and expert editor, Ms. Katharine
Leavitt, generously helped with final changes to the text. Above all, my
husband provided me with endless support and dedicated countless hours
helping me attend to the crises that accompany chairing a national conference and editing a book.

1

Introduction

Emily M. Douglas

WHAT IS CHILD AND FAMILY POLICY?

There has been considerable debate about the definition of child and family policy. The definition was intensely debated in the late 1970s, when there was an increase in the number of publications on family policy and some special issues of academic and professional journals that were dedicated to child and family policy. Some authors discuss family policy as a broad, but single, policy mission that would promote and reward particular behaviors.[1] For example, in 1979, Barbaro[2] argued against a national family policy, fearing that families that do not conform to a government-born definition of "family" would be excluded from benefits and services. This concern was well-warranted; thirty years later, some families are excluded, by state legislation, from adopting or fostering children because the heads of household are the same sex.[3]

Others have discussed family policy as a wide range of programmatic and policy initiatives that each address specific, but different, family issues. This is more of a patchwork approach to using public policy to promote child and family well-being.[4] In this case, government responds to individual problems by passing legislation that targets each problem, even though the policies may benefit the same families. For example, a government might pass legislation making child care more affordable and more available.

1

Families who would benefit from this might also benefit from funding for children's health insurance coverage, which a government could address as well. These would, however, usually be part of separate pieces of legislation. The vast majority of the child and family policies in the United States take this form.

Finally, still others discuss a "family perspective" in policy-making, which encourages stakeholders to consider how specific policy initiatives would have an impact on all families, regardless of composition, across the lifespan.[5, 6, 7] In other words, how does legislation around long-term care have an impact on a family system? How do tax breaks for married families with minor children affect all families?

The chapters in this book primarily adhere to the second approach to family policy: individual social and family problems are studied with targeted actions proposed to address that specific family problem. Thus, no national, broad, social safety-net is discussed as a solution to any of the family problems discussed by the authors in this volume, although many of them might benefit from such an approach. A few of the chapters utilize a family perspective in policy-making by trying to examine how a specific public policy, which might be intended to provide family support, actually has an impact on family systems (namely chapters 6 and 13).

Regardless of the type of policy initiative or definition of family policy, there is broad agreement that the function and purpose of family policy should be to strengthen families, although what constitutes a "family" is currently a heated argument in multiple areas of the public sphere: political, religious, and social. Nonetheless, family policy usually addresses at least one of four areas: (1) family creation, (2) economic support, (3) childrearing, and (4) family caregiving.

Family creation includes marriage, divorce, bearing children, adopting children, and providing foster care for children. Current family policies that address family creation include same-sex marriage, the legal rights of gays and lesbians to adopt, and the federal Adoption and Safe Families Act of 1997, which encourages states to place more maltreated children in adoptive homes.

Economic support includes providing for the needs of each member of a family. Legislation that addresses this area of family policy includes the Deadbeat Parents Punishment Act of 1998, legislation that makes it possible to incarcerate parents who move across state lines in order to avoid paying child support, a topic which is addressed in chapter 14 of this book. The Personal Responsibility and Work Opportunity Reconciliation Act of 1996, or what we know as "welfare reform," is another example of economic support. This legislation was intended to move families from welfare dependence to working independence.

Childrearing addresses educating and socializing the next generation. An example of this is the federal Child Care Development Block Grant Act of

1990 that provides funding for states to develop high-quality and afford-able care for children. Providing short-term, high-quality child care is the topic of chapter 4. Divorce education programs that are mandated in some states instruct parents about the impact of divorce on the family unit and specifically on children. Finally, home visiting services offered to families with newborns are often legislatively created and mandated for families. Such services are the topic of chapter 5.

Family caregiving includes caring for those who are ill, elderly, frail, or disabled. Our largest national policy that addresses this is the Family Medi-cal Leave Act of 1993, which permits individuals in the workforce to take a twelve-week (unpaid) leave from their employment to care for a family member in need, without losing their jobs. This initiative does not provide income replacement, but individual states in the nation do. Such policy initiatives are addressed in chapters 12 and 13. Family caregiving would also include the services that are available to families with special needs children; this is the topic of chapter 15.

A BRIEF (AND RECENT) HISTORY
OF CHILD AND FAMILY POLICY

The primary socio-behavioral EBSCOhost databases provided a context for better understanding of the history of child and family policy in the social sciences. Searching across six databases (ERIC, PsychARTICLES, Psychol-ogy and Behavioral Sciences Collection, PsycINFO, Social Work Abstracts, and SocINDEX), one of which dates back to 1887 (PsycINFO), we learn that the first reference to an article with "family policy" in the title was in 1948. This early postwar article focused on issues that continue to be fea-tured today: the instruction of interpersonal relations. In fact, in his article, Montagu[8] declares that the American education system should be reformed to be "institutes of teaching on human relations" and that the "other three r's" should be secondary to the concerns of teaching our nation's children good interpersonal skills. Sixty years later, this advice is being carried out today across the nation by schools, anti-bullying programs, and many local family support centers.[9]

In the twenty years that followed that first article in 1948, there were only four more references to articles with "family policy" in the title: fam-ily policy in Soviet Russia, Sweden, the United States, and a sociological article about sexual relations within the family. The first of these, published in 1951, focused on the increased stratification and restriction of mobility on Russian Soviet families.[10] In contrast, a 1955 article addressed the then-developing and comprehensive social welfare system that had been en-acted in Sweden.[11] The third article, from 1962, posited about the common goals that were then being established for families in the United States.[12]

The fourth and final article in that two-decade span of time, this one published in 1962, reviewed a book titled *Sex Ways in Fact and Faith: Bases for Christian Family Policy*, which ultimately focuses on sexuality in both traditional and diverse families.[13]

Granted, this methodology is a crude way to assess interest in family policy issues, but it provides a rough idea of the level of attention dedicated to a particular issue or area of specialization. A similar search for the twenty-year period of 1988–2008 yields 472 articles with "family policy" in the title, and the topics of the articles vary significantly: adoption,[14] family therapy,[15] equality between the genders,[16] work-family policy,[17] sex education,[18] child care services,[19] and fertility.[20] It is reasonable to say that our interests in child and family policies have both intensified and broadened over the past nearly sixty years, a trend that is common for any emerging academic and professional specialization.

A number of national, professional associations have also adopted a focus on or special committee dedicated to family policy issues. These associations include: National Council on Family Relations (www.ncfr.org), American Association of Family and Consumer Sciences (www.aafcs.org), American Family Therapy Academy (www.afta.org), and the Society for Child and Family Policy and Practice (Division 43 of the American Psychological Association, www.apa.org/divisions/div37/), just to name a few. In each of these instances the professional association has dedicated a point person or committee and resources to addressing ways to bring family issues to the attention of decision- and policy-makers. These are provided as further evidence that specializations in child and family policy continue to grow. Moreover, social scientists who research family problems want their findings to be used in meaningful ways to have an impact on family wellbeing. This evidence reflects a larger trend among researchers who strive to conduct "use-inspired basic research,"[21] or research that aims to solve everyday problems and improve the lives of humankind.

WHY AN EDITED BOOK ON CHILD AND FAMILY POLICY?

There are multiple ways to contribute to the growing, national conversation about solutions to child and family issues: editorials in newspapers, blogging, conferences, academic journals, political talk shows, and many more, including an edited volume that contains the contributions, research findings, and recommendations of multiple social scientists who are concerned about the well-being of children and families. *Innovations* affords us the opportunity to hear from scholars from multiple disciplines about how to understand the problems that families face, how to use research to strengthen the families in our nation, and how to assess the outcomes of policies and programs that are intended to improve child and family well-being. This book includes child and family programs, in addition to policies, because agency-, local-, or county-level programming often serves as a pilot phase before statewide reform is enacted.[22, 23] The same is true for federally funded state pilot projects that pave the way for national-level public policies.[24] This book captures child and family programming and policies at the widest point, with topics that cover all of the four definitional points of family policy previously mentioned: family creation, economic support, childrearing, and family caregiving.[25]

SNAPSHOT OF THE CHAPTERS

- Chapter 2: Patricia Hrusa Williams discusses the outcomes of literacy-focused home visiting services with Hispanic and non-Hispanic families in Massachusetts. She found that, generally speaking, families had high retention rates and that having younger children and being a newer immigrant are related to program retention.
- Chapter 3: Esther F. S. Carvalhaes uses a large-scale, national dataset to examine the impact of parental involvement on children's motivation to learn. She determines that there is a strong relationship between parents' expectations of their children and their motivation to learn.
- Chapter 4: In this chapter, Loretta L. C. Brady explores the need for short-term, high-quality child care in the state of New Hampshire. She finds that families are in need of such services and many of them miss important obligations because they are without childcare options.
- Chapter 5: Michelle P. Taylor and Karen McCurdy examined factors related to the retention of families engaged in home visiting services. They found that the relationship between the provider and parent was key to ensuring longer engagement with program services.
- Chapter 6: Amy D'Andrade explores the effect of child welfare legislation in California which states that families with children under the age of three only have six (as compared with twelve) months to comply with agency requests for parental behavior change. Using existing child welfare data, she finds few negative consequences of this policy.
- Chapter 7: Corey J. Colyer and L. Christopher Plein examine the processes of multidisciplinary review teams within the child welfare profession in West Virginia. They ultimately determine that the goal of multidisciplinary teams is met only in spirit and that most teams function under the directorship of one or two professions.
- Chapter 8: In this chapter Yvonne Wasileswki and her colleagues work with multiple domestic violence shelters in North Carolina to

incorporate screening for children's mental health problems. They describe the challenges to implementing this intervention and the outcomes of the follow-up stage of their project.

- Chapter 9: Terry A. Solomon and her colleagues tackle a common phenomenon in the child welfare profession—African American kinship caregivers and the impact that age has on their ability to provide care. Using child welfare data from the state of Illinois, they find that older caregivers rate their foster children as having fewer problems.

- Chapter 10: Anne Dannerbeck Janku's contribution to this book is a study of risk among those in "emerging adulthood" (age eighteen to twenty-five) who are incarcerated in the state of Missouri. She finds that when compared to individuals in other age groups, offenders in emerging adulthood face a number of risk factors; she makes recommendations that focus on assessment and intervention for this population.

- Chapter 11: Terry-Anne Craigie conducts a secondary data analysis of the Fragile Families and Child Wellbeing Study to examine the impact of parental incarceration on children's well-being. Using instrumental variables estimation, she finds that paternal incarceration has important and negative effects on children's development; she makes recommendations for assessment and intervention.

- Chapter 12: In this chapter, Melissa Brown provides a historical overview on the federal Family Medical Leave Act and takes account of 2007 state legislative action concerning family leave.

- Chapter 13: On a related topic, Stacy Ann Hawkins and her colleagues evaluate the level of knowledge and use among new mothers of California's paid family leave policy. They find that the policy does not provide enough financial coverage for all families and that there are still cultural barriers for taking a family leave, especially for men.

- Chapter 14: Jason Castillo examines the relationship between fathers' social networks, social capital, and the establishment of child support orders. He finds that relationships between mothers and fathers and that fathers' participation in formal networks of support are both important determinants of whether or not a father has a child support order.

- Chapter 15: In this chapter, Judy Doktor and her colleagues examine the perceptions of mothers of children in the autism spectrum. After investigating the online blogging of these special needs families, they make recommendations based on the experiences of families and their children.

For our novice and/or student readers, we hope that *Innovations* will help you to develop a greater sense of what academics, professionals, and politicians mean when they speak of "child and family policy," and also an appreciation for how social science research can contribute to policy-making to support children and families. For our more advanced readers, we hope that these chapters make a significant contribution to the conversations regarding how multidisciplinary social science research can inform policy recommendations in a number of different domains. For all of our readers, we hope that the use-inspired research presented in *Innovations* will help to strengthen and support the well-being of children and families through innovative child and family policies.

NOTES

1. Robert M. Rice, "A Preamble to Family Policy: Issues of the Past and Present," *Policy Studies Journal* 7, no. 4 (Summer 1979): 811–20.

2. Fred Barbaro, "The Case Against Family Policy," *Social Work* 24, no. 6, 455–58.

3. Taylor Gandossy, "Gay Adoption: A New Take on the American Family," *CNN*, 27 June 2007, www.cnn.com/2007/US/06/25/gay.adoption/index.html (20 Aug. 2009).

4. Shirley L. Zimmerman, "Policy, Social Policy, and Family Policy: Concepts, Concerns, and Analytic Tools," *Journal of Marriage & Family* 41, no. 3 (Aug. 1979): 487–95.

5. Karen Bogenschneider, "Has Family Policy Come of Age? A Decade Review of the State of Family Policy in the 1990s," *Journal of Marriage & the Family* 62, no. 4 (Nov. 2000): 1136–59.

6. Karen Bogenschneider, *Family Policy Matters: How Policymaking Affects Families and What Professionals Can Do* (Mahwah, NJ: Lawrence Erlbaum Associates, Publishers, 2002).

7. Theodora Ooms, "Families and Government: Implementing a Family Perspective in Public Policy," *Social Thought* 16 (1990): 61–78.

8. M.F. Ashley Montagu, "Human Values and Family Policy," *Marriage & Family Living* 10, no. 5 (1948): 5–11.

9. Jeffrey M. Jenson and William A. Dieterich, "Effects of a Skills-Based Prevention Program on Bullying and Bully Victimization among Elementary School Children," *Prevention Science* 8 (2007): 285–96.

10. Lewis A. Coser, "Some Aspects of Soviet Family Policy," *American Journal of Sociology* 56, no. 5 (March 1951): 424–37.

11. Anna-Lisa Kälvensten, "Family Policy in Sweden," *Marriage & Family Living* 17, no. 3 (August 1955): 250–54.

12. Alvin L. Schorr, "Family Policy in the United States," *International Social Science Journal* 14, no. 3 (1962): 542–67.

13. "Book Review: *Sex Ways—In Fact and Faith: Bases for Christian Family Policy*," *American Sociological Review* 27, no. 1 (February 1962): 135.

14. Barry Luckock, "Adoption Support and the Negotiation of Ambivalence in Family Policy and Children's Services," *Journal of Law & Society* 35, no. 1 (March 2008): 3–27.

15. John Pardeck, "Family Policy: An Ecological Approach Supporting Family Therapy Treatment," *Family Therapy* 9, no. 2 (1982): 163–65.

16. Patricia Spakes, "Reshaping the Goals of Family Policy: Sexual Equality, Not Protection," *Affilia: Journal of Women & Social Work* 4, no. 3 (Fall 1989): 7–24.

17. Susan G. Singley and Kathryn Hynes, "Transitions to Parenthood: Work-Family Policies, Gender, and the Couple Context," *Gender & Society* 19, no. 3 (June 2005): 376–97.

18. Richard Whitefield, "Sex Education," *Sexual & Marital Therapy* 5, no. 1 (1990): 5–24.

19. Joya Misra, Stephanie Moller, and Michelle Budig, "Work-family policies and poverty for partnered and single women in Europe and North America," *Gender & Society* 21, no. 6, 804–27.

20. Anne Gauthier, "The Impact of Family Policies on Fertility in Industrialized Countries: A Review of the Literature," *Population Research & Policy Review* 26, no. 3 (June 2007): 323–46.

21. Donald E. Stokes, *Pasteur's Quadrant: Basic Science and Technological Innovation* (Washington, DC: Brookings Institute Press, 1997).

22. Florida State Department of Children and Families, *Annual Report on Foster Care Privatization, District Four* (1997).

23. Richard Warchol, "County Tests Own Welfare Reform with Pilot Project," *Los Angeles Times*, 6 July 1997, articles.latimes.com/1997/jul/06/local/me-10185 (19 Aug. 2009).

24. Associated Press, "Georgia Wins Nod for Welfare Reform," *Boston Globe*, 2 November 1994, 4(A).

25. Bogenschneider, *Family Policy Matters*, 25.

EARLY CHILDHOOD
AND EDUCATION

2

Hispanic Families and Family Literacy Practices: Differences by Country of Origin*

Patricia Hrusa Williams

U.S. Census data shows trends in the growth of Hispanics in the United States.[1] The number of Hispanic children in the United States is increasing, with Hispanics under eighteen outnumbering non-Hispanic whites by 11.6 percent. Hispanics also account for half of the nation's growth in population from 2000 to 2006. Immigration is a heated and controversial issue in the United States. However, no matter what side of the debate one stands on, there is an overarching concern regarding the risks that new Hispanic immigrants in the United States face. Lower levels of education and limited competency in English are factors which may limit this group's economic well-being. National data shows lower rates of educational attainment for Hispanic adults and higher rates of poverty in children.[2] These factors jeopardize parents' ability to support their children's education and serve as barriers to their literacy development and potential for success within the U.S. educational system.

While most acknowledge that there are cultural and structural differences between non-Hispanic and Hispanic families, Hispanic families are not a homogeneous group, differing in country of origin and immigration history.[3, 4, 5] Hispanic families come to the United States from various parts of the world. Economic inequality exists since those who come to the United States from different countries encounter different immigration laws and job opportunities, leading to differences in socioeconomic status and family integration.[6] Additionally, it is important to examine differences in the

11

paths and patterns of established Hispanic immigrants (such as those who have traditionally immigrated to the United States from Mexico, Puerto Rico, and Cuba) and new or recent Hispanic immigrants coming from the Caribbean, Central, and South America.[7] The purpose of this study is to examine the literacy practices of Hispanic families with young children, contrasting differences in non-Hispanic families with Hispanic families who differ in their country of origin and wave of immigration. The goal is to understand the unique challenges and resources of diverse Hispanic families and how these factors affect children's educational and literacy development. Differences in receptivity to an intervention to promote children's school readiness and literacy development will also be examined.

HISPANIC FAMILIES IN THE UNITED STATES

There is an increased awareness of the diversity of Hispanic immigrants and subgroups. Population-based data suggests that 55–60 percent of Hispanics are native-born and 40–45 percent are foreign-born.[8, 9] Of Hispanics in the United States, 75 percent are first or second generation immigrants.[10] Tienda and Mitchell also make a distinction between established versus new Hispanic immigrants.[11] They state that 77 percent of Hispanics are considered traditional or established Hispanics (those originating from Mexico, Puerto Rico, and Cuba) and 11 percent are new or recent Hispanic immigrants, with 7 percent originating from the Caribbean and Central America (Dominican Republic, El Salvador, and Guatemala) and 4 percent from South America (Columbia, Peru, and Ecuador).

RISKS TO HISPANIC IMMIGRANTS IN THE UNITED STATES

Hispanic families in the United States face a range of socioeconomic risks. Their rate of poverty ranges from 15 to 26 percent and 30–50 percent have no high school degree, with these rates varying by their country of origin.[12] Further, data shows higher rates of poverty and lower educational attainment for Hispanic groups that originate from Mexico and Puerto Rico, which are considered Hispanic groups that are well established in the United States.

Hispanics coming to the United States also often face dismal job prospects. Stamps and Bohon note that immigrants face many risks to their social adaptation including discrimination, negative stereotypes based on race, and hostility directed at them due to the role immigrants play in the competition for jobs and resource demands in a community.[13] They add that new immigrant groups and those that settle in "traditional gateway cities" may encounter more hostility and therefore may be less optimistic about their prospects and their children's future.

Specific Concerns about Hispanic Children

Available data suggest that Hispanic children in the United States face multiple challenges. As previously mentioned, they face high rates of poverty and are more likely to be reared by parents who have not graduated from high school. Hernandez, Denton, and Macartney use data from the 2000 Census to illustrate how these risks may limit children's access to experiences that positively impact literacy development.[14] They discuss the challenges immigrant parents face in understanding the U.S. educational system, interacting with individuals within it, assisting their children with their academic work, and getting their children the support they need. They also find that immigrant children, particularly those originating from Mexico, Central America, and the Dominican Republic, are less likely to be enrolled in early childhood education programs than their white, native-born counterparts. Data from the National Survey of Early Childhood Health (NSECH) show that Hispanic parents are less likely to read to their children on a daily basis than white or black parents, whether Spanish- or English-speaking.[15] Children's exposure to print, verbal interaction, early childhood education, and home support for learning are all vital ingredients to children's literacy development and future educational success.

INTERVENTIONS TO PROMOTE THE DEVELOPMENT OF HISPANIC CHILDREN

Research suggests that there are several protective factors that may serve to help Hispanic families thrive in the face of risk and adversity. One set of factors are considered cultural and influence the structure and functioning of Hispanic families such as their cultural emphasis on familism, extended family networks, and tendency to be more permeable.[16, 17] Middlemiss and McGuigan suggest that Hispanic families have higher permeability because they emphasize *familism* and *compadrazgo*, the acceptance of nonrelated community members as family. They are less focused on individual concerns, as is more common in non-Hispanic families in the United States.[18] This results in Hispanic families relying on support from larger, extended family networks.[19] While it has been found that familism decreases across the generations, families who retain more traditional views may be more open to interventions, especially those that require outsiders to interchange with their family and come into their home.[20] This highlights the potential of home-based programs to help increase service use and access for Hispanic families with young children.

One means to reach Hispanic families is through the use of home visiting. In their meta-analysis examining the effectiveness of home visiting services with parents or primary caregivers, Sweet and Appelbaum found that home visiting services have the potential to strengthen caregiver-child relationships and exert a direct influence on caregivers' attitudes and behaviors associated with cognitive and socioemotional gains for children.[21] Research on models of home visiting like Healthy Families, which focuses on preventing child maltreatment, finds that Latinos are more likely to stay enrolled in these types of programs than their European American counterparts.[22]

Parent-Child Home Program (PCHP) Model of Home Visiting

One model of home visiting that has been utilized successfully with Hispanic families is the Parent-Child Home Program (PCHP). Founded in 1965 by Phyllis Levenstein and originally called the Mother-Child Home Program, the primary goal of PCHP is to strengthen verbal interaction and educational play between parents and their young children.[23, 24] PCHP is a nationally established model of home visiting located in over 150 communities and sixteen states. It is a home-based parenting, early literacy, and school readiness program. The intervention strategy utilized is to provide twice weekly home visits to toddlers and their families who are at-risk for school failure. PCHP targets families who experience one or more of the following risks for program inclusion: (1) those with a very low income (below $20,000), (2) those headed by a single parent, (3) those having a mother with less than a high school education, (4) those having a father with less than a high school education, and (5) families that speak a language other than English (which may present a communication barrier for the family). Visits are provided by paraprofessional home visitors who model behavior and interaction to show that learning can be fun. They bring a new toy or book each week that the family can keep. In most cases children receive two years of services, starting between eighteen and thirty months of age and continuing until the child reaches pre-kindergarten age.

Benefits and Challenges of Implementing Home Visiting Programs with Hispanic Families

Despite the promise of home visiting models such as PCHP to assist families, research on other models of home visiting such as Healthy Families and the Parents as Teacher (PAT) Program point to both benefits and challenges in service provision. Differences in program success have been noted based on factors such as family culture, socioeconomic status, and language use. For example, in contrast to other types of home visiting programs, literacy-focused interventions have been less successful in maintaining ethnic minority families. Studies of these types of programs have found that young, less educated Latinos are less likely to persist in programs.[25] This suggests that individual factors, like parental education, may outweigh beliefs about social support that are culturally ingrained. Landale, Oropesa, and Bradatan make the point that poverty may serve to erode and challenge some of the protective factors, such as familism, that once helped families function more effectively.[26] It is a question of whether these strains lead to disintegration or deterioration of these networks or force families to rely on them more heavily for survival.[27]

Research on the effects of socioeconomic status on family progress in home visiting has been less decisive. Some studies suggest that children and parents from families with very low incomes (less than $15,000 per year) experience more consistent positive benefits from literacy-focused home visiting programs.[28] Other work has found that there is more potential to change the quality of the home environment in middle-class samples.[29] It is important to consider, however, that for many immigrant Hispanic families multiple risks are intertwined with inequities in society making it more likely that they will also live in poverty, urban areas, and have language or educational barriers that compound the risks they face.

Acculturation or taking on the behavior of the dominant culture, as measured by language use, also seems to be an important factor in understanding success in home visiting. Data from Oregon's Healthy Start program show greater improvement in family functioning and parenting outcomes for Latinos. Those Latinos, however, who showed less evidence of acculturation, as evidenced by preferring to use Spanish, had greater increases in parenting skills.[30] Wagner and Clayton found that Parents as Teachers programs achieved better outcomes for Latinos who speak their native language in the home.[31] Acquisition of English improves Hispanics educational and job prospects, bringing many tangible benefits to families. However, Suro cautions that acculturation, as measured by the acquisition of the English language, serves as a vehicle by which Latinos begin to take on ideas and views that are more in line with non-Latinos.[32] This may lead to the erosion of important cultural values and family ties that promote individual and family well-being.

STUDY QUESTIONS

Research on Hispanic families reviewed here suggests that we need to not look at Hispanics as a single group, but rather as multiple groups based on country of origin and wave of immigration. While many Hispanic families in the United States are challenged by poverty and lack of educational opportunity, the question remains as to how differences in the risks and resources of Hispanic parents influence family literacy practices with their young children. Questions examined in this study include the following:

1. Are there differences between established Hispanic immigrants (those coming from Mexico, Puerto Rico, Cuba) versus new immigrants (those coming from the Caribbean, Central, and South America)? How do these two separate groups of Hispanics differ from their non-Hispanic counterparts?
2. Are there negative effects of acculturation? Do, as suggested in this review of the literature, established Hispanic immigrant groups with young children experience a greater number of risks to their children's literacy development than other Latinos?
3. How effective are home visiting services, such as PCHP, in helping promote literacy development in non-Hispanic versus Hispanic families? Does the use of families' native language, Spanish, in the context of intervention assist in families' retention in the program and growth in skills?

METHODS

Sample

A sample of 217 families participating in twenty-three state-funded Parent-Child Home Programs across the state of Massachusetts (PCHP) was tracked from program entry to exit. Programs were supported by a total budget of $900,000 for standard service provision. State grants of $40,000 were awarded per program. Programs were designed to serve fourteen families each. Some programs had additional funding resources and supported larger programs (twenty-two to thirty-five families). Data collection began in September 2004 and continued until June 2006. Data were collected from all families in the state receiving services between September 2004 and June 2005. Over time the size of programs increased. Due to this increase, starting in September 2005, programs were required to submit data on at least two families per program. Programs were required to complete an intake with families within the first month of services, with subsequent follow-ups at four to six months after entry, and at program exit (typically twenty months after entry) if families did not leave the program prematurely.

Families representing three distinct ethnic groups were compared. One group was non-Hispanic, comprising 39 percent (n = 85) of the sample. Additionally, 28 percent (n = 61) were Hispanic and could be considered established immigrants, with 42.6 percent born in the United States. If not born in the United States, they are either from Puerto Rico (37.7 percent) or Mexico (11.5 percent), traditional locations from which Hispanic immigrants to the United States originate. Finally, 33 percent (n = 71) were new Hispanic immigrants with 40.8 percent originating from the Dominican Republic, 18.3 percent from Guatemala, 11.3 percent from El Salvador, and 8.5 percent from Brazil.

Measures

Family Background Information

Data on individual families were gathered during home visits. Information collected included data on maternal/paternal education, family income, family configuration, ethnic background, the language families chose to use when data was collected (Spanish or English), and the language used in the home. Data on language use was used as a measure of family acculturation as suggested by Middlemiss and McGuigan, and Suro.[33, 34] Data collected on ethnic background included having families identify which racial/ethnic group they identify with and from what country the parents and/or child originated.

A family risk index was also created for each family based on risk factors identified by the PCHP National Center as criteria for program inclusion. Families were assigned one point for each risk including the following: (1) having a very low income (below $20,000), (2) having a family headed by a single parent, (3) having a mother with less than a high school education, (4) having a father with less than a high school education, and (5) speaking a language other than English (which may present a communication barrier for the family). Child information such as gender, date of birth, and age of child at program entry was recorded.

Individual Skills, Family Support, and Engagement outside of Visits

The Familia Inventory: A Questionnaire for the Assessment of Literacy Practices in Families (Infant-Toddler Version) was used to examine family literacy skills at the level of the individual, dyad, and within the support system used by the family.[35] The Familia Inventory is a fifty-one-item, parent self-report measure that examines the frequency of literacy-related activities in the family along nine dimensions. Statements regarding the frequency of family activities were rated using a five-point scale with responses ranging from "Never" to "Daily." Sample questions examining verbal interaction in the family are "We talk with our children as we play, work, or carry out our daily routine" and "We sing songs and say rhymes with our children." Sample questions examining shared reading are "We read color-ful infant/toddler books with our children" and "We have favorite books that we read over and over with our children." The tool is appropriate for use with families and children aged birth to five years and is available in English and Spanish. The measure was administered to families at program entry, four- to six-month follow-up, and at program exit.

Each subscale of the Familia Inventory contains six questions (some questions loaded on more than one subscale) for a total potential score of thirty points per subscale. Two subscales measure parents' individual skills (practical reading and writing in the home), three examine families' contacts with support systems (extended family, library use, and support of school), and four examine parent-child interaction around literacy activities outside of visits (family work and play, shared reading, parental modeling, and verbal interaction). Correlational analyses found strong associations between several of the subscales measured by the Familia Inventory such that two composite measures were created. One composite measure examines parents' individual literacy skills using the practical reading and writing subscales ($r = .575 - .661$), and another measures family literacy interaction for family work and play, parental modeling, shared reading, and verbal interaction subscales ($r = .455 - .756$).

Program Participation and Engagement

Families' program entry and exit dates were tracked, as was each family's program status (whether still enrolled, completed the program, or left be-fore completion) at each data collection point. Program participation was measured using a number of strategies. Length of enrollment in months was calculated using program entry and exit dates. Completing the program required that families receive the equivalent of seventeen weeks of service or thirty-four visits.

RESULTS

Differences in Risks and Acculturation

Table 2.1 contains the results of analyses examining differences in risks, family structure, and acculturation/social adaptation by families' ethnic-ity and country of origin. There were statistically significant differences in socioeconomic status, language use, and overall risks for the three groups examined. A greater percentage of Hispanic families had low incomes than non-Hispanic families. Established Hispanic immigrants were most likely to not have graduated from high school. New Hispanic immigrants were least likely to speak only English in the home and more likely to use Span-

Table 2.1. Differences in Risks and Social Adaptation by Country of Origin

| | Country of Origin | | | |
| | Non-Hispanic, Caucasian N = 85 | Established Hispanics N = 61 | New Hispanic Immigrants N = 71 | Statistic χ^2 or F |
Variable				
% Low Income (< $20,000)	44.7%[bc]	77.0%[a]	70.4%[a]	18.83, p < .001
% No HS Degree	16.5%[bc]	49.2%[a]	38.0%[a]	18.61, p < .001
% Single Parents	36.5%	52.5%	45.1%	3.76, p = .153
# of Children Under Ten	1.85	1.98	1.87	.371, p = .690
Family Size	3.48	3.46	3.42	.054, p = .948
English Only Used in Home	97.6%[bc]	26.2%[ac]	0.0%[ab]	161.55, p < .001
Spanish Used in Surveys	0.0%[bc]	43.3%[a]	59.2%[a]	68.17, p < .001
Overall No. of Risks	1.15[bc]	3.74	3.83[a]	138.89, p < .001

Note. Statistically significant differences between groups are indicated as follows:
[a] = significantly different from non-Hispanic Caucasians
[b] = significantly different from established Hispanics
[c] = significantly different from new Hispanic immigrants

ish in surveys, suggesting less acculturation. Overall, Hispanic families experienced a greater number of risk factors than non-Hispanic families.

Differences in Literacy Practices, Supports, and Response to Intervention

Table 2.2 contains the results of analyses examining differences in literacy practices by country of origin and wave of immigration prior to receiving

Table 2.2. Differences in Literacy Practices, Supports, and Response to Intervention by Country of Origin

| | Country of Origin | | | |
| | Non-Hispanic, Caucasian N = 85 | Established Hispanics N = 61 | New Hispanic Immigrants N = 71 | Statistic χ^2 or F |
Variable				
Individual Skills (max = 60)	44.71[bc]	39.11[a]	38.82[a]	8.55, p < .001
Family Interaction (max = 120)	106.83[bc]	90.52[a]	91.29[a]	26.33, p < .001
Supports and Resources (max = 30)				
External Family Support	20.79[bc]	16.38[a]	16.70[a]	14.39, p < .001
Library Use	9.86[bc]	6.93[a]	7.21[a]	.46, p = .630
Support of School	12.67	11.90	13.42	3.62, p = .028
Length of Enrollment HV Program (in Months)	14.7[b]	9.9[ac]	14.5[b]	7.473, p = .001

Note. Statistically significant differences between groups are indicated as follows:
[a] = significantly different from non-Hispanic Caucasians
[b] = significantly different from established Hispanics
[c] = significantly different from new Hispanic immigrants

intervention. There were statistically significant differences in use of individual literacy skills, family interaction involving literacy, external family support of literacy, and library use. Non-Hispanic families reported engaging in more of these activities and having greater access to these supports than either group of Hispanic immigrants. The three groups did not differ, however, in their self-reported support of their children's school activities. Additionally, despite the risks experienced, new Hispanic immigrants were more likely to remain involved in a home visiting intervention than non-Hispanic nonimmigrants; both of these groups remained in the PCHP intervention for five months longer than established Hispanic immigrants.

Association between Family Characteristics and Practices

For all three groups there were differences in the relation between family characteristics and literacy practices. For example, there was a statistically significant relationship between child characteristics such as age at entry and use of supports for non-Hispanic families. There was a positive relationship between age at entry and family support of school ($r = .27, p = .014$). Children who were younger at program entry also remained enrolled in the program longer ($r = -.32, p = .008$). For non-Hispanic families, experiencing more risks was associated with greater support of school ($r = .37, p = .001$).

For established Hispanics, family risks such as income, maternal education, and the overall risks faced were all related to literacy practices. Higher levels of maternal education and lower levels of overall risk were associated with increased use of individual literacy skills ($r = .27, p = .033; r = -.33, p = .041$). Lower levels of family income were associated with more external support of children's literacy, suggesting that in cases of low resources, external family members help compensate for the lack of resources available ($r = -.26, p = .041$). Higher levels of family income and maternal education were associated with increased use of resources like the library ($r = .28, p = .029; r = 339, p = .008$). Greater family risk was inversely related to library use ($r = -.42, p = .001$). Family income was positively related to length of service provision ($r = .44, p = .002$) and family risk was inversely related to retention ($r = -.329, p = .026$). For new Hispanic immigrants, family income and size were related to literacy practices. Higher family income was associated with more use of the library ($r = .27, p = .023$). Having more children under the age of ten was associated with remaining in a home visiting intervention longer ($r = .33, p = .038$).

Overall, these findings suggest that individual factors, such as the age of the child are important to understanding family practices in non-Hispanic families. For Hispanic families, family considerations, such as the number of risks present in the family context, family income, and family size are more important to understand family literacy practices and use of literacy support services.

Differences in Response to Intervention

Repeated measures MANOVA were utilized to examine family progress over the first six months of the intervention by country of origin and wave of immigration. Figure 2.1 contains data on the average change in literacy skills over the first six months of the intervention for the three areas families showed statistically significant progress. There were statistically significant changes over time in families' skills in the areas of using individual literacy skills, F $(1, 150) = 31.063$, p <.001; engaging in family literacy activities, F $(1, 150) = 15.039$, $p < .001$; and library use, F $(1, 150) = 10.840$, $p = .001$. Both Hispanic groups showed greater growth in family literacy interaction and library use than non-Hispanic families. Non-Hispanic families and new Hispanic immigrants reported greater increases in the use of individual literacy skills than established Hispanic families.

Figure 2.2 contains data on differences in length of retention in the program for Hispanics by language used. There was a statistically significant main effect by type of Hispanic immigrant and language use on program retention, F $(1, 82) = 7.84$ $p = .006$ and F $(1, 82) = 3.93$, $p = .078$, respectively. Hispanic families who preferred to use Spanish remained in the program longer than those who were more acculturated as evident in their

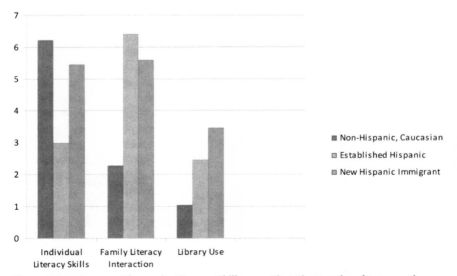

Figure 2.1.   Average Change in Literacy Skills over First Six Months of Intervention

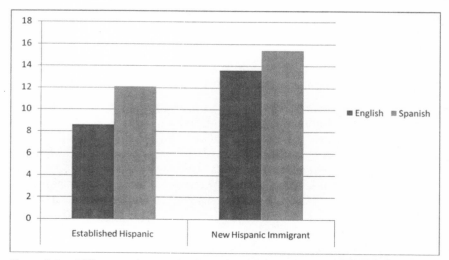

Figure 2.2. **Differences in Length of Enrollment in Months for Hispanic Families by Language Use**

preference for using English. New Hispanic immigrants also remained in the program longer than established Hispanic families.

CONCLUSION

Results revealed differences in the risks and resources of families by country of origin and wave of immigration. Hispanic families who enrolled in PCHP in Massachusetts, whether established or new immigrants, were more likely at program entry to have lower incomes, to use literacy skills less frequently (whether individually or in interaction with their children), and to utilize extended family and library resources less frequently in facilitating their children's literacy development. The findings regarding differences in the risks experienced by non-Hispanic and Hispanic parents are similar to what has been found in other studies.[36] This study did not, however, reveal like others that experiencing a greater number of risks is associated with a shorter length of engagement in literacy-focused home visiting services or less potential for family progress.[37, 38]

Findings from this study suggest that socioeconomic factors and cultural/ structural factors influence family literacy practices. Statistically significant differences exist between non-Hispanic, nonimmigrant, and Hispanic families. Despite facing fewer risks and having more advantages, non-Hispanic families were as likely to persist in a literacy-focused intervention program as new Hispanic immigrant families. Both groups received an average of five more months of service than Hispanic families from established immigrant groups. Family factors and language use in visits are important to understanding this pattern of results. For new Hispanic immigrants, family factors such as having more children under ten were associated with retention, indicating that familism or the needs of the group rather than the individual is a strong force in guiding family behavior.[39, 40] Programs working with Hispanic immigrants may be well served by developing strategies to incorporate siblings and extended family members into interventions to promote program use.

There is also another possible reason why new Hispanic immigrants were retained longer in programs than their established Hispanic immigrant counterparts. Since new immigrants experience far more risks in this sample than non-Hispanic families, program personnel such as home visitors may perceive them as being needier than the other Hispanic group in the study who are more established in the United States and provided them more assistance.[41] This may have enabled them to remain in the program longer. Further, our group of more established immigrants may be subject to more negative stereotypes based on race which consciously or unconsciously influence behavior in interaction with them.[42] Follow-up work should examine home visitor-parent interaction and how patterns differ across Hispanic immigrant groups to look for biases in interaction which may also account for the poorer outcomes of some Hispanic families in literacy-focused interventions.[43]

In general, Hispanic families were retained longer in programs if their native language was used in the context of early service provision, suggesting that less enculturation and more family permeability serves as a protective factor for high-risk families involved in intervention.[44, 45] It is also possible that when programs use a family's native language in service provision, they show individual families that they have a commitment to accommodate them and meet a family's needs. By providing a match between service context and program clients, it results in better outcomes for families.[46] Messages of support and information may be lost in translation for programs serving immigrants that do not have access to bilingual staff. This may be particularly important for new immigrant groups who are less likely to report using English exclusively in the home.

One of the more positive findings from this study is that there was no difference in families' support of school across ethnic groups or wave of immigration. This is particularly important given Hernandez, Denton, and Macartney's findings that suggest that Hispanics, especially those from Mexico, Central America, and the Dominican Republic, are less likely to be enrolled in early childhood education programs.[47] Recent work from the *Pre-K Now* study suggests that the majority of Latino parents are actually strong supporters of developing their children's literacy skills, with

96 percent supporting the use of pre-kindergarten services for children; almost half seeing the experience as important to developing children's academic skills and knowledge of letters, numbers, and colors.[48] This study highlights the fact that when Hispanic families receive outreach in communities, they are receptive to services. Similar outreach to encourage use of other community resources, such as the library, may be equally effective in helping immigrant Hispanic families.

Finally, another positive finding of this study is that home visiting programs like PCHP show great potential in helping to facilitate the literacy development of families, especially Hispanic immigrants. In this study, positive effects and family growth in literacy practices were evident even during the first four to six months of intervention. Sweet and Appelbaum noted that the effects of home visiting are greatest during the early stages of intervention.[49] Qualitative work by Perry, Kay, and Brown has taken a closer look at the types of literacy interventions and practices that are effective in working with Hispanic families.[50] They found that approaches like PCHP, which emphasize fun, enjoyable, entertaining activities provided in a relaxed setting, using modeling versus direct instruction, are more appealing to Hispanic families. Programs such as PCHP seem to fit their definition of "flexible, home-based curriculum materials that offer opportunities for pleasurable, bilingual literacy interactions in which multiple family members might participate (p. 111)." Programs and policies need to be further developed so that immigrant families have better access to services that help maintain their language and culture while still learning new skills. In addition, public awareness is needed to dispel some of the myths that exist about immigrant families and literacy practices so that we are creating a context that allows all children and families to succeed.

NOTES

*Acknowledgments: Dr. Williams would like to acknowledge the Massachusetts Department of Education and Massachusetts Department of Early Education and Care for their support. She would also like to recognize Emily Caille, M.S.W., of the Massachusetts Department of Elementary and Secondary Education and Julia Kane of Towson University for their assistance.

1. U.S. Census Bureau, *Hispanics in the United States* (Washington, DC: Author, 2006).

2. Roberto R. Ramirez and G. Patricia de la Cruz, *The Hispanic Population in the United States: March 2002*, Current Population Reports, P20-545 (U.S. Census Bureau: Washington, DC, 2002).

3. N. S. Landale, R. S. Oropesa, and C. Bradatan, "Hispanic Families in the United States: Family Structure and Process in an Era of Family Change," in *Hispan-*

ics and the Future of America, eds. Marta Tienda and Faith Mitchell (Washington, DC: National Academies Press, 2006), 138–78.

4. N. Sarkisian, M. Gerena, and N. Gerstel, "Extended Family Ties among Mexicans, Puerto Ricans, and Whites: Superintegration or Disintegration?" *Family Relations* 55 (July 2006): 331–44.

5. Marta Tienda and Faith Mitchell, "Uncertain Destinies," in *Multiple Origins, Uncertain Destinies: Hispanics and the American Future*, eds. Marta Tienda and Faith Mitchell (Washington, DC: National Academies Press, 2006), 113–28.

6. N. Sarkisian, M. Gerena, and N. Gerstel, "Extended Family Ties among Mexicans, Puerto Ricans, and Whites: Superintegration or Disintegration?" *Family Relations* 55 (July 2006): 331–44.

7. Marta Tienda and Faith Mitchell, "Uncertain Destinies," in *Multiple Origins, Uncertain Destinies: Hispanics and the American Future*, eds. Marta Tienda and Faith Mitchell (Washington, DC: National Academies Press, 2006), 113–28.

8. Roberto R. Ramirez and G. Patricia de la Cruz, *The Hispanic Population in the United States: March 2002*, Current Population Reports, P20-545 (U.S. Census Bureau: Washington, DC, 2002).

9. Marta Tienda and Faith Mitchell, "Uncertain Destinies," in *Multiple Origins, Uncertain Destinies: Hispanics and the American Future*, eds. Marta Tienda and Faith Mitchell (Washington, DC: National Academies Press, 2006), 113–28.

10. Marta Tienda and Faith Mitchell, "Uncertain Destinies," in *Multiple Origins, Uncertain Destinies: Hispanics and the American Future*, eds. Marta Tienda and Faith Mitchell (Washington, DC: National Academies Press, 2006), 113–28.

11. Marta Tienda and Faith Mitchell, "Uncertain Destinies," in *Multiple Origins, Uncertain Destinies: Hispanics and the American Future*, eds. Marta Tienda and Faith Mitchell (Washington, DC: National Academies Press, 2006), 113–28.

12. Roberto R. Ramirez and G. Patricia de la Cruz, *The Hispanic Population in the United States: March 2002*, Current Population Reports, P20-545 (U.S. Census Bureau: Washington, DC, 2002).

13. Katherine Stamps and Stephanie A. Bohon, "Educational Attainment in New and Established Latino Metropolitan Destinations," *Social Science Quarterly* 87, no. 5 (December 2006): 1225–40.

14. D. J. Hernandez, N. A. Denton, and S. E. Macartney, "Children in Immigrant Families: Looking to America's Future," *Society for Research in Child Development (SRCD) Social Policy Report* 22, no. 3 (October 2008): 1–23.

15. A. A. Kuo, T. M. Franke, M. Regalado, and N. Halfon, "Parent Report of Reading to Young Children," *Pediatrics* 113, no. 6 (June 2004): 1944–51.

16. N. S. Landale, R. S. Oropesa, and C. Bradatan, "Hispanic Families in the United States: Family Structure and Process in an Era of Family Change," in *Hispanics and the Future of America*, eds. Marta Tienda and Faith Mitchell (Washington, DC: National Academies Press, 2006), 138–78.

17. Wendy Middlemiss and William McGuigan, "Ethnicity and Adolescent Mothers' Benefit from Participation in Home Visitation Services," *Family Relations* 54 (April 2005): 212–24.

18. Wendy Middlemiss and William McGuigan, "Ethnicity and Adolescent Mothers' Benefit from Participation in Home Visitation Services," *Family Relations* 54 (April 2005): 212–24.

19. J. D. Coatsworth, L. G., Duncan, H. Pantin, and J. Szapocznik, "Differential Predictors of African American and Hispanic Parent Retention in a Family-Focused Preventive Intervention," *Family Relations* 55, no. 2 (March 2006): 240–51.

20. N. S. Landale, R. S. Oropesa, and C. Bradatan, "Hispanic Families in the United States: Family Structure and Process in an Era of Family Change," in *Hispanics and the Future of America*, eds. Marta Tienda and Faith Mitchell (Washington, DC: National Academies Press, 2006), 138–78.

21. M. A. Sweet and M. I. Appelbaum, "Is Home Visiting an Effective Strategy? A Meta-analytic Review of Home Visiting Programs for Families with Young Children," *Child Development* 75, no. 5 (September 2004): 1435–56.

22. K. McCurdy, R. A. Gannon, and D. Daro, "Participation Patterns in Home-Based Family Support Programs: Ethnic Variations," *Family Relations* 52, no. 1 (January 2003): 3–11.

23. Phyllis Levenstein, *Messages from Home: The Mother-Child Home Program and the Prevention of School Disadvantage* (Columbus: Ohio State University Press, 1998).

24. Phyllis Levenstein and S. Levenstein, *Messages from Home: The Parent-Child Home Program for Overcoming Educational Disadvantage* (Philadelphia: Temple University Press, 2008).

25. M. Wagner, M. I. Linn, S. Gerlach-Downie, and F. Hernandez, "Dimensions of Parental Engagement in Home Visiting Programs: Exploratory Study," *Topics in Early Childhood Special Education* 24, no. 4 (Winter 2003): 171–87.

26. N. S. Landale, R. S. Oropesa, and C. Bradatan, "Hispanic Families in the United States: Family Structure and Process in an Era of Family Change," in *Hispanics and the Future of America*, eds. Marta Tienda and Faith Mitchell (Washington, DC: National Academies Press, 2006), 138–78.

27. N. Sarkisian, M. Gerena, and N. Gerstel, "Extended Family Ties among Mexicans, Puerto Ricans, and Whites: Superintegration or Disintegration?" *Family Relations* 55 (July 2006): 331–44.

28. M. Wagner, D. Spiker, and M. I. Linn, "The Effectiveness of the Parents as Teachers Program with Low-Income Parents and Children," *Topics in Early Childhood Special Education* 22, no. 2 (Summer 2002): 67–81.

29. M. J. Bakermans-Kranenburg, M. H. van IJzendoorn, and R. H. Bradley, "Those Who Have Receive: The Matthew Effect in Early Childhood Intervention in the Home Environment," *Review of Educational Research* 75, no. 2 (Spring 2005): 1–26.

30. Wendy Middlemiss and William McGuigan, "Ethnicity and Adolescent Mothers' Benefit from Participation in Home Visitation Services," *Family Relations* 54 (April 2005): 212–24.

31. Mary M. Wagner and Serena L. Clayton, "The Parents as Teachers Program: Results from Two Demonstrations," *The Future of Children* 9, no. 1 (Spring/Summer 1999): 91–15.

32. Roberto Suro, "The Hispanic Family in Flux," *Center on Children & Families, Working Paper* (November 2007): 3–16.

33. Wendy Middlemiss and William McGuigan, "Ethnicity and Adolescent Mothers' Benefit from Participation in Home Visitation Services," *Family Relations* 54 (April 2005): 212–24.

34. Roberto Suro, "The Hispanic Family in Flux," *Center on Children & Families, Working Paper* (November 2007): 3–16.

35. Ronald L. Taylor, *The Familia Inventory: User's Manual and Infant/Toddler Supplement* (Grandview, MO: Family Reading Resources, 2000).

36. M. Wagner, M. I. Linn, S. Gerlach-Downie, and F. Hernandez, "Dimensions of Parental Engagement in Home Visiting Programs: Exploratory Study," *Topics in Early Childhood Special Education* 24, no. 4 (Winter 2003): 171–87.

37. A. K. Duggan, E. C. McFarlane, A. M. Windham, C. A. Rohde, D. S. Salkever, L. Fuddy, L. A. Rosenberg, S. B. Buchbinder, and C. C. J. Sia, "Evaluation of Hawaii's Healthy Start Program," *The Future of Children* 9, no. 1 (Spring/Summer 1999): 66–90.

38. M. J. Bakermans-Kranenburg, M. H. van IJzendoorn, and R. H. Bradley, "Those Who Have Receive: The Matthew Effect in Early Childhood Intervention in the Home Environment," *Review of Educational Research* 75, no. 2 (Spring 2005): 1–26.

39. N. S. Landale, R. S. Oropesa, and C. Bradatan, "Hispanic Families in the United States: Family Structure and Process in an Era of Family Change," in *Hispanics and the Future of America*, eds. Marta Tienda and Faith Mitchell (Washington, DC: National Academies Press, 2006), 138–78.

40. Wendy Middlemiss and William McGuigan, "Ethnicity and Adolescent Mothers' Benefit from Participation in Home Visitation Services," *Family Relations* 54 (April 2005): 212–24.

41. E. A. Sharp, J. M. Ispa, K. R. Thornburg, and V. Lane, "Relations among Mother and Home Visitor Personality, Relationship Quality, and Amount of Time Spent in Home Visits," *Journal of Community Psychology* 31, no. 6 (2003): 591–606.

42. Katherine Stamps and Stephanie A. Bohon, "Educational Attainment in New and Established Latino Metropolitan Destinations," *Social Science Quarterly* 87, no. 5 (December 2006): 1225–40.

43. M. Wagner, M. I. Linn, S. Gerlach-Downie, and F. Hernandez, "Dimensions of Parental Engagement in Home Visiting Programs: Exploratory Study," *Topics in Early Childhood Special Education* 24, no. 4 (Winter 2003): 171–87.

44. Wendy Middlemiss and William McGuigan, "Ethnicity and Adolescent Mothers' Benefit from Participation in Home Visitation Services," *Family Relations* 54 (April 2005): 212–24.

45. Roberto Suro, "The Hispanic Family in Flux," *Center on Children & Families*, Working Paper (November 2007): 3–16.

46. K. McCurdy, R. A. Gannon, and D. Daro, "Participation Patterns in Home-Based Family Support Programs: Ethnic Variations," *Family Relations* 52, no. 1 (January 2003): 3–11.

47. D. J. Hernandez, N. A. Denton, and S. E. Macartney, "Children in Immigrant Families: Looking to America's Future," *Society for Research in Child Development (SRCD) Social Policy Report* 22, no. 3 (October 2008): 1–23.

48. E. E. Garcia and D. M. Gonzales, "Pre-K and Latinos: The Foundation of America's Future," *Pre-K Now Research Series* (July 2006).

49. M. A. Sweet and M. I. Appelbaum, "Is Home Visiting an Effective Strategy? A Meta-analytic Review of Home Visiting Programs for Families with Young Children," *Child Development* 75, no. 5 (September 2004): 1435–56.

50. N. J. Perry, S. M. Kay, and B. Brown, "Continuity and Change in Home Literacy Practices of Hispanic Families with Preschool Children," *Early Child Development and Care* 178, no. 1 (January 2008): 99–113.

3

Effects of Parental Involvement on First Graders' Approaches to Learning*

Esther F. S. Carvalhaes

Does parental involvement affect their children's motivation to learn? There is little question about the critical role that parents play in helping their children succeed in school. But there is no reason to believe that all forms of parental involvement are equally beneficial for their children's academic development as can be learned from parental involvement studies in higher grades. Can the effects of parental involvement in their children's motivation be detected in early grades as well? If so, what types of activities yield the most benefit? This chapter investigates these questions by analyzing a nationally representative sample of first-grade students from a large-scale database, the Early Childhood Longitudinal Study (ECLS). An introduction to the topic is provided, followed by a review of the literature on types of parental involvement and the importance of the home learning environment. The chapter proceeds with presentation of the data and methods used, the results of the analysis and a final discussion including recommendations for further research and implications for policy.

INTRODUCTION

Parents, educators, school administrators, and the government easily reach consensus by asserting the importance of parental involvement not only for students' improved academic achievement, but also for improvement of schools. The federal government has taken the position that high academic standards are a matter of "shared responsibility" between the school system and the parents. Accordingly, it has incorporated innumerous provisions related to parental involvement in the Elementary and Secondary Education Act of 1965 (ESEA), which was reauthorized by the No Child Left Behind Act of 2001 (NCLB Act). States, school districts, and schools receiving federal funding to promote the education of low-income students (Title I, Part A) are mandated to take steps that ensure parental involvement in their children's education. The measures, accompanied by budgetary commitments, include encouraging parents to assist in their child's learning, proactively communicating with the parents regarding their child's progress, getting parents involved in the activities at school, including them in advisory and decision-making committees, among others.[1]

The general public seems to echo the need of getting parents involved: the 1997 Phi Delta Kappan/Gallup poll reveals that 86 percent of the respondents listed support from parents as the most important way to improve schools,[2] and in 2000 the same poll reports that lack of parental involvement was considered by elementary and secondary teachers the second largest obstacle to public school improvement, right after lack of funding.[3] The positive impact of parental involvement on their children's academic life from the early years of preschool and kindergarten until much later into their middle and high school years has also found strong support in research.[4, 5, 6, 7]

While much research has focused on the positive effects of parental involvement in their children's academic achievement, especially on elementary grades, limited research has focused specifically on the impact of parental involvement on children's motivation to learn. There is abundant support for the positive role of student's motivation on learning from a variety of theoretical perspectives.[8] Children who are motivated are more likely to engage in the types of practices that can help them learn. They pay attention, display effort, take initiative, are more persistent, and seek help, all of which can support the cultivation of the types of routines, attitudes, skills, and habits that not only facilitate higher academic performance, but also help them learn in the face of difficulties.[9, 10] Thus understanding the role that parents have on their children's motivation to learn can help parents and teachers to better assist students to succeed in school as well as generate insights into possible explanations as to why parental involvement works.

There is sufficient evidence supporting positive associations between parental involvement and a number of educational outcomes, including positive attitudes about school, better attendance, and work habits.[11, 12, 13]

These outcomes, though supporting the notion that parents can help their children engage in learning, are not particularly focused on systematically measuring motivation. The present study intends to add to the knowledge in this field by focusing specifically on the effects of parental involvement on children's motivation to learn. Many definitions of motivation have been proposed in the literature depending on the types of theoretical emphasis adopted by their proponents. In this study, motivation is defined as "the process whereby goal-directed activity is instigated and sustained."[14] This is a general definition that seems to be aligned with most of the current views and research on motivation. Although there are vast differences among motivational researchers about what processes cause children to be motivated, most researchers agree that certain instances of behavior (rather than simply attitudes) are better indicators of the presence of motivation; typically accepted indexes are: choice of tasks, effort, and persistence. Along these lines, our indicator of motivation, an index named "approaches to learning," measures teachers' ratings of children's attentiveness, task persistence, eagerness to learn, learning independence, flexibility, and organization.

To date, no large-scale study has been undertaken to examine the impact of parental involvement in children's motivation during the elementary grades. This is ironic since early grades is precisely the time when parental involvement is at its peak.[15] The release of the Early Childhood Longitudinal Study (ECLS), a database sponsored by the National Center for Education Statistics, provides us with a unique opportunity to address this question by using a nationally representative database. The study gathers data on an initial cohort of approximately twenty thousand children and follows them from kindergarten through first, third, and fifth grade, with extensive data on the children, their family, their school, and their community.

We need to better understand the link between parental involvement and their children's motivation to learn, but we also need to investigate what kinds of parental involvement "really count." The literature has revealed that not all types of parental activities have the same effect on their children's success in school.[16, 17] Reading to children, taking them to libraries, working together on crafts, singing with them, etc. might not all have a uniform impact on their children's approaches to learning. In the parent's effort to create a stimulating learning environment for their children, which activities seem to be more promising in obtaining the desired responses? These are the issues that motivated this study. Specifically, the research questions are:

1. Does parental involvement affect their children's motivation to learn?
2. If so, what types of activities yield the most benefit?

THE IMPORTANCE OF PARENTAL
INVOLVEMENT IN CHILDREN'S LEARNING

A body of research has demonstrated positive correlations between parental involvement and their children's learning and consequent academic success.[18, 19, 20] Reading to the child; singing with the child; interacting with the school teacher and personnel; taking the child to recreational events, museums, and libraries; giving children encouragement; and serving as role models are all different ways in which parents actively participate to make a difference in their education.

Typically, most of the parental involvement research has focused on school success, particularly academic achievement in elementary grades. Though individual studies do not always reveal consistent positive results, a meta-analysis[21] conducted by Fan and Chen[22] concluded that there was a positive, moderate relationship between parental involvement and student achievement. Other positive associations have also been found, such as positive attitudes towards school, better attendance and work habits, especially among high school students.[23, 24, 25]

Studies using large-scale national datasets exist, but they examine the impact of parental involvement in later grades. These studies are fewer in number than those looking at parental involvement and achievement in the elementary grades, and they yield results on both directions. Catsambis[26] reviews them in her own study of parental involvement on high school students: parents' higher levels of participation in their children's education were found to be positively related to higher GPAs, higher engagement, higher concentration, and attention across school subjects; some negative correlations were also found, indicating that not all types of parental involvement are equally beneficial, and that apparently, as the children grow, some developmental adjustment has to take place on the parents' side for the effects to continue in a positive direction. Among high school students only some indicators of parental involvement are related to students' test scores, and the most pronounced effects are on coursework completion and curriculum enrollment. The most consistent benefit to students in secondary education was associated with parents' aspirations for their children and encouragement provided.

Lee[27] has observed that the effects of parental involvement on secondary school students' behavior, attitudes toward school, and report card grades may be greater than its effects on achievement test scores. Reading habits and homework, attitudes toward school and teachers, and commitment to school work, in addition to a reduction in behavioral problems and absenteeism, are all positive outcomes related to parental involvement. A review of studies examining motivational outcomes shows the beneficial effects of parental involvement on time spent on homework, attitudes toward school, staying in school, and educational aspirations beyond high school.[28] These studies focused on high school students; there is a scarcity of studies on parental involvement and motivational outcomes during the elementary grades.

TYPES OF PARENTAL INVOLVEMENT

An important segment of the parental involvement literature is dedicated to understanding the different types of parental involvement and how they relate to their children's performance in school. Parental involvement can be manifested in a variety of ways, and there is a wide range of activities that involve the interrelationship between family-school-child; sorting out direct influences on the children might be a difficult task, since a number of these practices are intertwined and influence each other. To address this multifaceted reality, a typology of parental involvement was developed by Epstein[29] to identify differential effects of parental involvement depending on the types of activities they engage in. Use of national data on secondary school students by Catsambis[30] has given support to Epstein's typology, which consists of six types of involvement: activities related to parenting and creating a learning environment (type 1), communication with school (type 2), attending school activities and participating as volunteers (type 3), school work at home (type 4), parents' participation in decision-making at school (type 5), and parents' access to community resources (type 6).

For the purposes of this study, only the effects of parental involvement of type 1 will be studied—namely, parental activities related to the home learning environment that seem to favor children's approaches to learning. In addition, parental expectation with respect to their children's educational attainment (the highest level of education parents expect the child to complete) as well as some other home learning contextual variables will be examined (how many books the child has and whether there is a home computer that the child uses).

THE IMPORTANCE OF THE HOME LEARNING ENVIRONMENT

The family and the home environment play a key role in children's education as it sets up not only the expectations about school, the interest that children develop in school, but also how many years children will remain in school.[31] With recent changes in society in the past three or four decades, such as an increase in the number of mothers who are college educated, the home environment has become a powerful educational resource in supporting students' progress. The relationship between school and the home was also transformed as a result: if in the past the education of children was delegated to the specialized care of teachers, in more recent decades parents have played a more direct role in helping their children with school work, since it is not uncommon that parents have as much education as their children's teachers or even more.[32]

Concerns about school readiness and the importance of helping children acquire skills that would help them benefit from their early educational experiences gained central stage.[33] In recognition that disadvantaged families would have little chance to provide the sort of home learning environment that parents with higher education could offer to their children, federal funding was provided in the 1960s to provide this "head start."

A number of activities that happen at home are thought to be central to help young children transition into a successful school life: reading to the child, providing familiarity with print, helping the child develop a sense of story sequence, inquiring about understanding, making connections between letters and sounds, helping the child with basic numerical skills, providing opportunities for gross and fine motor skills development, encouraging their curiosity to explore the immediate environment, favoring the use of imagination, and observing the objects around them and how they work are just some of the ways in which parents can support children at home. But the home is not only central in playing a supportive role to the school work, it provides the child with a wealth of long-term benefits such as encouragement, the formation of aspirations, the perception of what can be accomplished, and the setting of standards of quality.[34]

Moreover, the home is a privileged space for learning stimulation, which is associated with early motor, cognitive, and social development, language competence, and achievement. There is support for the idea that parental responsiveness plays a role in early development of competence among preschoolers and provides the basis for building secure attachment, which has long-term implications for a child's sense of well-being.[35] All of these factors contribute greatly to how children perceive their educational opportunities and feel motivated about their school work, making the home environment a stage in which lifelong learning is fostered. Identifying empirically how some of these home learning factors can affect children's approaches to learning in early grades is the purpose of the current study. Specifically, we examine the impact of parental involvement on children's approaches to learn and try to identify the types of activities that are associated with increased motivation.

STUDY METHODS

Data

Data from the ECSL was used for this analysis. The survey instruments are questionnaires completed by teachers and school administrators, as well as parents in interview sessions. We focused on the parents' interview to gain information on parents' expectations for their children's educational attainment and their involvement in creating a learning environment for their children. Information on children's approaches to learning was taken from their teachers' assessment. Background information on the schools comes both from the teachers' questionnaire and from the school administrators' questionnaire. All data used was collected in Spring First Grade (2002). Only cases with information from all data points were included, which resulted in a subsample of 11,942 first-grade students.

Variables

Dependent Variable

Our motivational outcome is a variable called "approaches to learning" and corresponds to the student's score on the teacher social rating scale available in the ECLS. Specifically, *"the Approaches to Learning Scale . . . measures behaviors that affect the ease with which children can benefit from the learning environment. It includes six items that rate the child's attentiveness, task persistence, eagerness to learn, learning independence, flexibility, and organization."*[36]

Independent Variables

Our independent variables come from survey questions representing parental involvement. Parental expectation refers to what level of education the parent expects the child to complete. The activities that parents engage in with their child were grouped into two variables: "parental involvement/recreational activities" (combined questions about how often parent plays sports with child, plays games, sings songs, helps with art projects, talks about nature) and "parental involvement/academic activities" (combined questions about how often parent practices numbers, reads, and tells stories to child). The other home learning environment variables are how many books the child has and whether there is a home computer that the child uses.

Control Variables

A number of characteristics of the children, their family, and schools were used as control variables. *Family characteristics* included parents' socioeconomic status, parents' education, family type, and size. *Child's characteristics* included gender, race, language spoken at home, absenteeism and tardiness at school, and whether the child receives center-based day care. *Classroom characteristics* included variables related to class composition (proportion of gifted students/of students repeating first grade/of students who are reading below grade level/ of students whose math skills are below grade level), group behavior, and teacher's job satisfaction. *School characteristics* included whether the school is public or private, location, percent of minority students, and school climate as rated by the teacher.

Data Analysis

Multiple regression was used to analyze the data. In a regression equation, an outcome variable (in our case, first graders' approaches to learning) is conceptualized as the result of the simultaneous influence of a number of other variables that are judged to be related to it plus an error term to account both for errors of measurement and for potential variables that might be related to the outcome but are unknown. The variables whose effect we are interested in (here, parental involvement) are the independent variables, and the remaining variables are added as control variables, which allows one to hold the effect of background characteristics constant.

The complete set of variables utilized for the analysis is presented along with their descriptive statistics in table 3.1.

Table 3.1.   Weighted Descriptive Statistics of Sample (N = 11,942)

Variable Name/Description	Mean	SD	Min	Max	Type[a]
First Grade Approaches to Learning	3.02	0.71	1.00	4.28	C
Parental Involvement Variables					
Parental Expectation—High School	0.11	0.32	0.00	1.00	D
Parental Expectation—College	0.65	0.48	0.00	1.00	D
Parental Expectation—Master's Degree	0.12	0.33	0.00	1.00	D
Parental Expectation—PhD/Advanced Degree	0.11	0.32	0.00	1.00	D
Parental Involvement—Academic Activities	2.44	0.53	1.00	4.00	C
Parental Involvement—Recreational Activities	3.09	0.62	1.00	4.00	C
Number of Books Child Has	2.32	1.38	1.00	5.00	SC
Home Computer Access (Yes = 1; No = 0)	0.65	0.48	0.00	1.00	D
Student's Characteristics					
Male	0.51	0.50	0.00	1.00	D
White	0.62	0.49	0.00	1.00	D
Black	0.14	0.35	0.00	1.00	D
Hispanic	0.17	0.38	0.00	1.00	D
Asian	0.02	0.15	0.00	1.00	D
Other Race	0.05	0.21	0.00	1.00	D

Home Language of Child (English = 1; Other = 0)	0.89	0.31	0.00	1.00	D
Child's Absenteeism (Number of Days/ School Year)	9.21	10.98	0.00	182.00	C
Child's Tardiness (Number of Days/ School Year)	4.39	6.99	0.00	108.00	C
Child Has Center-Based Care (Yes = 1; No = 0)	0.17	0.37	0.00	1.00	D
Family Characteristics					
Parent Highest Education Level					
High School	0.43	0.49	0.00	1.00	D
Some or Complete College	0.45	0.50	0.00	1.00	D
Master's Degree	0.06	0.24	0.00	1.00	D
Doctorate or Professional Degree	0.04	0.20	0.00	1.00	D
Graduate/Professional Degree— Non-Degree	0.02	0.15	0.00	1.00	D
Family Type (Two-parents = 1; Single Parent/Other = 0)	0.77	0.42	0.00	1.00	D
Total Number in Household	4.55	1.35	2.00	15.00	C
Socioeconomic Status	–0.06	0.77	–2.96	2.88	C
Classroom Characteristics					
Teacher's Job Satisfaction	4.42	0.60	1.00	5.00	SC
Percentage of gifted/talented students	2.83	6.02	0.00	62.50	C
Percentage of Repeating 1st Grade	4.65	6.29	0.00	87.50	C
Percentage Reading Below Grade Level	22.01	16.15	0.00	100.00	C
Percentage Math Skills Below Grade	15.55	13.97	0.00	100.00	C
Teacher Rating of Class Behavior	3.40	0.91	1.00	5.00	SC
School Characteristics					
Public vs. Private (Public = 0; Private = 1)	0.14	0.34	0.00	1.00	D
Large and Mid-Size City	0.32	0.47	0.00	1.00	D
Large and Mid-Size Suburb	0.42	0.49	0.00	1.00	D
Small Town and Rural	0.26	0.44	0.00	1.00	D
Percentage of Minority Students	0.31	0.46	0.00	1.00	C
Teacher Rating of School Climate	0.82	0.38	0.00	1.00	SC

[a]Variable type is: continuous (C), dummy (D), and scale (SC).

The variables were entered into the equation in separate steps, one group of variables added at a time, generating a total of six models (forward regression). Entering sets of variables in separate steps allows us to observe whether or not any initially observed effects remain unchanged after inclusion of additional control variables. It is also of interest to observe which control variables, once entered into a model, seem to explain away previously observed effects. A baseline model including only "parental expectation" was estimated first (model 1). Subsequently, another group of variables representing "parental involvement activities" was added to the previous model, generating model 2; in the next step, the set of variables representing "student's characteristics" was added (model 3), and so on, until all the variables were included in the equation (model 6). (See table 3.2 to view all of the models.)

The main interest is to know whether parental involvement has a significant effect on children's approaches to learning and if so, how large the effect is and whether it persists after controlling for other characteristics. In addition, we are interested in knowing which types of parental involvement variables are associated with first graders' motivation to learn.

STUDY RESULTS

A comparison of the models tested in a series of multiple regression analyses is presented in table 3.2. The impact of each independent or control variable on children's approaches to learning is given by their respective coefficients in the final model. In order to assess the magnitude of each variable's impact, we ask ourselves: for a unit change in this independent/ control variable, how much does the variable "approaches to learning" change, holding all other variables constant? The answers are presented in this section in standard deviation units of the variable approaches to learning.[37] This gives us a practical way to compare the magnitude of the changes in the outcome variable associated with each independent and control variable. To convert the regression coefficients found in table 3.2 into standard deviations, we simply divide each regression coefficient by the standard deviation of the variable approaches to learning (Mean = 3.02; Standard Deviation = 0.71). For example, to know the effect of the variable "family SES," divide .093 by .71 = .13; this means that for a unit increase in the SES scale, the variable approaches to learning is expected to rise by .13 standard deviations. As a rule of thumb, we consider changes around .10 of a standard deviation to be small, around .30 of a standard deviation to be moderate, and half a standard deviation or above to be large.

Parental Involvement

A significant positive moderate effect was found for parental expectation, which persisted after controlling for all other variables. Children of parents who expect them to graduate from college score .31 standard deviations above the children whose parents expect them to finish high school only. Expectation of parents that their children will graduate at higher levels has an even greater effect: .40 of a standard deviation for expected master's degree completion, and a similar .39 of a standard deviation for expected PhD completion. What does this mean? Suppose that a child who is expected to

Table 3.2. Unstandardized Regression Coefficients for Spring 2000 First Graders' Approaches to Learning (N = 10,235). Standard Errors Presented in Parentheses.

Variables	Model 1		Model 2		Model 3	
Intercept	2.630***	(.021)	2.507***	(.043)	2.881***	(.05)
Parental Expectation						
Complete College	0.425***	(.023)	0.339***	(.024)	0.291***	(.024)
Master's or Equivalent	0.522***	(.029)	0.422***	(.03)	0.389***	(.029)
PhD/Advanced Degree	0.449***	(.03)	0.386***	(.03)	0.355***	(.029)
Parental Involvement						
Recreational Activities			-0.003	(.015)	0.031*	(.014)
Academic Activities			0.000	(.013)	-0.017	(.012)
How Many Books Child Has			0.037***	(.005)	0.022***	(.005)
Home Computer Access (Yes = 1; No = 0)			0.184***	(.016)	0.148***	(.016)
Student's Characteristics						
Male					-0.276***	(.013)
Black or African American					-0.213***	(.022)
Hispanic					-0.040	(.022)
Asian					0.101*	(.048)
Other Race					-0.080*	(.033)
Home Language of Child (English = 1; Other = 0)					-0.036	(.027)
Child's Absenteeism					-0.003***	(.001)
Child's Tardiness					-0.013***	(.001)
Child Attends Day Care Before/After School					-0.085***	(.018)

(continued)

*p < .05 **p < .01 ***p < .001

Table 3.2. (*continued*)

Variables	Model 4		Model 5		Model 6	
Intercept	2.874***	(.06)	2.817***	(.084)	2.836***	(.086)
Parental Expectation						
Complete College	0.238***	(.024)	0.227***	(.024)	0.225***	(.024)
Master's or Equivalent	0.309***	(.03)	0.293***	(.03)	0.289***	(.03)
PhD/Advanced Degree	0.296***	(.03)	0.286***	(.03)	0.279***	(.03)
Parental Involvement						
Recreational Activities	0.032*	(.014)	0.034*	(.014)	0.038**	(.014)
Academic Activities	−0.017	(.012)	−0.020	(.012)	−0.022	(.012)
How Many Books Child Has	0.007	(.006)	0.006	(.006)	0.006	(.006)
Home Computer Access (Yes = 1; No = 0)	0.077***	(.016)	0.069***	(.016)	0.073***	(.016)
Student's Characteristics						
Male	−0.279***	(.013)	−0.270***	(.013)	−0.270***	(.013)
Black or African American	−0.151***	(.022)	−0.139***	(.022)	−0.170***	(.025)
Hispanic	−0.005	(.022)	−0.009	(.022)	−0.037	(.023)
Asian	0.085	(.048)	0.066	(.047)	0.049	(.047)
Other Race	−0.057	(.033)	−0.040	(.033)	−0.058	(.034)
Home Language of Child (English = 1; Other = 0)	−0.053	(.027)	−0.068*	(.027)	−0.059*	(.027)
Child's Absenteeism	−0.002**	(.001)	−0.002**	(.001)	−0.002**	(.001)
Child's Tardiness	−0.012***	(.001)	−0.011***	(.001)	−0.011***	(.001)
Child Attends Day Care Before/After School	−0.096***	(.018)	−0.096***	(.018)	−0.097***	(.018)

Family Characteristics

	Model 1	Model 2	Model 3
Parents Education—College Completed or Not	0.058** (.019)	0.059** (.019)	0.058** (.019)
Parents Education—Master's Degree	0.076* (.039)	0.076* (.038)	0.072 (.038)
Parents Education—Doctorate/Adv. Degree	-0.066 (.048)	-0.061 (.048)	-0.063 (.048)
Parents Education—Other No Degree Program	0.065 (.049)	0.065 (.049)	0.061 (.049)
Family Type (Two-Parents = 1; Single Parent/Other = 0)	0.104*** (.018)	0.106*** (.018)	0.109*** (.018)
Total Number in Household	0.006 (.006)	0.008 (.006)	0.007 (.006)
SES—Continuous	0.099*** (.016)	0.083*** (.016)	0.093*** (.017)
Classroom Characteristics			
Teacher's Job Satisfaction		0.034** (.011)	0.037** (.012)
Percentage of Gifted/Talented Students		0.000 (.001)	0.000 (.001)
Percentage of Repeating First Grade		0.002* (.001)	0.002 (.001)
Percentage Reading Below			
Grade Level		-0.001* (.001)	-0.002* (.001)
Percentage Math Skills Below Grade Level		-0.003*** (.001)	-0.003*** (.001)
Group Misbehaves Very Frequently		-0.083 (.046)	-0.087 (.046)
Group Misbehaves Frequently		-0.047* (.024)	-0.048* (.024)
Group Misbehaves Occasionally		-0.045** (.016)	-0.050** (.016)
Group Behaves Exceptionally Well		0.098*** (.024)	0.095*** (.023)
School Characteristics			
Public vs. Private (Public = 0; Private = 1)			-0.072*** (.021)
Large and Mid-Size Suburb			-0.025 (.016)
Small Town and Rural			-0.013 (.019)
Percentage of Minority Students (less than 50% = 0; more than 50% = 1)			0.060*** (.019)
Teacher Rating of School Staff (Low = 0; High = 1)			-0.012 (.019)

*p < .05 **p < .01 ***p < .001

complete only high school scores at the fiftieth percentile in the distribution of approaches to learning scores. How much better are the other children doing? According to these results, a child expected to graduate from college will be at the sixty-second percentile of the same distribution, and a child expected to complete a master's degree or a PhD will be at the sixty-fifth percentile in their approaches to learn. This is a considerable difference in how children perform in their motivation level at such an early stage in their academic journey.

With regard to parental activities with the child, only the variable parental involvement/recreational activities reached statistical significance, and the effect is quite small (only .05 of a standard deviation). It should, however, be placed in the context of the scale used for the parental involvement/recreational activities, which asks parents the frequency at which they engage in these activities with their child: not at all, once or twice a week, three to six times a week, every day. This means that as parents move from one category of this scale to the next higher level, their child's score on approaches to learning will increase by .05 of a standard deviation. When comparing children whose parents report similar levels of engagement, the differences in approaches to learning might seem negligible; only if one compares a child whose parent is "not at all" involved to a child whose parents engage in these activities "every day," there should be a more clear contrast. All else being equal, assuming that the former child starts off at the fiftieth percentile, the latter is predicted to be at the fifty-sixth percentile, a small but noticeable difference.

Parental involvement in academic activities did not reach statistical significance. Similarly, how many books a child has shows no bearing on how the student scores in the approaches to learning variable. Having access to a home computer has a positive, significant, but small effect: an increase of .10 of a standard deviation in approaches to learning is expected for a child who has computer access at home as compared to a child who does not.

Student Characteristics

A significant gender and race effect were found in the analyses. The results show a negative effect for boys; they score much lower than girls with similar background characteristics in their approaches to learning (.38 of a standard deviation lower). This is a considerable effect in magnitude: compared to a girl who scores at the fiftieth percentile, a boy who is similar to her in other ways will score at the thirty-fifth percentile in their approaches to learn. This is a surprisingly large gender gap in motivation and is similar in magnitude to the parental expectation effects. A small but significant and negative effect was found for blacks/African Americans as compared to white students (-.24 standard deviations); this means that a black student is predicted to be at the fortieth percentile in his/her approaches to learning when a white student with similar background variables scores at the fiftieth percentile. The racial divide was not found among the other ethnicities when compared to white students, all else held constant.

Home language of the child and whether the child receives center-based care were also found to be related to children's approaches to learning. Non-native English speakers score .08 standard deviations higher than their native-English counterparts, all else being equal (though this is a slight advantage, it could be seen as an asset that teachers can tap on in trying to help these students improve achievement). Finally, children receiving day care score .14 standard deviations lower than the others who are equal on all other variables.

Family Characteristics

The results related to parental education show a positive, significant effect for college-educated, as compared to high-school-educated parents. Note that parents' actual education level plays a much smaller role in their children's motivation to learn (expected change is only .08 standard deviations) in comparison to the more pronounced impact of parental expectation as seen previously. A child whose parents graduated from college will score at the fifty-third percentile in the approaches to learning distribution, compared to a child whose parents have only a high school diploma and is at the fiftieth percentile. In addition, children who live in a two-parent household score .15 standard deviations higher in approaches to learning than those in a single-parent household; higher SES also predicts higher scores in motivation (.13 standard deviations increase for each unit increase in the SES scale).

Classroom and School Characteristics

With regard to classroom characteristics, small, significant and positive effects were found for teacher's job satisfaction (.05 of a standard deviation) and for the overall class behavior (.13 standard deviation). The effect of school sector is significant and in the unexpected direction; children in private schools are found to score slightly lower in approaches to learning than their peers in public schools (a difference of .10 of a standard deviation). This could be a function of the expectations that teachers in each type of school have for their children, which might cause them to rate children differently, but this cannot be ascertained. The proportion of minority students in a school also has a small effect on how children score in their approaches to learning: children in schools that have more than 50 percent of minority students score .08 standard deviations higher in their approaches to learning than those in other schools, all else held constant.

DISCUSSION OF STUDY FINDINGS

The primary research question investigated in this study was: does parental involvement have an effect on first graders' approaches to learning? The second research question focused on discerning which parental activities yield the most benefit for children's motivation to learn.

The results of the regression analyses reveal a significant positive effect of parental involvement on children's approaches to learning. Of all parental involvement indicators tested, parental expectations have the largest positive effect on how children approach the task of learning. From very early on, parents' high academic expectations for their children seem to have an impact on their children's motivation that is even greater than the parents' actual educational attainment levels, and other parental involvement variables. That children's approaches to learn can be influenced at such an early age by aspirations that seem to be projected so far ahead in the future is striking: it suggests that this might be a key ingredient for how parents can set off their children in a positive lifelong learning journey. Examining further other dimensions of this variable might be a worthwhile development as it might reveal other aspects of parents' involvement, such as how parental expectation is conveyed to the children.

Despite the well-documented evidence linking parental involvement to academic achievement, when turning our attention to motivational outcomes, the results show no significant effect for parental involvement/academic activities. Instead, it is the set of recreational activities that are significantly related to children's approaches to learning although their effect is relatively small in comparison to the more substantial effect of parental expectations. To think that parental engagement in recreational activities significantly predicts children's approaches to learning while engagement in academic activities does not is counterintuitive. As noted before, the interconnections between the determinants of student's motivation and student's academic performance are very difficult to disentangle. More sophisticated models specifying the paths by which possible common determinants affect both variables are needed. It is possible, however, that these results are tapping into the motivational nature of our dependent variable rather than its relation to academic performance.

CONCLUSION

Collectively, these findings underscore the importance of what parents expect of their children even beyond the activities that they might engage in on a regular basis with their child. As observed previously, lower expectations might be enough to represent a motivational gap among children at the onset of their academic life, which might have long-term consequences for how they perform in school. The importance of parental expectation had already been asserted in previous research with respect to their positive impact on children's academic performance; its motivational effect had also been found in small-scale studies, and in large-scale studies among high school students. The current study adds to this stream of findings by confirming the substantial impact that parental expectation has on children's motivation to learn in elementary grades with the particular advantage of having used a nationally representative database of first graders.

Some additional noteworthy and unexpected findings were revealed, namely, the presence of a gender gap and a racial gap in first graders' motivation to learn. The magnitude of these effects makes them worrisome. It raises questions about whether the motivation measure is biased (reflecting teachers' perceptions more than actual motivation) or whether classroom influences might be fostering this gender and racial gap, which calls for further investigation.

On the policy front, some of the parental variables that were found to be significant hold some promise for action in that they, unlike SES, represent factors in the children's environment that are more amenable to change and may represent a real improvement in children's early education. In principle, programs can be designed (or reformulated) to disseminate the findings on parental expectation. It would be important to evaluate these programs for further evidence that parental expectation has the potential to produce increases in students' motivation. Our analyses leave a lot of unanswered questions. What cannot be learned from this study, for example, is what the determinants of parental expectation are, how these aspirations are formed, and how difficult it is to change them. What does it take to have a parent change the academic expectation that they hold for their child? Is it something that can be fostered in a parental involvement training/program, or is it the result of a lifelong history of influences and solidified beliefs? Which is easier to alter: the parents' aspirations for their child or their routine habits with the child? Does improving one tend to improve the other as well? These are interesting questions for further study and should keep this discussion open to new evaluations of how parents can better help their children succeed in the lifelong task of learning.

NOTES

*The author extends her gratitude to Dr. Sophia Catsambis and Dr. Roger Peach for encouragement and generous feedback.

1. *Parental Involvement: Title I, Part A. Non-Regulatory Guidance* (No Child Left Behind: Department of Education, 2004).

2. *What Research Says about Parent Involvement in Children's Education in Relation to Academic Achievement* (Michigan Department of Education, March 2002).

3. Alissa R. Gonzalez, "Parental Involvement: Its Contribution to High School Students' Motivation," *Clearing House* 75, no. 3 (2002): 132.

4. Sophia Catsambis, "Parental Involvement in Education," in *Blackwell Encyclopedia of Sociology*, ed. G. Ritzer (Malden, MA: Blackwell Publishing, 2007).

5. Gonzalez, "Parental Involvement, High School."

6. Nancy E. Hill et al., "Parent Academic Involvement as Related to School Behavior, Achievement, and Aspirations: Demographic Variations across Adolescence," *Child Development* 75, no. 5 (2004): 1491–1509.

7. Adeline Villas-Boas, "The Effects of Parental Involvement in Homework on Student Achievement in Portugal and Luxembourg," *Childhood Education* 74, no. 6 (1998): 367–71.

8. Paul R. Pintrich and Dale H. Schunk, *Motivation in Education, Theory, Research, and Applications* (Upper Saddle River, NJ: Merrill Prentice Hall, 2002).

9. Paul R. Pintrich and E. De Groot, "Motivational and Self-regulated Learning Components of Classroom Academic Performance," *Journal of Educational Psychology* 82 (1990): 33–40.

10. Barry Zimmerman and J. Ringle, "Effects of Model Persistence and Statements of Confidence on Children's Self-efficacy and Problem Solving," *Journal of Educational Psychology* 73 (1981): 485–93.

11. Catsambis, "Parental Involvement in Education."

12. Joyce L. Epstein, *School, Family, and Community Partnerships: Preparing Educators and Improving Schools* (Boulder, CO: Westview Press, 2001).

13. Hill, "Parental Involvement, School Behavior, Aspirations."

14. Pintrich and Schunk, *Motivation in Education.*

15. Catsambis, "Parental Involvement in Education."

16. Joyce L. Epstein, "School and Family Partnerships," in *Encyclopedia of Educational Research*, ed. M. Alkin (New York: MacMillan, 1992).

17. Sophia Catsambis, *Expanding Knowledge of Parental Involvement in Secondary Education: Effects on High School Academic Success* (Center for Research on the Education of Students Placed At Risk, CRESPAR, 1998).

18. Katheline V. Hoover-Dempsey and Howard M. Sandler, "Why Do Parents Become Involved in Their Children's Education?" in *Review of Educational Research* 67, no. 1 (1997): 3–42.

19. Gonzalez, "Parental Involvement, High School."

20. Catsambis, "Parental Involvement in Education."

21. A meta-analysis provides a rigorous and systematic way to summarize the findings of multiple quantitative studies examining the same research question. In meta-analysis, a researcher is interested in the effect size of a particular intervention, program, or policy (or a relationship between variables) across a number of separate studies.

22. Xitao Fan and Michael Chen, "Parental Involvement and Students' Academic Achievement: A Meta-Analysis," in *Educational Psychology Review* 13, no. 1 (2001): 1–22.

23. Catsambis, "Parental Involvement in Education."

24. Epstein, *School, Family, Community Partnerships.*

25. Hill, "Parental Involvement, School Behavior, Aspirations."

26. Catsambis, *Expanding Knowledge, Parental Involvement.*

27. Quoted in Catsambis, *Expanding Knowledge, Parental Involvement.*

28. Gonzalez, "Parental Involvement, High School."

29. Epstein, "School and Family Partnerships."

30. Catsambis, *Expanding Knowledge, Parental Involvement.*

31. Kevin Marjoribanks, "Family Learning Environments and Students' Outcomes: A Review," *Journal of Comparative Family Studies* 27, no. 2 (1996): 373–94.

32. Epstein, *School, Family, Community Partnerships.*

33. Karen L. Bierman et al., "Behavioral and Cognitive Readiness for School: Cross-Domain Associations for Children Attending Head Start," *Social Development* 18 (2009): 305–23.

34. Marjoribanks, "Family Learning Environments."

35. Robert Bradley et al., "The Home Environments of Children in the United States Part II: Relations with Behavioral Development through Age Thirteen," in *Child Development* 72, no. 6 (2001): 1868–86.

36. *User's Manual for the ECLS-K Longitudinal Kindergarten-First Grade Public-Use Data Files and Electronic Codebook* (Washington, DC: U.S. Department of Education, National Center for Educational Statistics, 2002). Available at nces.ed.gov/pubsearch.

37. The scores observed on a given variable (say on "approaches to learning") vary from student to student. Some children score at the mean value of the scale (the average for the entire sample), some will be above the mean, and some will be below; the "distance" from the mean can be computed for each student and totaled for the entire sample. When the total amount of this variation around the mean is averaged across all the students, the value obtained is called a "standard deviation." A standard deviation has the advantage of corresponding to known probabilities in a normal curve, which allows for the computation of percentiles.

4

Frayed Patchwork: The Need for Public Policy to Address Short-Term Child Care Needs*

Loretta L. C. Brady

All parents face the challenge of finding reliable and quality care for their children when they want or need to be away for a few hours at a time. It seems likely that the naturally occurring social network in which a parent resides would be able to meet the demands of such short-term care, yet that is not always the case. Some communities are beginning to identify this as an unmet need and are finding ways to formally fill this gap in care. What drives this need? Which factors influence a family's need? What models exist for meeting these care needs, and what policies might address the need for such care most effectively? This chapter explores the need for short-term child care (STCC), identifies sources contributing to this need, and examines policies which may be altered or expanded to address the need that has been identified. Finally, U.S. and international models of short-term care are examined and considered in the context of existing U.S. child care policy.

BACKGROUND AND HISTORY

Mothers' workforce participation has steadily climbed since 1975, with 79 percent of U.S. women with children under the age of eighteen working at least part time.[1] Recent reports of the economic downturn[2] indicate a higher proportion of women than men who are employed during the current recessionary period, further cementing employment participation rates among women and heralding a new era in child care arrangement needs. Beginning in the 1990s, federal and state policies were enacted to assist working and nonworking low-income parents in their move from public assistance toward self-sufficiency. Included with these initiatives were tax benefits, vouchers, and subsidies designed to alleviate the expense of child care, which could take up to 30 percent of low-income earnings.[3] The 1996 Personal Responsibility and Work Opportunities Reconciliation Act (PRWORA) consolidated an array of subsidy programs, streamlining the administration of funds dedicated to improving access to and quality of formal child care. By 2002, U.S. federal spending on child care had risen to $11.8 billion per year.[4] Child care access has been largely credited as the single best predictor of women's workforce participation.[5]

Even as access to formal child care among low-income earners has expanded, the demands of child care needs have not been equally met; parents working nonstandard work hours, split shifts, or whose work shifts vary from week to week may find it difficult to establish formal care arrangements for their children. This in turn has an impact on the access and utilization of relevant child care subsidy benefits.[6] Families are often stuck using informal care providers or leaving children unsupervised for varying lengths of time. When parenting demands conflict with work demands, parents often have to face the untenable choice between job security and child safety.[7]

CHILD CARE POLICY

In seeking to address policy that would have the largest impact on the availability and utilization of STCC, existing child care subsidy policies could be influenced. Currently subsidies do not address short-term child care needs and in fact are structured in such a way that they discourage short-term care arrangements. Subsidies were created in part to offset the cost of child care for families and to increase workforce participation, but in their application they have also expanded the need and availability of child care centers and licensed providers.[8] Such expanded need has been met with an increase in professionalization, market rates for pay, and quality of care.[9] Licensure requirements, although varied by state, have also become more stringent in the face of such advances, and these factors have further constrained the availability of professional short-term care.[10] The funding increased quality; the increase in quality prompts new regulations, which then dictate the shape of further arrangements.

Payments for care are often pro-rated so that a provider receives a maximum payment benefit for providing four or more hours of care. Formal daycares meet this requirement with their own standards for enrollment, often requiring parents to enroll their child for a minimum of four hours per day. State child care licensing places reasonable limits on the maximum enrollment in both home and center-based care, and here we see the conflict between subsidy policy, daycare availability, and parent needs for short-term care. If a parent can locate a center or provider, he or she cannot use his/her subsidy to run an errand and leave the child for only a few hours without jeopardizing the child's enrollment status. A center or provider that does accept short-term stays would have to be willing to forgo the spot for a child who could attend full time.

SOCIAL NETWORKS AS SOURCES OF INFORMAL CARE

Social networks are one solution to meeting care needs, but several factors have influenced their availability, success, and utilization. Family estrangement, distance from family, or distance between social network members and children's school or parents' work location all limit the availability of such care solutions for some families.[11] Reports have found this to be particularly true for lower-income single-parent families[12] whose need for and use of such networks may be more intense, while their ability to access and reciprocate within such networks may be strained.[13] This disparity of access is no small matter. Research indicates that mothers who had documented cases of neglect due to lack of parental supervision also had fewer positive interactions within their own family networks and higher numbers of network members with unsafe conditions (i.e., mental illness, substance abuse problems, poor living conditions).[14]

While the need for short-term care is not the barrier to employment that prompted subsidy creation, the lack of formalized options for such care does present burdens for families. These are burdens that may be disproportionately shared by our lowest income earners, parents working variable shifts, and families who are estranged or otherwise isolated from kin networks. Although employment participation has increased with the use of subsidies among low- and median-income families, these programs have not and were not intended to address parent need for short-term flexible child care. Restrictions for using subsidies vary at the local level and often include limits on parent activities while accessing subsidized care; parents may be engaged in education- or job-related activities but often are not allowed to use subsidized care for time spent out of these activities. In fact, low-income parents seeking to increase self-sufficiency while using subsidies may place their child care vouchers in jeopardy should they use subsidized care to attend to non-employment-related activities. Parents address their need for short-term care through a combination of formal and informal care including bartering or trade for services, paid babysitters, and kin care.[15] Parents paying for their own child care and with flexible work schedules may accomplish time away without any extraordinary efforts, but for many families such activities require a complicated array of solutions.

RESPITE CARE

The impact of this burden for families, like the burden itself, is frequently invisible. A tiny fraction of parents trigger neglect cases for leaving their child un- or undersupervised,[16] while the number of parents forgoing important personal or professional time away due to lack of short-term care options is unevaluated. While for most families the need and benefits of this type of care arrangement is unknown, there are populations of families for whom such care is well established: those whose children have medical or developmental needs and those whose children have emotional or behavioral disorders.[17] Respite care programs designed for these special need populations do exist, and funding for such programs emphasizes the cost-effectiveness[18] of these care arrangements in the context of high resource utilization. Intervention-based respite care (IBRC) such as this can include overnight, in-home, and out-of-home child care for a specific high-needs child within a family.

One study of parents of emotionally and behaviorally disordered children found that the benefits of short-term respite care included decreased parent stress, decreased need for out-of-home placement, and improved child functioning.[19] Medical respite care programs have also been examined, and their use has generally been promoted as a way of restoring caregiving parents who might otherwise become overly taxed by their children's complex care needs.[20] Respite care in its various forms has been demonstrated to benefit families, children, and to have documented cost benefits by reducing out-of-home placement, decreasing crisis intervention needs, and increasing the ability of parents to remain functioning caregivers.[21]

Funding for IBRC generally flows from one of three sources: (1) mental health treatment funding for identified children; (2) health and social service funding for children with medical needs or developmental delays; and (3) child protection service funding for children at risk of abuse or neglect or for families of adopted children.[22] Support for funding generally comes from evidence that providing community-based support decreases the costs associated with crisis intervention, out-of-home placements, or more serious medical care and hospitalization. While these are not costs or benefits that one could expect of short-term care, there are likely tangible and intangible benefits to be derived from short-term care models. Indeed, the need and use of IBRC programs overlap the needs that parents of any child might cite as their reason for short-term care: time to attend to personal needs, time to attend to needs of other children, time to rest or restore themselves, and time to experience greater independence/flexibility in not having to plan outings based on a child's need, rhythms, or schedules.[23]

Child care is an established need with policies to insure access, quality, and funding. Short-term care for special-needs children and their families is also an identified need, with policies established to insure access and funding for those most in need of IBRC. The gap appears to be in policies that address the needs of families who are socially isolated, with few social capital and financial resources, or who prefer even short-term care to be provided by trusted professionals. No policies exist that address non-intervention-based short-term care needs. Researchers need to identify and quantify the need for this type of care and examine the impact that the lack of such programs and policies has on children, families, and communities. It is also important to explore models that might address the unmet needs for this type of care.

CURRENT STUDY

A community-based needs assessment was conducted in 2007–2008 in southern New Hampshire for the purpose of better understanding the interest and availability of short-term child care within this community. A group of professionals and community members initiated a local needs assessment to determine the type of non-intervention-based STCC that parents would be interested in, as well as the location, costs, and access preferences they would request if such care were available. The data from this community assessment are offered here as one example that further defines the need and role of respite care in current child care policy developments.

METHODS

Procedures

The survey instrument was collaboratively created and approved through a local and academic Institutional Review Board (IRB) process. The survey asked participants to describe the composition of their family and the ages and needs of their minor children. It also inquired as to their current options for short-term child care, their general experience and satisfaction with current options, and their interest and needs for community-based short-term respite care, as well as hours, location of care, barriers to utilization, and preferred costs for care if it were to be provided in their local community. Surveys were then distributed to five area agencies serving the state's largest city. A total of 250 surveys, including forty Spanish-language surveys, were distributed to five area agencies.

At the start of the assessment, the agencies reported that they served approximately 1,665 families with children under age fourteen. This age was selected by the members of the study group as it represented the age at which most families feel comfortable leaving a child unsupervised for short periods of time. In total, fifty-eight completed surveys were received from the five agencies, representing 20 percent of the surveys distributed, but only 3.5 percent of the reported families served. It is likely that many families interface with more than one of the agencies included in this selection process; given this, the selection rate may in fact be an underestimate as respondents were instructed to respond to the survey only once even if presented the survey at more than one location.

Sample Demographics

Sixty-eight percent of the sample were European American, 22.4 percent were Hispanic (12 percent of survey respondents completed Spanish-language surveys indicating a preference for Spanish-language materials), 5 percent reported being of African descent, 3 percent were multiracial, 3 percent were Asian, and 5 percent reported being Native American. These sociocultural demographics represent a more diverse sample than that found in the broader community from which the sample was drawn; the 2000 U.S. Census reported a population that was 91.75 percent European American.[24] This difference in sociocultural ratios may indicate a greater utilization or need for social service supports among the city's ethnic and racial minority population. Nine percent of respondents reported a live-in partner, 32.8 percent were married, 32.8 percent were single, 15.5 percent were divorced, 7 percent were separated, and 1 percent was widowed. The mean age for respondents was 33.18; 50 percent of respondents were the only adult in their household. Families reported an average of 2.41 children. Twenty-five percent reported one child, 28 percent reported having two children, and 44 percent reported three or more children. In total, parents reported on their care needs for 135 children between the ages of birth and fourteen years. Mean ages of children varied by position within the family. First born children were $M = 7.38$ years, while fifth- and sixth-born children were $M = 4.0$ years of age. Overall mean ages of children reported placed the children between pre-kindergarten and second grade ages.

Family income ranged from less than $5,000 to more than $100,000 with 75 percent earning less than $25,001 per year. Participants were able to indicate more than one source of income, and 60 percent of respondents obtained their income from paid employment, 24 percent reported receiving TANF benefits, 29 percent reported receiving disability benefits, and 19 percent reported receiving child support.

Parents reported that their children were enrolled in full- or part-time daycare (34 percent), preschool (53 percent), and school (75 percent). Some of the parents reported that their children needed special educational supports (45 percent), and at least a third of the children reportedly had emotional difficulties (31 percent), behavioral difficulties (35 percent), and medical needs (30 percent).

RESULTS

Parents indicated a strong interest in professional short-term child care with 60 percent being "somewhat" to "very interested" in seeing such care developed, and 54 percent indicating they would "regularly" or "always" utilize such care should it become available. As further support, parents indicated that their current STCC solutions were less than ideal with 33 percent indicating they could rely on their current care provider only "rarely." Although most respondents reported relying on a relative (45 percent) or partner (25 percent) to provide short-term child care, 38 percent of parents indicated they preferred professional care over in-home care, with an additional 31 percent reporting no preference in types of arrangements. For those who reported a preference between in-home and center-based care, they had this preference because they either liked their child to interact with other children when possible (31 percent) or their child preferred familiar surroundings (25 percent). Parents were asked to indicate the reason for their preference, and parents choosing "in-home care" most often reported their child's preference for familiarity, while parents indicating center-based care cited their desire for interaction.

With 76–80 percent of parents reporting they would access STCC if it were available, it is clear that a market existed within this community for such care. Eighty six percent of respondents indicated that they could afford no more than $5 per hour for such care, while a substantial minority indicated they could not afford any fee for such care.

Parents reported an interest in short-term care primarily to assist in getting to appointments (55 percent), running errands, or having a break (each endorsed by 45 percent of sample). When asked questions regarding difficulties faced because they did not have care available parents offered unsettling feedback. While overall parents felt they could rely on care provided by relatives or close friends, at least 33 percent indicated that they have left a child in care they felt uncomfortable using at least once, and nearly 20 percent of parents "sometimes" to "regularly" had this experience.

Table 4.1.   **What Are You Missing Out On?**

Event Missed	Reporting "Yes" (%)
Personal Time	56.9
Medical or Dental Appointment/Self	46.6
Medical or Dental Appointment/Child	24.1
Job Interview	20.7
Financial or Benefits Meeting	19
School Meeting	13.8
Court	8.6

Additionally when parents have decided not to utilize available care, they reported having to miss their own or other children's appointments. Table 4.1 presents the percentage of respondents who reported missing important events due to lack of dependable STCC. It is clearly a struggle for families to balance their children's care needs with their own efforts to improve their family's well-being, and there is little support currently to assist them in their efforts. One participant said when asked to comment on her experiences:

> I find it hard being a single mom trying to juggle work and my children's needs. Due to the fact that I don't have transportation to run errands and pick up my children, short-term child care would be very beneficial to single moms trying to do everything that needs to be done.

CONCLUSION

The results of the needs assessment within this one community reveal that across income levels, ethnic backgrounds, and child stages, families identify short-term care as a need that has a significant impact on their family's success. A substantial minority indicated they have had to choose uncomfortable care arrangements at least once to attend to life's demands, with one in five stating that they have to make this choice with some frequency. While these findings prompt a consideration of policy and policy revision, this study is not without its limitations. The sample, drawn from one small U.S. city in New England, was not reflective of other cities, and indeed may not have been representative, at least culturally, of the city from which it was drawn. Because surveys were not offered to all agency visitors, and because no note was made of how many refused participation, it is impossible to determine the response rate for this survey, a well-established technique in evaluating the generalizability of the findings. That said, this needs assessment appears to have captured well the population and the needs of those served by the agencies participating in the poll. As results were shared with the group which sought the assessment, their familiarity with the needs identified appear to support the generalizability of these findings within this community. Overall the findings support an examination of policies and practices across communities that might respond to the needs found within this community.

What revisions to current policy might result in solutions for this or similar communities? Expanding the current care network so that children do not have to change providers and parents can form the trusting relationship that predicts positive outcomes would be ideal.[25] Such a solution might be achieved by enabling those who provide full-time care that is paid for through subsidies to be reimbursed for care that is drop-in or "ad hoc" for existing client families. Costs for this expansion might be managed with limits on the number of hours per month or quarter that a family could use short-term care. Costs might be made up in the form of greater job stability as many parents with vulnerable networks also have low-tenure hourly wage jobs that are jeopardized by absences. For those parents utilizing subsidies to pay for child care, they would be able to access an existing resource in a manner that would provide minimal disruption for their children and would not imperil their continued subsidy access.

A second alternative may be to encourage providers to offer a minimum number of drop-in spots in their center, which they could then offer to the community for such purposes. These centers might be offered a partial subsidy or tax benefit for holding such spots open if they are underutilized, and they may be able to collect a fee from a family that does utilize the spot. Each of these possibilities would require minimal alterations to current models but would greatly expand the formal network of providers for families that are most in need of short-term care. Even these changes, however, may not fully address the needs cited in the community assessment for school-aged children or for nontraditional working hours. These changes may require legislative actions, and as such other alternatives need consideration. What local, national, or international models might serve as a guide to creating programs and changing policy so that short-term care is reliably available for families most in need?

Alternative Models of Short-Term Child Care

New Hampshire

On a local level, parents in one New Hampshire community are able to participate in a cooperatively run child and family resource center which offers parenting classes, "baby and me" activities, and also operates a drop-in child care center for infants to preschool age children which parents may utilize for up to two to three hours at a time, up to six to nine hours per week depending on children's ages.[26] Parents pay a nominal fee for the service ($3 to $5 per hour) and an annual membership fee based on a sliding scale depending on family income. Parents may also volunteer to provide care in exchange for use of the center. This long-standing community solution has been in existence for over twenty-five years and is one example of care, but its limitations are worth noting. For one, some parents with limited networks or unique circumstances might not be able to reciprocate in offering care for someone else's children. Another obstacle in this arrangement would be the age limitations imposed, with school-age children having to be cared for through other means. Finally, this center is not conveniently located to public transportation lines, a common limitation in the state of New Hampshire, but one which in all communities would greatly impact the success or utilization of any care arrangement, short-term or otherwise.

Ottawa, Canada

Parents in Ottawa, Canada, may access STCC, referred to by the operating agency as "backup" care, through a pilot public/private partnership.[27] Local businesses pay an enrollment fee to an established child care center. This fee enables each company to offer backup child care to employees as a work/life benefit. Care is provided flexibly, either in the child's home, in a center with available space, or in a licensed provider's home. The STCC service facilitates trainings as well as performs background and quality assurance checks on providers and acts as the central information agency, fielding calls from families in need of care and locating providers who can meet that need in a variety of settings.

This innovative solution began in the late 1980s and experienced periods of inconsistent use and funding. Once businesses in the community weighed the costs of replacing trained staff against the costs of facilitating short-term care, many businesses were eager to participate to make the service a sustainable offering. Over the years of operation, lessons about staff recruiting and retention, as well as information about the seasonal demands for such care, have assisted this center in managing its resources and providing the widest possible array of care services for their participating families. Recent initiatives have sought to link short-term child care with a similar model of elder care services, a need beyond the scope but intimately linked to the topic of this chapter.

North Carolina

Some communities with many affluent families have identified a market for providing structured short-term care and have established for-profit companies to meet the demand. Three such entities are Kidspot, Bizikids, and Right Time Kids, all located in North Carolina.[28] These for-profit centers provide hourly child care for preschool to school-aged kids in an environment staffed by safety-trained play facilitators. Although each has its own unique niche, children at each business are free to participate in a variety of activities and may be offered a nap area and a snack at specific times. Business models also vary, with some offering a yearly enrollment fee and a per-hour use charge, and others requiring a per-hour fee.

It is unclear whether these North Carolina models are sustainable since all three list company start dates since the late 1990s, but in the abstract these models provide short-term care solutions for those families who may have limited social networks but for whom occasional paid care is feasible. In order for profit-based models like those found in North Carolina to be more widely applied and to serve a wider array of families, other states' licensure requirements that enable such arrangements (drop-in centers) would need to be examined. Given that all three for-profit centers were located in only a small number of states, it is likely that some states have less stringent licensing requirements for their child care centers. While states may debate the appropriateness of loosening their requirements, some awareness of what requirements might impede or foster drop-in center care could expand service offerings in more communities.

Proposed Solutions

Expansion of current subsidy and professional care access, child care co-operatives, business and organizational commitment to privately subsidize short-term care, and for-profit centers may all individually contribute to reducing the apparent unmet need for safe short-term care solutions, but individually each is imperfect and insufficient to addressing the totality of need documented in at least one New England community. Fostering community awareness and collaborative partnerships is a first step that may enhance the success of those policy makers or community leaders seeking to address the issue of short-term care needs systemically.

Creating a program that offers professionally staffed and trained short-term care in a location that is conveniently located to transportation and school or work locations is ideal. A community may seek to partner with large employers or medical and educational centers to accomplish the task. These private enterprises would see a benefit in facilitating transportation to their location from a drop-in center in order to increase access or utilization of their own products and services, or could see a benefit to service that might enhance the stability of their workforce. Another collaboration might be with health and education service and training programs. Parents of some children report specialized needs either due to health or behavioral concerns. If such health-related respite care is not available in a community, an STCC center might augment center-based care with both provider training and family referral services so that families needing a provider in their home can request and locate appropriate care. Having a center that partners with area higher educational centers might insure a reliable stream of volunteers and students that could augment services provided by a smaller number of professional staff.

Much could be done to reinforce a frayed patchwork of care solutions, and in so doing, policy-makers would strengthen families, improve economic well-being of those most marginalized, and decrease disparity in child care access. There appears to be a desire and need for STCC solutions, and a significant minority of families with fewer economic and social resources have had to make difficult choices in where to leave their children. Parents with few options for care are currently left to settle with poor quality or unreliable short-term care, or forgo necessary appointments, treatments, and training experiences that would otherwise benefit their family. Short-term care structured to respond to their needs would greatly alleviate this forced choice for families. While the need for non-intervention-based respite is newly emerging, there are models for such care that might assist communities in addressing this need more systematically and successfully. A comprehensive examination of child care policy must include questions related to short-term care needs. Without such questions, the need will remain unaddressed even as social and economic changes indicate increasing need.

NOTES

*Special thanks to members of the Respite Care Group who organized and requested this research. In particular, thanks are extended to Beth Prince, Sue Wall, and Wendy Garrity, members of the group that were instrumental in accessing the participants and carrying the torch for the project. Great appreciation is also due to Craig Whitney, who was instrumental in leading the team to manage the data collected for this project. He worked closely with Christopher Tremblay and Kristen Allard, all students at Saint Anselm College who deserve to be recognized for their contributions.

1. (n.d.) Bureau of Labor Statistics, "Working in the 21st century," www.bls.gov/opub/working/home.htm (accessed February, 2009).

2. Rampell, Catherine, "As layoffs surge, women may pass men in the job force." *New York Times*, February 6, 2009, 1.

3. Meyers, Marcia K., and Theresa Heintze, "The performance of the child care subsidy system." *Social Science Review* 39 (1999): 37–68.

4. Schexnayder, Deanna, Daniel Schrodeder, Ying Tang, Laura Lein, Julie Beausoleil, and Gina Amatangelo, June 2004, "The Texas Child Care Subsidy Program

after devolution to the local level." Ray Marshall Center for the Study of Human Resources. www.utexas.edu/research/cshr (accessed January 5, 2009).

5. Danzinger, Sandra K., Elizabeth Oltmans Ananat, and Kimberly Browning, "Childcare subsidies and the transition from welfare to work." *Family Relations* 53 (2004): 219–28

6. Le Bihan, Blanche, and Claude Martin, "Atypical working hours: Consequences for childcare arrangements." *Social Policy & Administration* 38 (2004): 565–90

7. Henly, Julia, and Sandra Lyons, "The negotiation of child care and employment demands among low income parents." *Journal of Social Issues* 56 (2000): 683–706

8. Blau, David, ed., *The Economics of Child Care* (New York: Russel Sage Foundation, 1995); Blau, David, and Erdal Tekin, "The determinants and consequences of child care subsidies for mothers in the USA." *Journal of Population Economics* 20, no. 4 (October 2007): 719–41.

9. Drentea, Patricia, Suzanne Durham, Norman Mwaria, Emily Norman, and Juan Xi, "Day care hopping: stabilizing day care options for low income mothers through subsidies." *Child Care in Practice* 10 (2004): 381–93. Kisker, Ellen, and Rebecca Maynard, "Quality, cost, and parental choice of child care," in *The Economics of Child Care*, ed. David Blau.

10. Brooks, Fred, "Impacts of child care subsidies on family and child well-being." *Early Childhood Research Quarterly* 17 (2002): 498–512.

11. Zippay, Allison, and Anu Ragarajan, "Child care 'packaging' among TANF recipients: Implications for social work." *Child & Adolescent Social Work Journal* 24 (2007): 153–72.

12. Henly and Lyons (2000), "Negotiation of Childcare."

13. Coohey, Carol, "Social networks, informal child care, and inadequate supervision." *Child Welfare* 86 (2007): 53–66.

14. Coohey, Carol (2007), "Social networks."

15. Beeman, Sandra, "Reconceptualizing social support and its relationship to child neglect." *Social Science Review* 71 (1997): 421–40.

16. Coohey, Carol (2007), "Social networks."

17. MacDonald, H., and Patricia Callery, "Different meanings of respite: A study of parents, nurses, and social workers caring for children with complex needs." *Child: Care, Health, & Development* 30 (2003): 279–88.

18. Bruns, Eric J., and John D. Burchard, "Impact of respite care services for families with children experiencing emotional and behavioral problems." *Children's Services: Social Policy, Research & Practice* 3 (2000): 39–61.

19. Bruns and Burchard (2000), "Impact of respite care."

20. MacDonald and Callery (2003), "Different meanings of respite"; Bruns and Burchard (2000), "Impact of respite."

21. Openden, Daniel, Jennifer B. Symon, Lynn Kern Koegel, and Robert L. Koegel, "Developing a student respite provider system for children with autism." *Journal of Positive Behavioral Interventions* 8(2) (2006) 119–23; Bruns and Burchard (2000), "Impact of respite."

22. Cowen, Slavik Perle, and David A. Reed, "Effects of respite care for children with developmental disabilities: Evaluation of an intervention for at risk families." *Public Health Nursing* 19 (2002): 272–83.

23. MacDonald and Callery (2003), "Different meanings of respite."

24. "Manchester, NH Demographics," manchester.areaconnect.com/statistics.htm.

25. Pearlmutter, Sue, and Elizabeth Bartle, "Participants' perceptions of the childcare subsidy system." *Journal of Sociology and Social Welfare* 30 (2003): 157–73; T. Toroyan, A. Oakley, G. Laing, I. Roberts, M. Mugford, and J. Turner, "The impact of day care on socially disadvantaged families: An example of the use of process evaluation within a randomized controlled trial." *Child: Care, Health, and Development* 30 (2004): 691–98.

26. "Concord, New Hampshire Children's Place," www.thechildrensplacenh.org. (accessed May 14, 2008).

27. "The Story of Short Term Child Care," www.afchildcare.on.ca/stcc/program.html (accessed February 10, 2009).

28. For-profit child care centers with drop-in and short-term care were identified through an Internet search using the search term "short-term child care center" with the Internet search engine Google. The for-profit centers that were identified were located throughout North Carolina, and additional operations were identified in Arizona and Pennsylvania. These included Kidspot, Bizikids, and Right Time Kids. Fitzsimon, Chris, and Jeanne Sturiale, November 29, 2006, "STCC growing in popularity." *North Carolina Journal,* www.ncpolicywatch.com/cms/2006/11/29/short-term-child-care-growing-in-popularity/ (accessed June 10, 2008).

5

The Contribution of the Helping Relationship in Promoting Retention in a Home Visitation Program to Prevent Child Maltreatment*

Michelle P. Taylor and Karen McCurdy

Child abuse and neglect pose significant challenges to the healthy development of young children in the United States. In 2004, almost 1,500 child fatalities were reported to the National Child Abuse and Neglect Data System (NCANDS), while almost nine hundred thousand children experienced abuse or neglect in 2002.[1] Beyond short-term physical and emotional injuries, children can develop problems that cut across multiple domains and generate long-term effects that often persist into adulthood. Examples include elevated risk for school failure and delinquency; physical problems, such as brain injury, fractures, and burns; low self-esteem, learning disabilities, aggressive or withdrawal behaviors; difficulties in establishing or maintaining relationships;[2, 3, 4] and other serious health problems.[5]

Fortunately, evidence suggests that home visitation programs can be effective in preventing child abuse and neglect. Parents in Healthy Families America (HFA) Arizona had significantly fewer substantiated cases of maltreatment as compared to a demographically similar comparison group.[6] Another study found a significantly lower incidence of infant death in visited families versus a matched control sample of nonvisited families in an HFA related program in Ohio.[7] A randomized controlled study of the Healthy Families New York (HFNY) program found that, relative to control mothers, HFNY mothers reported significantly fewer instances of severe physical abuse[8] and were significantly less likely to deliver a low-birth-weight infant.[9] Finally, HFA Texas parents had significantly fewer substantiated cases of child maltreatment as compared to parents who refused participation or dropped out prematurely.[10] Other studies, however, have not found similar impacts of HFA home visiting on child maltreatment indicators.[11, 12]

Despite the promise of voluntary home visiting programs such as HFA, many parents who could benefit from services choose not to participate in or not complete these programs. In the above studies of HFA programs, twelve-month dropout rates ranged from 35.5 percent to 50 percent.[13, 14] Low retention rates have been noted in a variety of other home visitation programs as well,[15] demonstrating the challenge programs face in retaining their parents. As early dropout has been associated with poor treatment outcomes in therapeutic settings and lowered effectiveness among visited families, identifying factors that contribute to a parent's decision to end home visiting services is crucial to improving the efficacy of home visiting programs.[16, 17]

Most attrition research has focused on whether demographic variables, such as race/ethnicity, marital status, maternal age, and education status, explain participation patterns, and has produced inconsistent results.[18, 19] Recent work, however, has begun to acknowledge the role of the provider in this dynamic,[20] with increasing attention paid to the quality of the provider-parent "helping" relationship as a key factor in increasing retention in home visiting programs[21, 22] and other treatment settings.[23, 24]

Research on the parent-provider relationship primarily comes from the fields of counseling and psychotherapy. This relationship, alternatively referred to as a "therapeutic alliance" or "helping relationship," has been found to be the most important factor in promoting favorable therapeutic outcomes.[25, 26] A review of the literature linked the therapeutic alliance to compliance with various aspects of treatment, including disposition plans, medication regimens, and completion of treatment.[27] This review concluded that the quality of the therapeutic relationship was critical to the success of programs for families at risk of child abuse and neglect.

Studies directly comparing the relative impacts of the client versus the provider view of the helping relationship have varied in their findings. A study of 125 client-therapist dyads found that perceived improvement was predicted by both client and therapist aspects of the therapeutic alliance.[28] In contrast, another study found that only the client's perspective of the therapeutic alliance predicted retention in psychiatric care and clients tended to rate the quality of the relationship better than did therapists.[29] Additionally, younger clients were more likely to drop out than older clients. These findings reinforce results from an earlier meta-analysis that client perceptions of the helping alliance most strongly correlated with ratings of their symptoms and problems and only the client perceptions of the relationship predicted early dropout.[30]

While less extensive, research among home visiting programs also supports the importance of the parent-provider relationship, though these studies typically captured only the participant's view of the relationship.[31] An earlier study using the current sample found that higher parent ratings of the helping relationship significantly correlated with the receipt of more visits.[32] Similar results were found in a recent study of home visiting in Early Head Start programs[33] while a national study of HFA programs found that, for some ethnic groups, similarity between the parent and provider on characteristics such as parity status and racial background increased retention rates.[34]

Evidence from the above studies demonstrates the importance of the helping relationship for retaining parents in programs, yet less is known about variables that may influence the quality of the helping alliance. Available studies have generated several characteristics that may create a strong "helping relationship," such as mutual respect, acceptance, trust, warmth, liking, understanding and collaboration,[35] provider empathy,[36] and friendliness and caring.[37] Work-related characteristics of the home visitors, such as their ability to meet participant expectations,[38] may also contribute to more productive relationships.

In summary, theory suggests that the quality of the provider-participant relationship will influence retention in home visiting programs; however, few home visiting studies have fully examined this hypothesis. The current study addresses this shortcoming by explicitly testing (1) whether participant and provider perceptions of the helping relationship explained retention rates among parents receiving home visiting services. We also tested the hypotheses that (2) maternal perceptions of the helping relationship would be a stronger predictor of retention than home visitor perceptions, and (3) that greater demographic similarity between the parent and home visitor would predict increased retention. Last, (4) we sought to identify significant factors that helped to explain parent or home visitor perceptions of the helping relationship.

METHODS FOR STUDY

Healthy Families America (HFA), created in 1992 by Prevent Child Abuse (PCA) America, is a nonmedical, home-visiting program designed to reduce child abuse and neglect and provide a variety of supports and services to maximize childhood development.[39] Typically, HFA sites offer an array of services that include: (1) weekly home-based visits during the first year of services; (2) an individualized family service plan; (3) linking of families to a medical "home;" (4) provision of a curriculum that teaches critical child development information and promotes healthy parent-child interactions; and

(5) connecting families to other services to address both parent (e.g., employment) and child (e.g., health screenings) needs. Home visitors, known as family support workers (FSWs), come from a variety of educational backgrounds and receive intensive training from experienced HFA trainers.

Procedures

This study used secondary data from a study of nine HFA programs in six states.[40] These HFA programs offered services to pregnant or new mothers who scored 25 or more on the Kempe Family Stress Inventory (KFSI). The KFSI assesses ten factors associated with parental dysfunction, such as negative impressions of the child, parental depression, and isolation. KFSI scores of 25 or greater are associated with high-risk parenting behavior.[41] Independent evaluators invited all eligible mothers, regardless of acceptance or refusal of HFA services, to participate in a twelve-month study of program services. In-depth interviews with participating parents were conducted at three points in time: enrollment into the study, either during pregnancy or within two weeks of the child's birth; three months later for all parents regardless of whether they had ever received a home visit; and, for parents who received a visit, at twelve months post-enrollment or within one month of service termination if services ended prior to twelve months. FSWs completed measures on all visited families at three months post-enrollment, and at twelve months or service termination. This study utilizes data from the initial and three-month parent interviews, the three-month FSW interview, and service data from the twelve-month/termination FSW interview. These procedures were approved by the Internal Review Board at the University of Chicago.

Sample

Each HFA program consecutively enrolled eligible mothers until at least thirty parents had agreed to participate in the retention study. Of the 430 eligible parents, 343 (80 percent) agreed to participate in the overall study, including seven who declined visits and ten who reported no intention to receive services. Overall, 309 mothers received at least one visit from ninety-eight FSWs. For the purposes of this study, this sample was narrowed further to those 261 (85 percent) parents with complete data on the outcome measure of the parent-FSW relationship, and their eighty-eight FSWs. Bivariate analyses indicated no significant demographic differences between visited parents with ($n = 261$) and without ($n = 48$) complete data.

Table 5.1 provides demographic characteristics of the parents and their home visitor or FSW. The two groups shared some demographic similarities as one-third of parents and FSWs was African American, while about

Table 5.1. Parent and Family Support Worker (FSW) Demographics

Demographic Attribute	Parent (n = 261)	FSW (n = 88)	Parent & FSW Match
Age			
% Under Thirty	90 (235)	30.7 (27)	
% Thirty-one or older	9.6 (25)	68.2 (60)	
% Missing	0.4 (1)	1.1 (1)	
% Age Match			31.4 (82)
Race/Ethnicity			
% African American	32.2 (84)	31.8 (28)	
% White	31.0 (81)	36.4 (32)	
% Hispanic	27.2 (71)	25.0 (22)	
% Other	9.6 (25)	4.5 (4)	
% Missing		2.3 (2)	
% Race Match			66.7 (174)
Education			
% Less than High School	51.3 (134)	0.0 (0)	
% High School/ GED	34.5 (90)	11.4 (10)	
% More than High School	13.4 (35)	83.0 (73)	
% Missing	.8 (2)	5.7 (5)	
% Education Match (Ed Match)			8.8 (23)
First baby/No other children			
% Yes	70.5 (184)	21.6 (19)	
% No	29.5 (77)	78.4 (69)	
% Parity Match			40.6 (106)
Mn # of Other Children (*SD*)	1.7 (.94)	2.0 (1.9)	

one-fourth of each group was of Hispanic ethnicity. Both parents and FSWs had, on average, two children. However, parents were substantially younger than FSWs, and were less likely to be educated beyond high school. Finally, a substantial portion of FSWs (21.6 percent) had not raised any children.

Measures

This study used multiple definitions of retention to better capture parent involvement in services. Similar to other studies, service dosage was measured by the number of visits the parent received from the FSW,[42, 43] and service duration was assessed as the number of weeks the parent was enrolled in the program.[44] Service intensity, or the number of visits divided by the number of weeks in the program, is included as a standardized measure of service concentration. Service data for these variables were collected by the FSWs at three and twelve months post-program intake.

The helping relationship was assessed with the Helping Relationship Inventory (HRI), which measures the subjective experiences of the participant and provider associated with the development of a collaborative, interpersonal relationship.[45] The twenty-item measure is comprised of two scales: a ten-item structural scale which measures the degree of parent involvement in determining program services, and a ten-item interpersonal scale which assesses emotional qualities of the relationship. The parent completed the participant version of the HRI (HRI-C), while the FSW completed the provider version (HRI-W). Minor variations exist in the participant and provider versions to make them more relevant to the individual completing the instrument. Each item is rated on a Likert-type scale of 1–5, with 1 indicating the lowest level of agreement with the item and 5 indicating the highest level of agreement. Items are typically summed. Young and Poulin report that the full HRI scale has high internal reliability ($\alpha = .92$) and support for good construct validity.[46] The parent HRI and FSW HRI were completed at three and twelve months post-enrollment, but only the three-month scores were utilized in this study. For these analyses, we included only those parents with fewer than two missing responses on the twenty items, and calculated mean scores for all parents. This study found high internal reliability ($\alpha > .90$) for parent and FSW HRI scores and subscales.

To assess the degree to which the parent felt that the FSW lived up to her expectations (e.g., Perceived FSW Effort), we utilized a single Likert-type item from the three-month survey which asked parents "Do you think your FSW has done . . ." with three choices (i.e., less than expected, about what was expected, more than expected). To assess provider characteristics that may influence maternal perceptions of the helping relationship, we used the project-developed Provider Personality Index (PPI), consisting of eleven items assessing personality attributes (e.g., depressed/cheerful, warm/cold, unfriendly/friendly). Mothers selected from three options: a positive personality characteristic, a negative personality characteristic, or "neither." Of the eleven items, six were worded positively and five negatively. The ratings were recoded into a Likert scale such that 1 = positive assessment, 2 = neutral assessment, and 3 = negative assessment. The eleven items were summed, with possible scores ranging from 11 to 36. Lower scores indicated more positive personality attributes. The total scale had acceptable internal consistency ($\alpha = .82$). Initial analyses of the PPI, however, revealed a highly skewed distribution (–3.4) as 65 percent of parents gave the FSW high ratings on all eleven attributes. To address this bias, we created a dichotomous PPI variable—High PPI—with 1 = highest rating on all attributes and 0 = all else. The new variable, High PPI, had an acceptable distribution (skew = –.55, kurtosis = –1.7).

Demographic data on both parent and FSW were collected at entry to the study and included race/ethnicity, education, parity status, and age. These variables were used to construct parent-level items reflecting the parent's similarity to the FSW. For ethnic match, parent and FSW reports were scored in the following manner: 1 = same ethnicity, 0 = different ethnicity. For education match, a match was defined if both parent and FSW had less than a high school degree or less than twelve years of education, if both had a high school degree (twelve years of education), or if both had more than twelve years of education. Parity match was coded as 1 if the parent's parity status matched that of the home visitor (e.g., either both parents or both not parents) and a 0 if they differed. Age match was coded 1 if both parent and FSW were under twenty-one, twenty-one to thirty, thirty-one to forty, or if both were over age forty; otherwise, age match was coded as 0.

Data Analysis

Basic descriptive analyses and correlations were conducted for all variables. Next, *t*-tests and one-way analysis of variance (ANOVA) assessed whether retention rates or HRI scores varied by parent demographic attributes. Second, ordinary least squares (OLS) linear regression equations were calculated to predict factors associated with dosage, duration, and intensity. In each equation, parent and FSW HRI scores were entered on the first step. Next, we entered demographic variables with significant associations with either retention or HRI scores, followed by all parent-FSW match variables. Finally, exploratory forward regression analyses were run to identify correlates of parent and FSW HRI scores. In these exploratory regression equations, the following variables were examined: all parent demographic characteristics, all parent-FSW match variables, Perceived FSW Effort, and High PPI.

RESULTS OF STUDY

Services Received, Parent and FSW Characteristics

For the 261 parents with dosage data, the typical parent received 18.9 visits ($SD = 13.5$). For the 226 parents with duration data on the number of weeks in program, the average parent was enrolled for 37.6 weeks ($SD = 19.1$). Thus, the average intensity was .53 visits/week ($SD = .26$), or less than half of the planned amount of visits. One-way ANOVAs and *t*-tests noted several significant demographic differences in retention rates. Older parents were more likely to have a higher number of visits, $t = 2.48$, $p < .05$, and first-time mothers had fewer visits than experienced mothers, $t = -2.07$, $p < .05$. One-way ANOVAs indicated no significant retention differences based on maternal education; however, race influenced both dosage and intensity. Hispanics received significantly more visits than whites, African Americans, and those from other racial/ethnic backgrounds, $F (260)$

= 9.67, $p < .001$. Additionally, Hispanics enjoyed greater intensity of visits than whites and other races, while African Americans had a higher intensity of visits than parents whose race or ethnicity fell into the "other" category, $F (225) = 6.03, p = .001$.

Parent-FSW Relationship

In terms of the parent-FSW helping relationship, FSWs gave slightly higher scores than parents. For example, the typical parent mean rating was 3.2 ($SD = .71$) on the HRI, which translates to an average of 12.7 on the twenty-item parent HRI, while FSW HRI mean scores averaged 3.91 ($SD = .62$), the equivalent of 15.6. Parent and FSW HRI ratings were moderately correlated, $r = .22, p < .01$. For the parent, HRI scores did not vary by demographic characteristics such as parent age, education, parity status and race. For the FSW, parent race had a significant relationship with HRI scores such that FSWs gave higher ratings when the parent was of Hispanic ethnicity as compared to whites, $F (260) = 6.1, p < .01$. Because the HRI interpersonal and structural scales were highly correlated for the parents (Pearson's $r = .67$) and FSWs (Pearson's $r = .69$), the analyses utilized the full scale for both the parent and FSW.

Finally, variation in the correlation between parent HRI scores and FSW HRI scores with the three retention variables showed that the three definitions captured different aspects of retention. While both parent and FSW HRI scores were significantly associated with dosage ($p < .01$), only FSW HRI was significantly related to duration of visits ($p < .01$) and intensity of visits ($p < .05$).

The Helping Relationship and Parent Retention

To test the hypothesis that HRI scores influence retention, we conducted separate multiple regression analyses with each retention variable (table 5.2). We entered parent and FSW HRI scores on the first step, followed by parental age, parity status, and race/ethnicity, and all parent/home visitor match variables. Parent education was excluded as it did not predict retention or HRI scores. Across these models, this combination of factors better explained dosage (Adjusted $R^2 = .20$) than duration (Adjusted $R^2 = .05$) or intensity (Adjusted $R^2 = .07$). For dosage, both parent HRI scores ($\beta = .14$, $p < .05$) and FSW HRI scores ($\beta = .22, p < .001$) emerged as significant predictors, along with Hispanic ethnicity ($\beta = .22, p < .01$). Perceptions of a better helping relationship by the parent or FSW, and Hispanic ethnicity corresponded to more visits. Age of parent had a trend relationship with visits as younger mothers received somewhat fewer visits than older mothers ($p < .10$). No other demographic or match variable influenced dosage.

Table 5.2. Linear Regression Analyses Predicting Retention (Only Step 2 Shown)

Variable (Omitted Category)	Dosage (n = 261)			Duration (n = 226)			Intensity (n = 226)		
	B	SE	β	B	SE	β	B	SE	β
(Constant)	-8.12	6.7		.67	11.6		.30	.2	
HRI									
Parent	1.35	.6	.14*	.50	.9	.04	.00	.0	.06
FSW	2.5	.7	.22***	2.54	1.1	.16*	.00	.0	.09
Maternal age (≥ 30)									
< 30	-.471	2.7	-.10[a]	4.48	4.3	.07	.00	.1	-.11[a]
Parent ethnicity (white)									
African American	-.96	2.0	-.03	-1.34	3.4	-.03	.00	.0	.17*
Hispanic	6.77	2.1	.22**	2.60	3.4	.06	.11	.0	.20*
Other	-.37	3.1	-.01				.00	.1	-.07
Parent-FSW Similarity									
Age match	1.72	1.8	.06	-.46	2.9	-.01	.00	.0	.02
Ed. match	.00	2.7	-.00	3.07	4.5	.05	.00	.1	.06
Race match	2.52	1.9	.09	10.43	3.2	.25***	.00	.0	.05
Parity match	-1.86	1.7	-.07	1.14	2.8	.03	.00	.0	.00
F score	6.28***			2.08*			2.57**		
Df	10,250			10,215			10,215		
Adjusted R^2	.169			.046			.06		

[a]$p < .10$, *$p < .05$, **$p < .01$, ***$p < .001$

For duration, higher FSW HRI scores, $\beta = .16$, $p < .05$, and a racial/ethnic match between the parent and FSW ($\beta = .25$, $p < .001$) corresponded to more weeks in the program. Unexpectedly, parent HRI scores did not significantly influence duration. Results for the third retention variable, intensity, also contradicted our hypotheses. For intensity, neither parent nor FSW HRI scores significantly affected the number of visits per week that the parent received. African American ($\beta = .17$, $p < .05$) and Hispanic parents ($\beta = .20$, $p < .05$) received more intense visits as compared to whites. As with dosage, mothers under age thirty had somewhat fewer visits per week than mothers over age thirty ($p < .10$).

Factors Related to the Helping Relationship

The next set of analyses examined predictors of parent and FSW HRI scores (table 5.3). For parent HRI scores, forward regression analyses indicated that perceived FSW effort ($p < .001$) and High PPI ratings significantly explained parent HRI scores ($p = .001$), accounting for a large portion of the explained variance (Adjusted $R^2 = 32$) in these scores. Thus, when the FSW received the highest parent ratings on perceived effort and on personality attributes, the parent also assessed the helping relationship as stronger. In contrast, parent demographic characteristics and demographic similarity to the FSW did not significantly explain parent HRI scores. Using these same variables, forward regression analyses predicting the FSW

Table 5.3.   Exploratory Forward Regressions Predicting HRI Scores

Variable (Omitted Category)	Parent HRI Score[1]			FSW HRI Score[2]		
	B	SE	β	B	SE	β
Constant	3.58	.28		6.87	.31	
Perceived FSW Effort	0.99	.12	.463***	.62	.18	.220**
High PPI[3] (Low PPI)	0.57	.17	.196**	ns		
Hispanic Parent (white)	ns			.33	.13	.168**
F score		55.7***			10.1***	
Df		2,239			2,225	
Adjusted R^2		.320			.082	

ns = non-significant; ** $p < .01$; *** $p < .001$

[1] Variables excluded from the final equation: parent ethnicity (African American, white, Hispanic, other), maternal education, maternal age, maternal parity status, age match, race match, education match, and parity match.

[2] Variables excluded from the final equation: High PPI parent African American, parent other race, maternal education, maternal age, maternal parity status, age match, race match, education match, and parity match.

[3] High PPI = High Provider Personality Index

HRI yielded two significant predictors. Similar to parent HRI scores, higher ratings of perceived FSW effort corresponded to higher FSW HRI scores ($\beta = .22$, $p < .01$). In addition, Hispanic ethnicity was significant ($\beta = .168$, $p < .01$), such that FSWs rated their relationship with Hispanic parents more highly than their relationship with white parents. These two variables explained 8 percent of the variance in FSW HRI scores, substantially less than for parent HRI scores. No other variable, including high scores on the PPI, was significant.

DISCUSSION

The hypothesis that higher parent and home visitor ratings of the quality of the helping relationship would predict longer retention was fully supported only when retention was defined as dosage, or number of visits. When retention was operationalized as duration (i.e., length of time in services), higher home visitor ratings of the helping relationship were significantly associated with longer stays. In contrast, the parent's view had no significant effect on duration. Finally, while bivariate correlations demonstrated significant associations between intensity of services with parent and home visitor ratings of the helping relationship, this association disappeared in the multiple regression analyses, once parent demographic characteristics and demographic similarity with the home visitor were controlled. These results indicate that the helping relationship does guide some aspects of service involvement, and that research should utilize multiple indicators of parent involvement in home visiting services to best understand how and why parents utilize services.

Unexpectedly, maternal perceptions of the quality of the helping relationship proved to be a less significant predictor of retention than home visitor perceptions. In contrast to studies of therapeutic settings, the home visitors' evaluation of the helping relationship made a stronger contribution to dosage than parent perceptions, and only home visitor HRI scores significantly predicted duration of services. Why the home visitors' assessment of the quality of the helping relationship is the strongest predictor of retention is puzzling. As the HFA model calls for persistent outreach and continued efforts to enroll and retain families in services,[47] these findings may indicate that duration of service involvement reflects the willingness of the home visitor to continue to pursue the parent, and perhaps also the parent's unwillingness or inability to clearly terminate services. In contrast, both the parent and home visitor appear to negotiate the number of visits received by the family.

In thinking about why these findings differ from existing research in the field of psychotherapy, it is important to consider the nature of the services themselves. Therapeutic services are often initiated by the client, who has identified that he/she is experiencing a problem. Even when services are court-ordered or "strongly encouraged" by a significant other, the person is still motivated to solve a problem (i.e., eliminate the court's punishment or pacify the significant other). Beyond personal motivation, the client can more easily end services by failing to show up for treatment, as a therapist typically will not attempt to visit the client at home. With prevention services, such as a home visitation program, the parent may be less motivated to participate as he/she may not recognize a need for services, especially when enrollment is based on a risk assessment tool. And, unlike a therapist, the home visitor has greater incentive and opportunity to find and deliver services to the parent.

Overall, demographic similarity between the parent and home visitor exerted few effects on retention rates in this sample. In contrast to findings from a qualitative study of home visiting[48] and an analysis of racial/ethnic differences in retention,[49] similarity in parity status, age, and education did not explain amount of visits, duration of services, or intensity of services. However, ethnic match significantly influenced one aspect of retention. Parents served by home visitors of similar ethnic background stayed in services for longer periods of time than unmatched parents, though dosage and intensity were unaffected. Other studies also have found that ethnic match influenced retention, but only for African American families.[50, 51] Overall, however, the findings indicate that demographic similarity had limited effects on creating a more enduring service partnership between the parent and visitor for the typical study parent. Thus, program efforts to hire providers with similar demographic attributes as the target population may be less effective than efforts to ensure that the home visitor involves the parent in decisions regarding service, and provides consistent emotional support and encouragement to the parent.

Of parent demographic attributes, only race/ethnicity influenced retention once parent and home visitor assessments of the helping relationship were considered in the multiple regression analyses. Similar to other studies,[52, 53] parents who were Hispanic received more visits and more intense services, as compared to white parents. African American parents received greater service intensity than white parents, though differences did not exist in number of visits or length of services. This latter finding conflicts with another home visiting study that noted reduced engagement by African American parents.[54] As it is unclear why these retention differences occur, further research is needed, especially qualitative studies that can identify key barriers that may impact ethnic groups in different ways, such as perceived intrusiveness of visits,[55] fear of further social service involvement,[56] or social norms that may favor program participation.

Another way to investigate this issue is to evaluate how race/ethnicity, as well as the match between parent and home visitor characteristics, impact the quality of the helping relationship. Our analyses revealed that parent ethnicity did not impact the parent's perception of this relationship. In contrast, home visitors were significantly more likely to rate the helping relationship higher when parents were Hispanic, as compared to whites. While perhaps an anomaly related to this particular sample, these findings suggest that this more favorable rating may help explain why Hispanics received more visits as well as greater intensity of visits by their home visitor. If this finding is confirmed by other research, future investigators need to examine home visitor perceptions of parent ethnicity and whether those perceptions affect outreach activities used by the home visitor. The findings also suggest that expanding professional development opportunities to encompass cultural beliefs and practices that influence service participation may be warranted, including assisting home visitors to explore their personal biases about race/ethnicity, both positive and negative.

The exploratory analyses noted other significant determinants of the helping relationship. For both parent and home visitor, high ratings on the single item measure of perceived FSW effort corresponded to better HRI scores. While one could reasonably expect that the greater effort by the home visitor would play a strong role in predicting the parent's assessment of the quality of the helping relationship, the finding that it also significantly predicts the home visitor's assessment of the relationship is a little more surprising. This is especially true given the relatively low correlations between the parent and home visitor HRI scores. Even so, this finding does suggest a level of awareness and responsiveness on the part of the home visitor about how well the parent perceives that the visitor has met the parent's expectations. Thus, the parent's assessment of the home visitor's effort is a critical element in determining the quality of the helping relationship. Because it may not be feasible for home visiting programs to administer a validated measure of the helping relationship, such as the HRI, this single item might serve as a quick, proxy measure that can determine if there are potential problems from the parent's perspective. This item could be used to test the quality of the helping relationship at frequent intervals in the home visitation process, thereby allowing the visitor to "readjust" and better meet the parent's expectations, possibly preventing the parent from dropping out of services. Of course, programs considering the use of this item should be aware that parents may be less likely to respond negatively if interviewed by an FSW, and therefore, should use third-party interviewers, if possible. Further research would have to evaluate whether such procedures reduce the value of this question.

Several study limitations argue for caution in interpreting these results. While parents who dropped out of services before the three-month interview were not demographically different from those who stayed, some bias may exist that could influence these results. Further, while all nine programs adhered to the core program elements of the HFA framework, variations in service delivery across sites cannot be ruled out and may affect these findings in unknown ways. Similar to most studies of home visiting, this research focused on one form of home visiting programs known as Healthy Families America. Thus, the findings may not generalize to non-HFA sites, which may utilize dramatically different approaches in their efforts to prevent child abuse and neglect. The three definitions of retention did not cover all notable aspects, such as length of visit, nor address other critical components of engagement that may influence parent and child outcomes, such as the level of familial involvement during the visits.[57] Finally, this study could not assess whether parents with higher retention rates had improved outcomes though such results have been found in other HFA studies with similar populations.[58, 59]

CONCLUSION

This study provides one of the first examinations of how parent and home visitor perceptions of the helping relationship shape parent involvement in home visiting services. The finding regarding the importance of the home visitor's evaluation of the quality of the helping relationship in predicting long-term retention is in direct contrast to therapeutic studies suggesting that the client or service recipient is more important.[60, 61] While parent factors may be the most important in promoting enrollment in home visiting service, the burden of maintaining long-term participation may indeed shift to the service provider. From a program management perspective, these results represent good news as home visitors' beliefs clearly influence parent service involvement. Close supervision that involves regular evaluations of FSW perceptions of each parent, along with in-depth discussions as to how these beliefs may impact the quality of the parent-FSW relationship, may help to improve this alliance and lead to greater engagement in services by the parent. From a research perspective, this study adds to the growing literature seeking to understand long-term service retention in the hopes of reducing the incidence of child abuse and neglect. Future work needs to verify these findings and provide more insight into how the helping relationship is co-constructed, as well as its effect, over time, on participation in home visiting services.

NOTES

*This study was partially supported by grants from the William T. Grant Foundation and the Annie E. Casey Foundation to Deborah Daro, University of Chicago; Karen

McCurdy, University of Rhode Island; and Carnot Nelson, University of South Florida. Lead investigators participating in the evaluation include: Elizabeth Anisfeld, Columbia University College of Physicians and Surgeons; Aphra Katzev, Oregon State University; Ann Keim, University of Wisconsin; Craig LeCroy, University of Arizona; Courtney McAfee, Georgia Council on Child Abuse; and Carnot Nelson, University of South Florida. Special thanks to Lydia Falconnier and Carolyn Winje for their assistance with data set construction.

1. Child Welfare Information Gateway, *Child Abuse and Neglect Fatalities: Statistics and Interventions* (Washington: U.S. Department of Health and Human Services, 2006).

2. J. Harder, "Prevention of Child Abuse and Neglect: An Evaluation of a Home Visitation Parent Aide Program Using Recidivism Data," *Research on Social Work Practice* 1, no. 4 (2005): 246–56.

3. C. Huebner, "Evaluation of a Clinic-Based Parent Education Program to Reduce the Risk of Infant and Toddler Maltreatment," *Public Health Nursing* 19 (2002): 377–89.

4. National Research Council, *Understanding Child Abuse and Neglect* (Washington: National Academy Press, 1993).

5. J. Galano and C. Schellenbach, "Healthy Families America® Research Practice Network: A Unique Partnership to Integrate Prevention Science and Practice," *Journal of Prevention and Intervention in the Community* 34 (2007): 39–66.

6. J. Krysik and C. LeCroy, "The Evaluation of Healthy Families Arizona: A Multisite Home Visitation Program," *Journal of Prevention and Intervention in the Community* 34 (2007): 109–27.

7. E. Donovan, R. Ammerman, J. Besl, H. Atherton, J. Khoury, M. Altaye, F. Putnam, and J. Van Ginkel, "Intensive Home Visiting Is Associated with Decreased Risk of Infant Death," *Pediatrics* 119 (2007): 1145–51.

8. K. DuMont, S. Mitchell-Herzfeld, R. Greene, E. Lee, A. Lowenfels, M. Rodriguez, and V. Dorabawila, "Healthy Families New York (HFNY) Randomized Trials: Effects on Early Child Abuse and Neglect," *Child Abuse & Neglect* 32 (2008): 295–315.

9. E. Lee, S. Mitchel-Herzfeld, A. Lowenfels, R. Greene, V. Dorabawila, and K. DuMont, "Reducing Low Birth Weight Through Home Visitation: A Randomized Controlled Trial," *American Journal of Preventive Medicine* 36 (2009): 154–60.

10. Harder, "Parent Aide Program," 246–56.

11. A. Duggan, E. McFarlane, L. Fuddy, L. Burrell, S. Higman, A. Windham, and C. Sia, "Randomized Trial of a Statewide Home Visiting Program: Impact in Preventing Child Abuse and Neglect," *Child Abuse & Neglect* 28 (2004): 597–622.

12. K. Harding, J. Galano, C. Martin, L. Huntington, and C. Schellenbach, "Healthy Families America Effectiveness: A Comprehensive Review of Outcomes," *Journal of Prevention and Intervention in the Community* 34 (2007): 149–79.

13. Harder, "Parent Aide Program," 246–56.

14. A. Duggan, A. Windham, E. McFarlane, L. Fuddy, C. Rohde, S. Buchbinder, and C. Sia, "Hawaii's Healthy Start Program of Home Visiting for At-Risk Families: Evaluation of Family Identification, Family Engagement, and Service Delivery," *Pediatrics* 105 (2000): 250–59.

15. D. Gomby, P. Culross, and R. Behrman, "Home Visiting: Recent Program Evaluations—Analysis and Recommendations," *The Future of Children* 9, no. 1 (1999): 4–26.

16. H. Johansson and M. Eklund, "Helping Alliance and Early Dropout from Psychiatric Out-Patient Care," *Social Psychiatry and Psychiatric Epidemiology* 41 (2006): 140–47.

17. H. Raikes, B. Green, J. Atwater, E. Kisker, J. Constantine, and R. Chazan-Cohen, "Involvement in Early Head Start Home Visiting Services: Demographic Predictors and Relations to Child and Parent Outcomes," *Early Childhood Research Quarterly* 21 (2006): 2–24.

18. S. Greenfield, A. Brooks, S. Gordon, C. Green, F. Kropp, R. McHugh, M. Lincoln, D. Hien, and G. Miele, "Substance abuse treatment entry, retention, and outcome in women: A review of the literature," *Drug and Alcohol Dependence* 86 (2007): 1–21.

19. W. McGuigan, A. Katzev, and C. Pratt, "Multi-Level Determinants of Retention in a Home-Visiting Child Abuse Prevention Program," *Child Abuse & Neglect* 27 (2003): 363–80.

20. K. McCurdy and D. Daro, "Parent Involvement in Family Support Programs: An Integrated Theory," *Family Relations* 50 (2001): 113–21.

21. J. Korfmacher, B. Green, M. Spellman, and K. R. Thornburg, "The Helping Relationship and Program Participation in Early Childhood Home Visiting," *Infant Mental Health Journal* 28 (2007): 459–80.

22. J. Korfmacher, B. Green, F. Staerkel, C. Peterson, G. Cook, L. Roggman, R. Faldowski, and R. Schiffman, "Parent Involvement in Early Childhood Home Visiting," *Child Youth Care Forum* 37 (2008): 171–96.

23. R. Cotter, J. Burke, R. Loeber, and J. Mutchka, "Predictors of Contact Difficulty and Refusal in a Longitudinal Study," *Criminal Behavior and Mental Health* 15, no. 2 (2005): 126–37.

24. J. Green, "Annotation: The Therapeutic Alliance—A Significant but Neglected Variable in Child Mental Health Treatment Studies," *Journal of Child Psychology and Psychiatry and Allied Disciplines* 47 (2006): 425–35.

25. A. Horvath, "The Alliance," *Psychotherapy* 38 (2001): 365–72.

26. T. Young and J. Poulin, "The Helping Relationship Inventory: A Clinical Appraisal," *Families in Society: The Journal of Contemporary Human Services* (March-April 1998): 123–33.

27. M. Dore and L. Alexander, "Preserving Families At Risk of Child Abuse and Neglect: The Role of the Helping Alliance," *Child Abuse and Neglect* 20 (1996): 349–61.

28. A. Clemence, M. Hilsenroth, S. Ackerman, C. Strassle, and L. Handler, "Facets of the Therapeutic Alliance and Perceived Progress in Psychotherapy: Relationship between Patient and Therapist Perspectives," *Clinical Psychology and Psychotherapy* 12 (2005): 443–54.

29. Johansson and Eklund, "Helping Alliance," 140–47.

30. A. Horvath and B. Symonds, "Relation between Working Alliance and Outcome in Psychotherapy: A Meta-analysis," *Journal of Counseling Psychology* 38 (1991): 139–49.

31. Raikes, Green, Atwater, Kisker, Constantine, and Chazan-Cohen, "Involvement in Early Head Start," 2–24.

32. D. Daro, K. McCurdy, L. Falconnier, C. Winje, E. Anisfeld, A. Katzev, A. Keim, C. LeCroy, W. McGuigan, and C. Nelson, "The Role of Community in Facilitating Service Utilization," *Journal of Prevention & Intervention in the Community* 34 (2007): 181–204.

33. Korfmacher, Green, Spellman, and Thornburg, "The Helping Relationship," 459–80.

34. K. McCurdy, R. Gannon, and D. Daro, "Participation in Home-Based, Family Support Programs: Ethnic Variations," *Family Relations* 52 (2003): 3–11.

35. D. Orlinsky, M. Ronnestad, and U. Willutzki, "Fifty Years of Psychotherapy Process-Outcome Research: Continuity and Change," in *Bergin and Garfield's Handbook of Psychotherapy and Behavior Change, fifth edition*, ed. M. J. Lambert (New York: Wiley, 2004), 307–89.

36. B. Drake, "Relationship Competencies in Child Welfare Services," *Social Work* 39 (1994): 595–602.

37. H. Winefield and J. Barlow, "Child and Worker Satisfaction in a Child Protection Agency," *Child Abuse and Neglect* 19 (1995): 897–905.

38. McCurdy and Daro, "Parent Involvement," 113–21.

39. R. Ammerman, F. Putnam, J. Kopke, T. Gannon, J. Short, J. Van Ginkel, M. Clark, M. Carrozza, and A. Spector, "Development and Implementation of a Quality Assurance Infrastructure in a Multisite Home Visitation Program in Ohio and Kentucky," *Journal of Prevention and Intervention in the Community* 34 (2007): 89–108.

40. K. McCurdy, D. Daro, E. Anisfeld, A. Katzev, A. Keim, C. LeCroy, C. McAfee, C. Nelson, L. Falconnier, W. McGuigan, J. Park, J. Sandy, and C. Winje, "Understanding Maternal Intentions to Engage in Home Visiting Programs," *Children and Youth Services Review* 28 (2006): 1195–1212.

41. S. Murphy, B. Orkow, and R. Nicola, "Prenatal Prediction of Child Abuse and Neglect: A Prospective Study," *Child Abuse and Neglect* 9 (1985): 225–35.

42. McCurdy et al., "Maternal Intentions," 1195–1212.

43. M. Wagner, D. Spiker, M. Linn, S. Gerlach-Downie, and F. Hernandez, "Dimensions of Parental Engagement in Home Visiting Programs: Exploratory Study," *Topics in Early Childhood Special Education* 23 (2003): 171–87.

44. R. Ammerman, J. Stevens, F. Putnam, M. Altaye, J. Hulsmann, J. Lehmkuhl, J. Monroe, T. Gannon, and J. Van Ginkel, "Predictors of Early Engagement in Home Visitation," *Journal of Family Violence* 21 (2006): 105–15.

45. Young and Poulin, "Helping Relationship," 123–33.

46. Young and Poulin, "Helping Relationship," 123–33.

47. Healthy Families America, *Critical Elements: Rational and Supporting Research* (Chicago: Prevent Child Abuse-America, 2001), www.healthyfamiliesamerica.org/downloads/critical_elements_rationale.pdf (19 July 2009).

48. S. Brookes, J. Summers, K. Thornburg, J. Ispa, and V. Lane, "Building Successful Home Visitor-Mother Relationships and Reaching Programs Goals in Two Early Head Start Programs: A Qualitative Look at Contributing Factors," *Early Childhood Research Quarterly* 21 (2006): 25–45.

49. McCurdy, Gannon, and Daro, "Participation," 3–11.

50. McCurdy, Gannon, and Daro, "Participation," 3–11.

51. S. Sue, D. Fujino, L. Hu, D. Takeuchi, and N. Zane, "Community Mental Health Services for Ethnic Minority Groups: A Test of the Cultural Responsiveness Hypothesis," *Journal of Counseling Psychology* 59 (1991): 533–40.

52. McGuigan, Katzev, and Pratt, "Multi-Level Determinants," 363–80.

53. McCurdy, Gannon, and Daro, "Participation," 3–11.

54. Ammerman et al., "Predictors of Early Engagement," 105–15.

55. D. Slaughter-Defoe, "Home Visiting with Families in Poverty: Introducing the Concept of Culture," *The Future of Children* 3 (1993): 172–83.

56. J. Stevens, R. Ammerman, F. Putnam, T. Gannon, and J. Van Ginkel, "Facilitators and Barriers to Engagement in Home Visitation: A Qualitative Analysis of Maternal, Provider, and Supervisor Data," *Journal of Aggression, Maltreatment & Trauma* 11 (2005): 75–93.

57. Korfmacher, Green, Staerkel, et al., "Parental Involvement in Early Childhood Home Visiting," 171–96.

58. Harder, "Parent Aide Program," 246–56.

59. McGuigan, Katzev, and Pratt, "Multi-Level Determinants," 363–80.

60. Johansson and Eklund, "Helping Alliance," 140–47.

61. C. Rucker-Whitaker, K. Flynn, G. Kravitz, C. Eaton, J. Calvin, and L. Powell, "Understanding African-American Participation in a Behavioral Intervention: Results from Focus Groups," *Contemporary Clinical Trials* 27 (2006): 274–86.

GOVERNMENT INTERVENTION:
FAMILY VIOLENCE,
CHILDREN'S WELFARE,
AND JUSTICE CONCERNS

6

Exploring the Effects of California's Shortened Reunification Time Frames for Children under Three

Amy D'Andrade

As mandated by federal law, parents whose children have been removed due to abuse or neglect receive reunification services for up to twelve months. In 1996, California passed AB 1524, limiting the length of time parents of very young children can receive reunification services to only six months. The effects of this shift in child welfare policy are unknown. While some have heralded restrictions on reunification timelines as better meeting the developmental needs of children, others have expressed concern that shortened time frames may not accommodate realistic recovery processes for substance-abusing parents or facilitate reunification for African American children, who historically have experienced poorer permanency outcomes. This study addresses those issues.

BACKGROUND

One of the few instances in which the state may intrude upon family life occurs when a parent has neglected or maltreated a child, and that maltreatment has been reported to the state child protective services agency (CPS). If the investigating CPS agency social worker determines that the child is unable to safely remain in the parent's home, a juvenile court dependency judge can order the child to be removed from the parent's custody and placed in foster care. The federal Child Welfare Act of 1980 (P.L. 96-272)

83

required states to create reunification services programs, and make "reasonable efforts" to assist parents to reunify by providing or paying for treatment services to address the parents' problems. These efforts were to last for no more than eighteen months. A "permanency hearing" was held after this period, at which the dependency court judge determined whether the parents had adequately improved their parenting deficiencies, and the child could be returned home. If not, reunification services to the parents were terminated, and the child was given a "permanent plan"—a guardianship or adoptive home would be found for the child, or the child would be placed in "long-term foster care."[1]

In the decade following passage of the Child Welfare Act, concerns in the field focused upon parents' rights to due process and treatment services.[2] However, increased understanding of the importance of attachment for young children,[3, 4] along with a body of research suggesting that prolonged stays in foster care and multiple placements had detrimental effects on children,[5, 6, 7] shifted the focus of concern away from parental rights and towards children's rights to timely permanency and stability.[8] This shift culminated in passage of the Adoption and Safe Families Act of 1997 (ASFA) (P.L.105-89). ASFA reduced the amount of time parents had to receive reunification services to twelve months, down from the eighteen months set by the 1980 Child Welfare Act. To decrease the likelihood that children would linger in permanent foster care if parents failed to reunify, ASFA provided incentives to states that increased the number of adoptions: $4000 was paid to states for every child adopted over the number adopted in the baseline year.[9]

In California, Assembly Bill 1524 further reduced time frames for reunification to six months for parents of children three years old or younger. (In 1999, time frames for siblings of children under three were also reduced to six months.) California is one of a relatively small group of states that have reduced reunification time frames to a period of time shorter than the federally imposed twelve months. As of 2006, Connecticut, New York, Oklahoma, Pennsylvania, and Louisiana had limited reunification time frames for all parents to a period of between six and nine months. Two other states have taken California's approach and created age-based distinctions in reunification time frames: Minnesota limited reunification time frames for parents of children under eight to six months, and Colorado limited reunification for parents of children under six to only three months.[10, 11]

While many agree that timely permanency is important for very young children,[12, 13] policies reducing reunification time frames may have unintended consequences. Reducing time frames could result in fewer reunifications overall, as parents who might have resolved their problems with another six months of services would lose the opportunity to do so. But for several populations in particular, concerns about the possible unintended effects of this policy are heightened.

Children of color are more likely to be removed from their parents, receive fewer services while in care,[14] and are less likely to be reunified with their families of origin.[15, 16] While causal factors behind these disparities remain unclear, policy changes limiting access to services may have a greater negative impact on African American families than on other families. Similarly, parents with substance abuse issues also are less likely to be reunified.[17, 18] Complicating the issue further, recovery from substance abuse is generally understood to be a long-term process often involving relapse,[19] and there are concerns that reduced time frames may not accommodate realistic recovery processes.[20] Additionally, the availability of services and coordination of services can be problematic for parents with substance abuse problems.[21] For these parents too, reductions in time frames might have a greater negative impact on reunification than they do for other parents.

The research literature does suggest that parents who reunify more quickly are more likely to have their children removed again than are parents who reunify more slowly;[22] however, we know very little about the effects of reducing the time frames themselves. Therefore, the questions for this study were the following:

1. What are the effects of AB 1524 for children under three?
2. Are there negative consequences of the policy for either

   a. African American children, or
   b. Children of substance abusing parents?

Specific hypotheses were the following:

1. The likelihood of reunification will decrease subsequent to the policy.
2. The likelihood of adoption will increase subsequent to the policy.
3. Children of substance abusing parents will have a decreased likelihood of reunification subsequent to the policy.
4. African American children will have a decreased likelihood of reunification subsequent to the policy.

METHODS

Research Design

This study is a secondary data analysis. A before/after design is used to assess the effects of AB 1524 on outcomes of young children under three. Outcomes for a cohort of children under three entering care before passage of the legislation were compared to outcomes of a cohort of children entering care after passage of the legislation using multivariate survival analysis.

Sample

The original study used case file data from six California counties to examine the effects of various child welfare reforms on child outcomes (for more information on this study and the data source see[23, 24]). A random sample was drawn from each of two cohorts of children under ten entering foster care, the first cohort entering care 1993–1994 and the second entering care 1998–2000. Data were collected from each case file for the three-year time period after the child's removal from home, or until adoption or reunification (if this event occurred before three years passed). A subset of children from this dataset—those under three years of age whose parents received reunification services—make up the sample for this study (n = 507).

Measures

Data for the original dataset came from court reports and documents within child welfare case files written by social workers to inform the juvenile court judge of case happenings. Court reports included information on family problems such as substance abuse, domestic violence, and mental health problems, and client characteristics such as ethnicity, age, and custodial status. Court reports allowed a longitudinal understanding of each case: social studies, written for the jurisdictional-dispositional hearing held within thirty days of the child's entry to care, described client and case characteristics at the outset of the case; subsequent reports required for ongoing review hearings held at least every six months described client progress and case outcomes. A team of two to four student research assistants in each county extracted data from case files via a data collection form. Inter-rater reliability for the data collection effort was estimated at .88.[25] For this study, analyses were conducted using SPSS statistical software version 16.

A categorical variable indicating whether the child reunified, was formally adopted, or left care for other reasons was used in conjunction with a time-in-care variable to estimate the outcome. Entry cohort was measured with a dichotomous variable coded 1 if the child entered care after the passage of the policy (1998–2000) and 0 if the child entered care before passage of the policy (1993–1994).

Child ethnicity was coded as African American, white, Latino, or other. Child age was measured as a dichotomous variable coded 1 if the child was an infant under the age of one year, and 0 if the child was between the ages of one and three. Three maltreatment severity variables were used to measure the severity of different types of maltreatment suffered by the child: physical abuse, parental failure to provide, and lack of supervision. Item scores were five-point Likert-like items estimating the type and severity of maltreatment based upon the social worker's description of the incident prompting the child's entry into care in the jurisdictional dispositional report or the screening narrative. Reliability estimates for these measures were: for physical abuse (.90), failure to provide (.83), and lack of supervision (.90).[26] These measures were used rather than the legal reason for entry to care, as that measure does not address maltreatment severity and reflects what parties stipulated to in court rather than the actual maltreatment experienced by a child.

Parent characteristics were measured in regard to the primary custodial parent of the child. These characteristics included current substance use, current mental health problem, developmental delay, and incarceration during the first three months of the case. These characteristics were captured with a set of dichotomous variables coded 1 if the condition was noted by the worker as present on the jurisdictional dispositional court report, and 0 otherwise.

Analyses

Reunification and adoption are likely to have different pathways and predictors, so each of these outcomes was considered separately in the analysis. To examine the effects of the policy on the reunification of children of substance abusing parents and African American children, separate analyses were run just on these specific populations.

Proportional hazards regression analysis was used. Using the occurrence and timing of events, proportional hazards regression estimates the "hazard" of experiencing an event. The hazard is often referred to as the instantaneous probability of experiencing an event, given the subject is still at risk of the event. The analysis produces estimated hazard ratios (HR), showing the multiplicative effect of a one-unit increase in an independent variable on the hazard of the event of interest.[27] A hazard ratio greater than 1 indicates an increased risk, while a hazard ratio less than 1 indicates a decreased risk. The nature of the sample was such that the observation period varied by county in the second cohort; proportional hazards regression analysis allows for this situation, censoring cases at the end of the observation period and using available information in estimates of risk without requiring any assumption that the event of interest did or did not happen[28] (cases were also censored when the child moved out of the county, or died).

A competing risks model was used to test hypothesis 1 (the likelihood of reunification would decrease subsequent to passage of the legislation) and hypothesis 2 (the likelihood of adoption would increase subsequent to passage of the legislation). This model is employed in proportional hazards regression when there are more than two possible outcomes or events, the experience of any one of which removes a subject from the risk of experiencing any other event. For example, a child who has been reunified is no longer "at risk" of being adopted. Separate analyses are run for each outcome, and in each case, observations are censored at the end of the observation period or at the point the subject experiences any one of the other possible outcomes. This strategy is advantageous because it allows for the timing, occurrence, and influences of different permanency outcomes to vary; subsuming all permanency outcomes into a single "exit" event can obscure important differences that may exist in predictors and processes.[29] For testing hypothesis 3 (children of substance abusing parents would have a lower likelihood of reunification after passage of AB 1524), only children of substance abusing parents (n = 334) were included in the analysis. For testing hypothesis 4 (African American children would have a lower likelihood of reunification after passage of AB 1524), only African American children (n = 135) were included in the analysis. The same multivariate model (with county as the stratification variable) was used for the first three analyses; a somewhat reduced model without the stratification variable was used for the last analysis due to the smaller number of African American children in the sample. The assumption of proportional hazards was checked and no major violations found.

RESULTS

Of the 507 children in the sample, 40 percent were reunified after three years, 21 percent were adopted, and almost 30 percent remained in care. Sixty-one percent were infants under the age of one. Approximately 27 percent of the sample was African American, 22 percent Latino, and over 40 percent were white. Almost 66 percent of the children had parents with current substance abuse problems. Forty-eight percent of the children entered care before the passage of the policy, and 52 percent entered care after passage of the policy (see table 6.1).

Hypothesis 1 (the likelihood of reunification would decrease after passage of the policy) was not supported by the data. Variables with a statistically significant relationship with the hazard of reunification in the multivariate analysis included ethnicity (African American children were less likely to be reunified than white children, HR = .61), parental failure to provide (HR = .89), parent's current substance abuse (HR = .61), and parent's developmental delay (HR = .39) (see table 6.2).

Hypothesis 2 (the likelihood of adoption would increase after passage of the policy) was supported by the data. This relationship is statistically

Table 6.1. Total Sample Characteristics

Variables	Values	n	%
Case Outcome	Reunification	205	40.4
	Adoption	106	20.9
	Other	53	10.5
	Still in Care	143	28.3
County	1	126	24.9
	2	30	5.9
	3	36	7.1
	4	80	15.8
	5	172	33.9
	6	61	12.0
	Missing	2	0.4
Child Age	<1	311	61.3
	1-3	196	38.7
Child Ethnicity	African American	135	26.6
	Latino	109	21.5
	Other	44	8.7
	White	219	43.2
Child Gender	Male	280	55.2
	Female	226	44.6
	Missing	1	0.2
Parental Substance Abuse	Yes	334	65.9
	No	170	33.5
	Missing	3	0.6
Parental Mental Health Problem	Yes	83	16.4
	No	403	79.5
	Missing	21	4.1
Parent Developmental Delay	Yes	28	5.5
	No	457	90.1
	Missing	22	4.3
Parent Incarcerated First 3 Months	Yes	91	17.9
	No	400	78.9
	Missing	16	3.2
Entry Cohort	Before AB 1524	244	48.1
	After AB 1524	263	51.9

significant in the multivariate analysis (HR = 1.94). Also found to be associated with adoption in the multivariate analysis was ethnicity, with African American children less likely to be adopted than white children (HR = .37), and age, with infants about twice as likely as children one through three to be adopted (HR = 2.12) (see table 6.3).

Hypothesis 3 (children of substance abusing parents would be less likely to reunify after the policy) was not supported by the data. In the

Table 6.2.   Survival Analysis of Likelihood of Reunification—Full Sample

Variable	Values	HR	p-value
Child Age	<1	0.79	.123
	1–3	1.00	
Child Gender	Male	0.99	.951
	Female	1.00	
Child Ethnicity	African American*	0.61	.014
	Latino	0.72	.106
	Other	0.73	.225
	White	1.00	
Maltreatment Severity Scale— Failure to Provide*		0.89	.014
Maltreatment Severity Scale— Lack of Supervision		1.05	.338
Maltreatment Severity Scale— Physical Abuse		1.08	.229
Parent Substance Abuse	Yes*	0.61	.003
	No	1.00	
Parent Developmental Delay	Yes*	0.39	.020
	No	1.00	
Parent Mental Health Problem	Yes	0.90	.599
	No	1.00	
Parent Incarcerated First 3 Months	Yes	0.82	.301
	No	1.00	
Entry Cohort	After AB 1524	0.82	.083
	Before AB 1524		

* = p < .05; ** = p < .01; *** = p < .001

Note: Reference category in italics

multivariate analysis using just children of substance abusing parents, children entering care after passage of the policy were not less likely to reunify than children entering care prior to passage of the policy (see table 6.4). In fact, while not statistically significant, the hazard ratio is in the opposite direction to the one hypothesized. In this population, African American children (HR = .51) and Latino children (HR = .50) were only half as likely to reunify as white children; children whose parents failed to provide for them also had a lower likelihood of reunification (HR = .87).

Hypothesis 4 (African American children would be less likely to reunify after passage of the policy) was not supported by the data. The multivariate analysis using just African American children shows that entry after passage of the policy doubled the likelihood of reunification (HR = 2.17) (see table 6.5).

Table 6.3. Survival Analysis of Likelihood of Adoption—Full Sample

Variable	Values	HR	p-value
Child Age**	<1	2.12	.008
	1–3	*1.00*	
Child Gender	Male	1.05	.817
	Female	1.00	
Child Ethnicity	African American***	0.37	.001
	Latino	0.77	.349
	Other	0.86	.690
	White	*1.00*	
Maltreatment Severity Scale— Failure to Provide		1.15	.067
Maltreatment Severity Scale— Lack of Supervision		1.00	.975
Maltreatment Severity Scale— Physical Abuse		1.12	.416
Parent Substance Abuse	Yes	1.14	.644
	No	1.00	
Parent Developmental Delay	Yes	0.50	.111
	No	*1.00*	
Parent Mental Health Problem	Yes	1.23	.424
	No	*1.00*	
Parent Incarcerated First 3 Months	Yes	0.73	.307
	No	*1.00*	
Entry Cohort	After AB 1524**	1.94	.004
	Before AB 1524	*1.00*	

* = p < .05; ** = p < .01; *** = p < .001

Note: Reference category in italics

CONCLUSION

Overall, the hypothesized negative effects of the policy were not found in this study. Children were not less likely to reunify after passage of the policy; this was true for the whole sample as well as for African American children and children of substance abusing parents when considered separately. In fact, outcomes generally improved after the policy: adoption was more likely overall, and the likelihood of reunification increased for African American children.

One explanation may be that counties did not pursue the policy aggressively. A contingency in the law allows agencies to extend services to parents of very young children an additional six months if parents appear to be making good progress with reunification services, and counties may have decided to use this option.

Table 6.4. Survival Analysis of Likelihood of Reunification—Children of Substance-Abusing Parents

Variable	Values	HR	p-value
Child Age	<1	0.76	.200
	1–3	*1.00*	
Child Gender	Male	0.84	.380
	Female	1.00	
Child Ethnicity	African American**	0.51	.009
	Latino*	0.50	.018
	Other	0.59	.191
	White	*1.00*	
Maltreatment Severity Scale— Failure to Provide*	0.87	.023	
Maltreatment Severity Scale— Lack of Supervision	1.04	.597	
Maltreatment Severity Scale— Physical Abuse	0.99	.944	
Parent Developmental Delay	Yes	0.71	.645
	No	*1.00*	
Parent Mental Health Problem	Yes	0.97	.920
	No	*1.00*	
Parent Incarcerated First 3 Months	Yes	1.13	.605
	No	*1.00*	
Entry Cohort	After AB 1524	1.38	.108
	Before AB 1524	*1.00*	

* = p < .05; ** = p < .01; *** = p < .001

Note: Reference category in italics

A second possibility relates to ASFA. A before/after research design is vulnerable to the threat of history; something in the environment other than the policy might have produced the changes in adoption and reunification rates seen here. ASFA is the most obvious candidate. Passed in 1997 and implemented in California state policy in 1998—roughly the same time period as AB 1524—it included a variety of actions intended to spur adoption and emphasize child safety. Studies of ASFA's effects have been mixed: some research has noted a recent decrease in reunification rates;[30, 31] another study found that reunification was more likely for children entering care in 1997, 1998, or 1999 (after ASFA) than for children entering in 1996 (before ASFA);[32] and still another study found no change in reunification rates pre- and post-ASFA.[33] Adoption has generally been seen to increase post-ASFA.[34, 35]

While there is no indication the AB 1524 law negatively affected the likelihood of reunification for children of substance abusing parents or African

Table 6.5.   Survival Analysis of Likelihood of Reunification—African American Children

Variable	Values	HR	p-value
Child Age	<1	0.65	.255
	1-3	*1.00*	
Maltreatment Severity Scale— Failure to Provide	0.83		.092
Maltreatment Severity Scale— Lack of Supervision	0.99		.930
Parent Substance Abuse	Yes	0.72	.410
	No	1.00	
Parent Developmental Delay	Yes	1.82	.330
	No	*1.00*	
Parent Mental Health Problem	Yes	0.80	.652
	No	*1.00*	
Parent Incarcerated First 3 Months	Yes	0.36	.023
	No	*1.00*	
Entry Cohort	After AB 1524*	2.17	.023
	Before AB 1524	*1.00*	

* = p < .05; ** = p < .01; *** = p < .001

Note: Reference category in italics

American children, these children were less likely to reunify than other children. Similarly, in this study African American children were much less likely to be adopted, as has been found in other studies.[36, 37]

Study Limitations

As noted above, the before and after research design cannot rule out the threat of history. Additionally, only rough measures of parental problems and maltreatment were possible given the data source. Case files and court reports are not created for research purposes; they vary in depth, content, and quality by both county and worker.[38] In addition, they hold only the perspective and observations of the child welfare agency social worker, which may not always accurately reflect the true circumstances of the case. In addition, important characteristics of interest that are not required by the agency for payment or accountability reasons may not be detailed.

Future Research and Conclusions

Future studies evaluating this policy intervention should incorporate an assessment of implementation, perhaps via qualitative interviews with key stakeholders, and/or observations of courtroom processes. In addition, a useful strategy would be to take a difference-in-difference approach, and compare outcomes before and after passage of the policy between the population of very young children targeted by AB 1524 and the population of older children. Another alternative might be to look at policy changes using states as the units of observation. Finally, given the association of quicker reunifications with increased reentry to care,[39] consideration of foster care reentry should be incorporated into future examinations of the policy's effects.

Too often changes in child welfare policy are not based on research or data, and reporting requirements are limited or absent.[40, 41] While the negative effects of AB 1524 hypothesized here were not found, the concern about possible unintended consequences of child welfare policy reform remains. It is important for policy evaluation research in child welfare and other fields to consider not just whether policies have their intended effects, but also whether there may be unintended consequences for certain particularly vulnerable groups.

NOTES

1. The Adoption and Child Welfare Act of 1980.

2. Wulczyn, Fred. "Family Reunification." *The Future of Children* 14, no. 1 (2004): 95–114.

3. Carlson, E.A. "A Prospective Longitudinal Study of Attachment Disorganization/Disorientation." *Child Development* 69 (1996): 1107–28.

4. Lyons-Ruth, K. "Attachment Relationships among Children with Aggressive Behavior Problems: The Role of Disorganized Early Attachment Patterns." *Journal of Consulting and Clinical Psychology* 64, no. 1 (1996): 64–73.

5. Eckenrode, J., E. Rowe, M. Laird, and J. Brathwaite. "Mobility as a Mediator of the Effects of Child Maltreatment on Academic Performance." *Child Development* 66 (1995): 1130–42.

6. McDonald, T. P., R. I. Allen, A. Westerfelt, and I. Piliavin. *Assessing the Long-term Effects of Foster Care: A Research Synthesis* (Washington, D.C.: Child Welfare League of America Press, 1996).

7. Newton, R., A. Litrownik, and J. Landsverk. "Children and Youth in Foster Care: Disentangling the Relationship between Problem Behavior and Number of Placements." *Child Abuse and Neglect* 24, no. 10 (2000): 1363–74.

8. Testa, M. F. "When Children Cannot Return Home: Adoption and Guardianship." *The Future of Children* 14, no.1 (2004): 115–29.

9. ASFA 1997; reauthorized in the Adoption Promotion Act of 2003.

10. U.S. Department of Health and Human Services, Administration for Children and Families, Administration on Children, Youth and Families, Children's Bureau. "Reasonable efforts to preserve or reunify families and achieve permanency for children: Summary of state laws." *Child Welfare Information Gateway* 2006. www.childwelfare.gov/systemwide/laws_policies statutes/planningall.pdf (24 Feb. 2009).

11. U.S. Department of Health and Human Services, Administration for Children and Families, Administration on Children, Youth and Families, Children's Bureau. "Court hearings for the permanent placement of children: Summary of state laws." *Child Welfare Information Gateway* 2006. www.childwelfare.gov/systemwide/laws_policies/statutes/planningall.pdf (24 Feb. 2009).

12. Berrick, Jill D., Barbara Needell, Richard P. Barth, and Melissa Jonson-Reid. *The Tender Years: Toward Developmentally Sensitive Child Welfare Services for Very Young Children* (New York: Oxford University Press, 1998).

13. Goldstein, J., A. Freud, and A. J. Solnit. *Beyond the Best Interests of the Child* (New York: The Free Press, 1979).

14. Hill, Robert B. "Synthesis of Research on Disproportionality in Child Welfare: An Update," *Casey-CSSP Alliance for Racial Equity in the Child Welfare System* 2006, www.racemattersconsortium.org/docs/BobHillPaper_FINAL.pdf (24 Feb 2009).

15. Connell, C. M., K. H. Katz, L. Saunders, and J. K. Tebes. "Leaving Foster Care—The Influence of Child and Case Characteristics on Foster Care Exit Rates." *Children and Youth Services Review* 28 (2006): 780–98.

16. Kortenkamp, K., Rob Geen, and M. Stagner. "The Role of Welfare and Work in Predicting Foster Care Reunification Rates for Children of Welfare Recipients." *Children and Youth Services Review* 26 (2004): 577–90.

17. Brook, J., and T. P. McDonald. "Evaluating the Effects of Comprehensive Substance Abuse Intervention on Successful Reunification." *Research on Social Work Practice* 17, no. 6 (2007): 664–73.

18. Eamon, M. K. *The Effect of Economic Resources on Reunification of Illinois Children in Substitute Care* (Urbana: University of Illinois at Urbana–Champagne, Children and Family Research Center, 2002).

19. Fenster, J. "Substance Abuse Issues in the Family." In Gerald Mallon and Peg McCartt Hess (Eds.), *Child Welfare for the 21st Century: A Handbook of Practices, Policies and Programs* (335–48) (New York: Columbia University Press, 2005).

20. Stein, T. J. "The Adoption and Safe Families Act: Creating a False Dichotomy between Parents' and Children's Rights." *Families in Society: The Journal of Contemporary Human Services* 81, no. 6 (2000): 586–92.

21. Young, Nancy K., Sidney L. Gardner, Brook Whitaker, Shaila Yeh, and Cathleen Otero. "A Preliminary Review of Alcohol and Other Drug Issues in the States' Children and Family Service Reviews and Program Improvement Plans." *National Resource Center for Child Welfare Data and Technology* 2005. www.ncsacw.samhsa.gov/files/SummaryofCFSRs.pdf (27 Feb. 2009).

22. Wulczyn, Fred. "Family Reunification." *The Future of Children* 14, no. 1 (2004): 95–114.

23. Berrick, Jill D., Young Choi, Amy D'Andrade, and Laura Frame. "Reasonable Efforts? Implementation of the Reunification Exception Provisions of ASFA." *Child Welfare* 87, no. 3 (2008): 163–82.

24. D'Andrade, Amy. "The Differential Effects of Concurrent Planning Practice Elements on Reunification and Adoption." *Research on Social Work Practice* 19, no. 4 (2009): 446–59.

25. D'Andrade, Amy. "The Differential Effects of Concurrent Planning Practice Elements on Reunification and Adoption." *Research on Social Work Practice* 19, no.4 (2009): 446–59.

26. Manly, J. T., D. Cicchetti, and D. Barnett. "The Impact of Subtype, Frequency, Chronicity, and Severity of Child Maltreatment of Social Competence and Behavior Problems." *Development and Psychopathology* 6 (1994): 121–43.

27. Allison, Paul D. *Survival Analysis Using the SAS System: A Practical Guide*. Cary, NC: SAS Institute Inc, 1995.

28. Allison, Paul D. *Survival Analysis Using the SAS System: A Practical Guide*. Cary, NC: SAS Institute Inc, 1995.

29. Courtney, Mark E., and Y. I. Wong. "Comparing the Timing of Exits from Substitute Care." *Children and Youth Services Review* 18, nos. 4/5 (1996): 307–24.

30. Wells, K., and S. Guo. "Reunification of Foster Children Before and After Welfare Reform." *Social Service Review* 78, no. 1 (2004): 74–95.

31. Wulczyn, Fred. "Family Reunification." *The Future of Children* 14, no. 1 (2004): 95–114.

32. Eamon, M. K. *The Effect of Economic Resources on Reunification of Illinois Children in Substitute Care* (Urbana: University of Illinois at Urbana–Champaigne, Children and Family Research Center, 2002).

33. Rockhill, A., B. L. Green, and C. Furrer. "Is the Adoption and Safe Families Act Influencing Outcomes for Families with Substance Abuse Issues?" *Child Maltreatment* 12, no. 1 (2007): 7–19.

34. Rockhill, A., B. L. Green, and C. Furrer. "Is the Adoption and Safe Families Act Influencing Outcomes for Families with Substance Abuse Issues?" *Child Maltreatment* 12, no. 1 (2007): 7–19.

35. Wulczyn, Fred. "Family Reunification." *The Future of Children* 14, no. 1 (2004): 95–114.

36. Berrick, Jill D., Barbara Needell, Richard P. Barth, and Melissa Jonson-Reid. *The Tender Years: Toward Developmentally Sensitive Child Welfare Services for Very Young Children* (New York: Oxford University Press, 1998).

37. Courtney, Mark E., and Y. I. Wong. "Comparing the Timing of Exits from Substitute Care." *Children and Youth Services Review* 18, nos. 4/5 (1996): 307–24.

38. Fanshel, D., S. J. Finch, and J. F. Grundy. *Foster Children in a Life Course Perspective* (New York: Columbia University Press, 1990).

39. Wulczyn, Fred. "Family Reunification." *The Future of Children* 14, no. 1 (2004): 95–114.

40. Berrick, Jill D., Young Choi, Amy D'Andrade, and Laura Frame. "Reasonable Efforts? Implementation of the Reunification Exception Provisions of ASFA." *Child Welfare* 87, no. 3 (2008): 163–82.

41. D'Andrade, Amy, and Jill D. Berrick. "When Policy Meets Practice: The Untested Effects of Permanency Reforms in Child Welfare." *Journal of Sociology and Social Welfare* 33, no. 1 (2006): 31–52.

7

The Multidisciplinary Misnomer: A West Virginia Case Study of Multidisciplinary Treatment Teams in Child Welfare*

Corey J. Colyer and L. Christopher Plein

Contemporary child welfare practice recognizes the complexity of issues facing children and their families. Best practices call for interventions that are multifaceted and multidisciplinary. Indeed, the U.S. government recognizes and repeats this important principle in Department of Health and Human Services' *Child Abuse and Neglect User Manual Series*. "No single agency, individual, or discipline has all the necessary knowledge, skills, or resources to provide the assistance needed by abused and neglected children and their families."[1] While specialized public agencies evolved in the twentieth century to protect children's welfare, a diverse array of others outside of these agencies also maintain stakes in the well-being of children. These stakeholders are important resources for the child. "To be effective in addressing this complex problem, the combined expertise and resources of interdisciplinary agencies and professionals are needed."[2]

Multidisciplinary teams (MDTs), similar in nature to "family group conferencing," evolved over the past half-century in an effort to systematically promote interdisciplinary collaboration in response to child abuse and neglect.[3, 4, 5, 6] This chapter explores the use of MDTs in West Virginia abuse and neglect proceedings. The case study provides a reference point to consider the overall purposes and normative ideals of the MDT concept. Drawing on data from a comprehensive study of MDT proceedings and outcomes, we argue that rather than being truly interdisciplinary, MDTs are organized around two distinct institutional cultures: one relating to the state's child welfare agency and the other relating to the state's court system. Put differently, to describe these MDTs as multidisciplinary is to perpetuate a misnomer.

THE UNDERLYING PURPOSES OF MDTS: PRACTICE PARADIGMS AND POLICY IMPERATIVES

By the 1970s, a new practice paradigm emphasizing a multidisciplinary approach influenced case management and treatment planning in child welfare. This multidisciplinary response was predicated on the realization that child welfare is complicated by innumerable factors that frustrate the efforts of single agencies or treatment applications. This paradigm asserted that child welfare is best promoted through a mechanism of interdisciplinary collaborative effort. Inspired by the models used in medicine and by initial demonstration projects, the ideal of the MDT became an established norm in child welfare. Both professionals and policy-makers advocated this approach. However, there were few efforts to critically assess the implementation and effectiveness of these multidisciplinary interventions. Accordingly, the efficacy of multidisciplinary collaboration has largely unquestioned as a foregone conclusion.

MDTs were pioneered in two distinct settings. Most of the early literature (e.g., prior to 1980) examined the creation of child abuse and neglect detection and response teams in hospital settings.[7, 8, 9] Hospital-based MDTs were formed to assist in the diagnostic detection of abuse and planning an appropriate treatment response. They were organized to address the circumstances of physical and sexual abuse, the types of cases most likely to present in a hospital setting.[10, 11] In contrast, community-based child protection agencies had different challenges amenable to multidisciplinary response. In the community setting, allegations of abuse or neglect mobilized different agencies with overlapping jurisdiction. Multidisciplinary teams were developed to coordinate the activities of these agents to promote efficiency and sensitivity.[12]

The early scholarship on multidisciplinary teams in child welfare focus on the diffusion and variety of the application.[13, 14] Much of this literature offers taxonomies of MDT types, the geographical distribution of MDT policies, and a synopsis of the policy or program implemented through multidisciplinary efforts. Over the course of three decades, this literature has helped to flesh out the theoretical purposes of MDTs and to document the specific dimensions of child welfare casework where MDTs are used most often. However, these theoretical models and descriptive accounts rarely offer empirical evidence of effectiveness.

Broad surveys of application have helped us understand how MDTs have been applied various ways in child welfare services. Lalayants and

Epstein's[15] review of the literature identifies four conceptual categories of application: (1) Treatment teams collaborate on diagnosis and treatment of the child and/or the family; (2) case consultation teams collectively advise child protection agencies on specific cases; (3) resource development or community action teams provide ongoing treatment planning, service coordination, and resource mobilization; and (4) mixed model teams combine features of the other three models.

In addition to these four models, investigatory MDTs formed for the purpose of sharing resources and information in abuse and neglect investigations.[16, 17, 18, 19] Many point to the effectiveness of investigatory MDTs as the ideal model for interdisciplinary collaboration.[20] However, investigatory MDTs operate with a clearly defined purpose on well-defined cases. Their objective is unambiguous: was the child abused, by whom, and by what method? This is quite different from those applications of MDTs where the objective is to identify the underlying cause(s) of a family's difficulty in order to plan and monitor a treatment response. As child welfare scholars well know, these problems defy simple diagnoses or treatments.[21] The present chapter is concerned with treatment MDTs rather than multidisciplinary investigation panels.

A careful reading of this literature also suggests consistent challenges that confront multidisciplinary collaboration. Cross-disciplinary interactions lead to clashes of culture. These challenges are familiar to scholars of organizational and professional cultures. The only empirical assessment report available from the 1970s suggests that early MDTs were plagued by breakdowns in communication and role confusion. The National Center on Child Abuse and Neglect surveyed the members of fourteen multidisciplinary teams in 1978 and found "intellectual conflict" between members to be a significant barrier to achieving consensus in more than half of the sample. This survey identified conflict over the members' locus of control or "turf" to be an issue in slightly less than half the sample.[22] Other problems highlighted in that study are similar to those experienced today and bear relevance to contemporary MDT practice.

> Four teams reported difficulty in developing treatment plans which realistically reflected the available resources, and four reported that confidentiality of client records was a problem. Problems related to scheduling team meetings and the geographic location of the meetings were also reported.[23]

These challenges are instructive. Though intended to promote professional collaboration, MDTs also spawn interdisciplinary conflict. The MDTs bring people to the same table to discuss problems and propose solutions, but these efforts can be frustrated by several predictable factors. Those factors of frustration have not diminished over the past thirty years. For instance, in the most thorough review of the literature on MDTs to date, Lalayants and Epstein[24] write:

> Although respondents perceived MDTs as helping lessen the burden on CPS workers, some were confused about leadership roles, questioned ownership of the case, and felt uncomfortable about additional scrutiny of their work. Others commented that, at least at first, interdisciplinary decision making was more time-consuming than traditional approaches.

As we will describe, the issues of leadership, ownership, and antagonistic relations between the heterogeneous members of multidisciplinary teams continue to challenge practitioners. The West Virginia experience provides an opportunity to pull together various strands of literature and compare them to MDT processes in action. Our case study confirms some of the concerns already described, elaborates on others, and identifies new dimensions of the MDT concept. Such a case study can provide both a "reality check" and a platform for further exploration, as well as practical improvements in the application of MDTs to child welfare.

THE WEST VIRGINIA STUDY: BACKGROUND AND METHODOLOGY

West Virginia's MDT process was established by court rules that were codified into state code (§49-5D-3) by legislative statute. The precipitating causes of MDT adoption were widespread perceptions of poor performance in the child welfare system that led to a series of high-profile cases in the 1980s and remedial legal actions by the courts to improve child abuse and neglect investigation and treatment practices in the state.[25] West Virginia's MDT system is characterized by two types of teams: investigatory and treatment teams. MDTs were imposed by legislative action rather than being homegrown in most jurisdictions.

State law requires that each county establish multidisciplinary teams (MDTs) to assist the courts and the Department of Health and Human Resources (DHHR) in child abuse and neglect proceedings. The treatment MDT advises the court on treatment and placement recommendations and monitors the delivery of services. State code specifies that MDTs in West Virginia are to be convened and directed by the family's caseworker from the DHHR and consist of (1) the child, when deemed appropriate[26]; (2) the child's custodial parent(s), guardian(s), and/or other immediate family members; (3) legal counsel for the child (e.g., a guardian ad litem), parents, and DHHR, who is also the prosecuting attorney; and (4) when appropriate and available, a court-appointed special advocate (CASA), a member of the local child advocacy center, appropriate school officials, and "any other person or an agency representative who may assist in providing recommendations for the particular needs of the child and family."

This chapter draws from a study of the West Virginia MDT policy that we conducted in 2007–2008. The study was commissioned by West Virginia's Court Improvement Program, an initiative of the Administrative Office of the West Virginia Supreme Court of Appeals, to assess the efficacy of team activity. Specifically the study gauged satisfaction of various participants concerning MDT processes and outcomes and identified: (1) institutional and other structural barriers that limited MDT performance, (2) processes and practices that translate into conduits for success, and (3) areas amendable to training and development.

Constructed as a multiphased study, the project utilized a mixed methodology of direct observation and survey research. In the first phase several MDT sessions were observed in locations across West Virginia. Because child welfare functions are coordinated through regional field offices across the state, we observed team activities in ten separate sites across the state. This also allowed for observations of proceedings in different court jurisdictions which are customarily organized along county lines. This phase of the study allowed the research team to observe patterns of consistency and variation in the MDT process. It also allowed for the development of questions and topics to be investigated in the second phase of the inquiry.

In the second phase of the study, all professional MDT participants from across West Virginia were invited to complete a Web survey. A link to the survey was distributed through the DHHR's internal email system, through the state's bar association listserv, and through a private mailing list of MDT participants maintained by the court improvement program. In all, 432 completed responses were received.[27] The questionnaire was designed to capture data on two important concerns: how do MDT practices vary across West Virginia; and how do MDT participants experience the MDT process? These issues were measured through a battery of questions relating to:

(1) The respondent's background, experience, and exposure to training on MDT policy;
(2) The respondent's recollection of MDT logistics (location, scheduling, frequency and duration, facilitation, etc);
(3) The respondent's perception of the MDT's adequacy in terms of:

  (a) treatment planning
  (b) meeting the needs of various constituents
  (c) building consensus and achieving desired outcomes
  (d) maximizing stakeholder participation and contribution

Additionally, the surveys asked respondents to offer thoughtful answers to four open-ended questions which we draw from frequently in the remainder of this chapter:

(1) What should MDTs accomplish?
(2) How can the MDT process be improved?
(3) Who is not currently involved in MDTs that should be?
(4) What things haven't we asked about that are important for understanding MDT?

In the presentation of results that follows we draw largely on the qualitative observational data and from the open-ended survey responses. We summarize the trends identified through statistical analysis of the quantitative survey responses in narrative form. Readers interested in the more detailed statistical analysis of these responses are encouraged to consult the technical report from the larger study.[28] Unless otherwise indicated, quotes that follow are open-ended survey responses. Descriptions of MDT dynamics and interview quotes are drawn from field note records of our site visit observations.

BRIEF SUMMARY OF FINDINGS

The study findings were submitted to the board of West Virginia's Court Improvement Program in the form of a technical report.[29] These findings touched on four key observations. First, though guided by a uniform policy, MDT practice varies across administrative jurisdictions. Second, the constitution and makeup of MDTs varies considerably from one location to the next. Third, the leadership of MDTs is uneven. Some were led by child welfare professionals; others were led by prosecutors. Interesting dynamics hinged on the institutional home of the leaders. Fourth, MDT participants are strongly influenced by their institutional home. That is, attorneys and social workers differed in terms of perspective on the purpose of MDTs and their efficacy.

Perhaps the most interesting of these findings relevant to the present chapter concerns the patterns of participation and the accountability structure regulating participant behavior. We found that these patterns suggest a bidisciplinary rather than multidisciplinary structure for West Virginia MDTs. These MDTs attempt to bridge the chasm of two cultures which drive conflict, disagreement, and misunderstandings. This behavior, we believe, is rooted in entrenched professional subcultures that are further reinforced by external institutionalized mandates. Social work professionals (inclusive of caseworkers, agency supervisors, and service providers) tend to desire less formality in the process while legal professionals (prosecutors, defense counsel, and guardian ad litems) seek to expand the formality. Our conclusions about this dynamic are based on both direct observation and results from the survey encompassing both phases of the study.

BI-DISCIPLINARY DYNAMICS

As stated, West Virginia law stipulates that MDTs involve specific stakeholders in a child and family's case. Our study suggests that the inclusion and involvement of these stakeholders varies across jurisdictions. One factor that doesn't vary is the participation of the DHHR child welfare caseworker. In fact, caseworkers were the only participants to consistently contribute to the MDT in each of the ten jurisdictions we visited. Accordingly, the MDT proceedings often revolve around their efforts and needs. Most MDTs convene at a DHHR office, and in most jurisdictions the caseworker is responsible for scheduling and notifying the other members of the meeting. A battery of survey questions attempted to ascertain "the involvement" of various MDT participants. All of the survey respondents indicated that the caseworker is always present, and more than 80 percent rated the caseworker's involvement as "extremely active" in the MDTs.

Lawyers are the other dominant group of institutional participants in West Virginia MDTs. As noted, three separate legal counsels are necessary for child abuse and neglect cases (see West Virginia Code 49-5D). DHHR acts on behalf of the state, and thus, is represented by the circuit's prosecuting attorney. A guardian ad litem is assigned to protect the children's rights in these proceedings, while counsel is also assigned to the caretaker accused of abusing or neglecting children.[30] In nearly every MDT that we observed, the guardian ad litem and parents' counsel were present and involved in the proceedings. Thus, every primary party in the case also has legal counsel who should be present and involved in the MDT.

Viewed in the abstract, West Virginia's MDTs are bi-institutional. That is, the majority of active participants in the MDT are representatives of two sponsoring institutions. The concept of a sponsoring organization was clearly articulated by Eisenstein and Jacob[31] in their work on courtroom workgroups. "Such organizations determine who will be on the workgroup staff, and how long the staff members will stay."[32] Sponsoring organizations confer staff, resources, and perhaps most importantly institutional norms and culture onto the workgroup. An MDT is very much like Eisenstein and Jacob's courtroom workgroup; the difference is in application, where the DHHR and the state legal system are sponsoring organizations for MDTs.

These institutions exert influence over the MDT process and group dynamics. Each participant has been steeped in the institutional culture of his or her sponsoring agency. Aspects of these cultures infiltrate the formal procedure and informal expectations within the MDT. When cultures clash, one institution often becomes dominant, which is a conduit for frustration and discord. In MDTs, the dominant institution varies by locality. In most jurisdictions the culture and norms of DHHR shape MDT dynamics; however, some MDTs are more court-driven.

In court-dominated MDTs, the prosecutor's office runs the meeting and sets the agenda. In these MDTs, the agenda appeared to focus on timelines and compliance with the terms set forth in the court order(s) more so than on treatment planning and progress. While treatment plans were discussed, these discussions were couched within the context of pending court hearings.[33] One prosecutor described the purpose to be a pretrial hearing: "There should be no surprises when this case appears before the judge. We are getting our ducks in a row and clarifying the issues in advance." Thus, in this prosecutor's eyes, the purpose of the MDT is to serve the circuit court. The following observation illustrates a typical court-oriented MDT:

DHHR Caseworker: We made arrangements to start counseling with [a local provider] but [the adult respondent] didn't go to her scheduled appointment.

Respondent: I didn't know it was scheduled; my phone has been turned off.

Caseworker: It has been over a month now and they need to complete your intake testing. We also need you to complete the MMPI (a personality inventory). We can't start the program until we do this. This is important; the judge is going to expect you to follow through!

Respondent's Attorney: May I remind everyone that the department has not filed its treatment plan yet. Therefore, everything my client has done has been voluntary and I would think the judge would be happy with that.

Caseworker: Yes, that's true about the treatment plan. But your client's voluntary performance is an indicator of things to come.

The emphasis in this discussion was on compliance with court-ordered directives. While the department's caseworker was reviewing the respondent's failure to live up to a treatment plan, the respondent's attorney argued that this treatment plan did not actually exist. That is, until the plan is formally filed with the court, it is not an actionable plan. By extension, this attorney argued, the MDT may not draw inferences about the respondent's performance in relation to a treatment plan that has not been formally recognized by the court.

In contrast, department-driven MDTs focused on progress reports from the treatment providers. The discussions alternated between sharing of information and reviewing progress on the treatment plan's objectives. The following field note from one of the sites typifies this.

> The caseworker passed out notes from the counseling provider. They indicate that the parents are doing well in therapy (both as couples and in individual sessions). Then the caseworker informed the MDT that the father's paternity tests are in and he has been confirmed as the child's father. She was unsure what to do next because the child's birth certificate lists a different father. An attorney said that this problem could easily be resolved with a Judge's order and that she could take care of that. Next, the parenting class instructor reported that the couple completed her curriculum and has done well with supervised visits. She recommends that the family begin unsupervised visitation in the home. The DHHR supervisor ended the meeting by telling the couple that they are doing well and everything was on track for reunification.

In this MDT, the court was not mentioned at all. While a prosecutor was present, he did not actively participate in the discussions. The focus of the meeting was placed on the couple, their progress in court-mandated programs, and how they might resolve the administrative inconvenience of getting a birth certificate record corrected. In contrast to the court-oriented example, this MDT was responsive to the dynamics of the improvement period[34] and to communicating the next step in the treatment plan.

The bidisciplinary dynamic is by no means always harmonious and collaborative. Indeed, the process can be adversarial with battle lines drawn along an axis of institutional alignment. Consider an attorney's response to a survey question concerning the purpose of MDTs.

> MDTs are supposed to provide a free exchange of information and brain-busting to come up with solutions to the problems facing the family. In our area they often are more like an inquisitor trial from the Middle Ages, with the DHHR and the GAL (guardian ad litem) acting as the main interrogators of parents whose attorneys fail to show up or show up late.

The purpose of the MDT should be to collaboratively seek solutions to the problems that face families. But that ideal is blocked by inequities in influence. At least in this jurisdiction, the child protective service personnel appear to dominate the activities and set the agenda. Presumably more formality in the process would limit the opportunities for dominant members to mount an inquisition. This sense is offered by another attorney articulated a similar complaint in her survey response.

> I like the process overall, but it still remains somewhat of a sham, as the DHHR runs the show and almost always gets what it wants. In our area, my advice to clients is to do everything the DHHR tells you to do, or else you may lose your

kids. The DHHR personnel are typically not open to compromise, and refuse to believe they may have wrongly assessed a case. Therefore, MDTs mostly consist of everyone finding out what DHHR expects of them, and whether or not they are meeting those goals. I think it is a very rare occasion that an MDT fundamentally changes the viewpoint of the DHHR with respect to a case.

The language used in these answers is instructive. In contrast to the idyllic scenario of mutually edifying collaboration set forth in much of the literature, these comments describe a conflict dynamic. Words like inquisition and sham are evocative. They suggest that the MDTs, rather than being a truly collaborative endeavor where professionals from multiple disciplines collectively join together to discover solutions, become contests reflecting fundamental disagreements anchored to disciplinary world views. Without the mediating structure of formal rules, these disagreements can become institutionalized within the MDT framework. Note that this dynamic cuts both ways. DHHR survey respondents similarly complained about lawyers and their failure to respect the collaborative mission of the MDT. Many of these respondents described lawyers to be uncooperative participants who push the proceedings in an unnecessary adversarial direction. For instance, in a survey response this caseworker describes the lawyers as overly argumentative.

> We need less legal intervention and more social intervention to identify and address the issues that rise to level of abuse and neglect. Oftentimes progress is impeded due to legal conflicts and haggling by the lawyers. A productive treatment team is aware of the changes necessary to bring about changes for the family and eliminate safety concerns.

These tensions are anchored to disciplinary points of view. The DHHR personnel, tasked with formulating a family case plan while concurrently planning alternative arrangements for the child should the treatment fail are under specific pressures. The attorneys seeking to protect the parents' due process rights are driven by other pressures. While these points of conflict are clearly present and active, they are rooted in institutional origins. Therefore the conflicts are, in some ways mechanical rather than philosophical. They can be remedied.

OVERCOMING BI-INSTITUTIONAL BIAS: REVISITING AND REENVISIONING THE MDT

> MDTs are available to bring about optimal child placement. Since MDTs bring together multiple disciplines, children may be able to be better served; deciding child placements and outcomes should be a team effort. Important decisions about the future of our children should not be left

to individuals, as there are many different aspects and viewpoints that must be considered.

— *DHHR caseworker* (survey response)

The best things about MDTs is the face-to-face, informal exchange. While many respondents are displeased being told of the requirements of the Family Case Plan (or of their shortcomings in that respect), the meetings usually provide an opportunity to air problems, etc.

—*Attorney* (survey response)

Our study illustrates some of the challenges and pitfalls that compromise multidisciplinary collaboration in child welfare cases; it also provides ample evidence that most MDT members are united by a common purpose. The MDT process can be reconfigured to minimize disciplinary conflict and leverage the collective mission of these teams. We believe that the ideal MDT format to accomplish this goal relies on a neutral third-party facilitator. The facilitator's task is to guide the MDT and referee its process. A truly neutral facilitator will be positioned to recognize differences in professional culture and guide the proceedings to respect these differences. Moreover, a neutral facilitator has the capacity to encourage broader participation.

West Virginia has begun to experiment with different facilitation models. We observed four variations in approach to facilitating MDTs. The first two variations are most typical and do not involve specialized facilitators. Most commonly, the MDT is facilitated by the family's DHHR caseworker or caseworker's supervisor. In contrast, an assistant prosecuting attorney facilitated MDTs in other jurisdictions. Generally, MDTs facilitated by DHHR personnel demonstrated the department's institutional biases; MDTs facilitated by prosecuting attorneys were more heavily influenced by the institutional culture of the court system.[35] Each of these models requires a participant to engage in two roles. Neutral facilitation models have been implemented in two jurisdictions to avoid such challenges. One jurisdiction hired a DHHR caseworker whose sole responsibility was to facilitate MDTs. This staffer was responsible for coordinating schedules, sending out notifications, taking detailed notes of the meetings, and preparing meeting summary reports for court. She did not carry her own caseload, nor was she expected to participate in the MDT meeting as a full participant. The other jurisdiction utilized its county Child Advocacy Center (CAC) for MDT meetings. The center's director facilitated the MDT process.

Both innovations were conceived through multidisciplinary dialog. The jurisdiction that hired a new professional to facilitate MDTs did so because the leadership within DHHR recognized the burden placed on caseworkers who were trying to simultaneously participate in and facilitate the meeting. A supervisor told us that "it is nearly impossible to do both of those tasks well." In the other jurisdiction, hosting MDTs by the CAC was the product of collaborative dialog within a county-wide child abuse taskforce. The taskforce was concerned that MDTs were becoming too adversarial and attorney driven. They reasoned that meetings held at a neutral site under the leadership of a neutral facilitator would be more conducive to all the parties. The CPS supervisor in this jurisdiction believes the neutrality of the location and facilitation opens the proceedings and makes them more productive: "It is a lot less intimidating to the family for the CAC to facilitate these meetings. They're on neutral ground." Since adopting this model, caseworkers in this county believe they are under less pressure and are able to be more effective with families. Since neither DHHR nor the prosecutor's office runs the meeting, the caseworkers perceive families to be less guarded under this new model than in the past. According to one caseworker, "Now, fewer families view me as an enforcer."

We spoke to a prosecuting attorney who regularly participates in MDTs in this jurisdiction. She told us, "I am free to focus on the case. She [the CAC director] will keep the meeting on task and us in line." As a neutral participant, the CAC director begins the meeting and then retreats to background. She only becomes an active participant when the meeting needs to be redirected or ended. We observed this dynamic in action and offer an extended account of this observation below. This case involved a family nearing the end of an allocated treatment period and DHHR was concerned about their progress:

Caseworker: We have concerns about the home. . . .

Prosecutor: Yes, I've seen the photographs and, well, we're not there yet. We've been at this nine months and we're approaching the disposition. The best case scenario is that the Judge might grant a post-dispositional improvement period but...

Respondent's Counsel: Some of the pets have been sold.

Caseworker: It does appear that they're trying . . . the problem is that this house is just not clean. It smelled horrendous. It was horrible . . . despicable. I can hardly describe it. It's just not acceptable. We also have concerns about how they are going to feed both the animals and the children.

The respondents disagreed with the assessment and protested the criticism. The mother began to cry, insisting that she could care for her pets and children. The parenting class counselor, who had earlier reported on the parents' progress in therapy, reframed the discussion.

Counselor: You have made a lot of progress over the months that we've worked together. I remember when we first started you had an unclean smell. We talked about this and put a plan in motion, and when you worked hard on cleaning your house the smell went away. Well, when you came in for our last session, the smell was back. I think we need to do some more work.

Guardian ad litem: I have no problem pushing things back, but only if this is going to improve. I have to tell you that I'm not optimistic; we've been at this for a few years now.

Caseworker: We still have some major concerns that you have not addressed. Yes, you've followed the case plan for employment and getting appropriate housing, but the condition of the house is deplorable and not acceptable.

Guardian ad litem: Would them getting a bigger place help things?

Prosecutor: Size might help the organizational problems, but not the cleanliness.

Respondent's Counsel: Wait a minute now, the house has been a problem from the start and they've been working hard at resolving that. The kids have made substantial improvements and the parenting has improved as well. We should recognize these things!

Prosecutor: Look, I'm going to be forthright. The judge can go a couple of ways. He can say that the improvement is insufficient and make a disposition. Or he could look at what's improving and order another improvement period. It's a 50/50 thing so I don't know which way he will go. And honestly, I don't know what our position is going to be. I'm going to have to sit down and talk about this with the department.

Then, the mother asked for clarification. The prosecutor explained that potential legal outcomes at the next hearing included a dispositional improvement period which would order continued services but end the court's supervision; "an alt 5" which would rule that the parents are not presently capable of caring for the children, but would not terminate their parental rights;[36] or last, termination of parental rights. The prosecutor further explained, "Termination is exactly what it sounds like; there is no contact with the children unless they explicitly ask for it."

Guardian ad litem: Will the department go out and take more photos before the hearing?

Caseworker: I'm not sure that would do any good. We've done this before and there was improvement while we were taking photos; but then they backslide. This has been a pattern for a long time; because of that, we have a real problem with a post-dispositional improvement period.

Prosecutor: The state cannot recommend a dispositional improvement period. You have to act now. Get rid of the pets! They should be the first to go! I hate to be this harsh. But at this point, that's where we're at. Or maybe knock it down to one pet . . . or . . .

By now the mother was sobbing, and everyone appeared to be frustrated. The CAC director interrupted the prosecutor in mid-sentence, effectively stopping the meeting. She said, "I believe the point has been made and it's time for everyone to discuss this privately with their counsel. I think it's time to close off the discussion." The group confirmed the pending court date and the meeting ended. After the meeting, the CAC director explained that part of her role is to close off discussion that has outlived its usefulness. The prosecutor nodded in agreement and said, "She has a vantage point that I don't; sometimes we all need to be told to stop."

As the extended example shows, MDTs have the potential to veer off course or to pursue an agenda item beyond its utility in the case. At different points, each disciplinary participant advances a position reflective of his or her institutional culture. Yet none of those institutional cultures dominated the MDT meeting. The caseworker expressed her concerns about the children's well-being in the home, the parents' counsel advocated for his clients, the guardian ad litem suggested recommendations, and the prosecutor explained the state's position. The neutral facilitator effectively balanced these cultures allowing the meeting to retain productivity.

RESTRICTIONS OF HOMOPHILY

The ideal MDT model is also one of clearly defined and shared purposes. Each participant brings an important perspective to the table that adds to collaborative engagement. However, the ideal MDT model also recognizes that disciplinary pluralism implies heterogeneity of approach, perspective, and temperament. This diversity brings predictable challenges to the MDT concept. Social groups typically form around the adhesive of similarity. Nearly every social network ranging from friendship to professional association is regulated by the principle of homophily.[37] Briefly, homophily refers to a concentration of similarity in social networks. The groups to which we belong strongly shape our worldviews, and normative expectations. In consequence, homophily restricts information access and constrains attitude formation.

As demonstrated, MDTs are not immune to these dynamics. The constituent members of the MDT affiliate first with their institutional homes. One's tacit understanding of the MDT, its purposes, and its processes is shaped by professional subcultures nurtured by sponsoring institutions. MDTs operating without the benefit of neutral facilitation unwittingly run the risk of reorganizing activities through a unidisciplinary framework. Left unchecked, homophily undermines the MDT's effectiveness. When the culture of a dominant institution becomes entrenched, it is difficult for minority viewpoints to be considered.

MDTs are designed to minimize the effects of homophily by including a variety of viewpoints unified through the shared quest to achieve the best interests of the children. But the design breaks down in application when one institution is allowed to dominate the team's dynamics. Unfortunately, the state code on MDTs lacks clear guidelines to offset the dynamics of homophily. That is, the state law lacks explicit guidance concerning the expected relationships between MDT participants. Theoretically, each member of the MDT should be an equal contributor. However, studies in the sociology of small groups suggest that normal group dynamics create divisions and inequities which magnify over time. The law's list of potential MDT participants should bring together a diverse group of people representing different organizations and institutions. However, the state law also only assigns responsibility for the MDT to one agency. Structurally, this sows the seeds of homophily. The best corrective is to assign additional responsibilities along with the expectation for neutral facilitation.

The challenges facing MDTs are enhanced when they are imposed by legislation without concern for local conditions, traditions, and practices. It is clear from our survey of participants, that some jurisdictions treat MDTs as an administrative burden. As the literature has noted and our fieldwork confirms, compliance-driven MDTs generate little in the way of lasting legacy. If team members are simply "going through the motions," the MDT is yet another administrative burden imposed on families, rather than being a resource for families. In addition, such burdens consume time and other resources that are already too scarce in the child welfare system.

It is important that MDTs value shared accountability of the members. If the MDT is viewed as belonging to one institution, it will be difficult to maximize effective participation of all parties. When all members of the MDT believe that their role is valuable and they share responsibility in the outcome, the approach can be effective. At one of the site visits, a prosecutor explained that the diversity of participants in the MDT shows families that the process is for their benefit.

> These meetings help parents see this as a collaborative process, rather than an adversarial hearing. Things go wrong and we address them. When we do this, the parent can see that we're trying to work with them and not against them.

This prosecutor recognizes that in abuse and neglect cases many parties enter the MDT process distrustful and with caution. The team must actively work to build trust. Adult respondents have good reasons to be suspicious of the initial MDT meetings since few enter this process voluntarily. Many begin the process with a mind-set that DHHR has taken (or wants to take) their children, and therefore, they participate under duress. The team must convince these parents that they are, in fact, all on the same team. This is a difficult message to communicate, made even more challenging when the MDT is dominated by one institution. Our observation of early-stage cases suggests that many adult respondents distrust the other members of the MDT. Bi-institutional conflicts undermine the process.

CONCLUSION

Nearly every jurisdiction in the United States relies on some form of multi-disciplinary case planning in child abuse and neglect cases.[38, 39, 40] Moreover, policy experts agree that the most effective way to address the challenges facing families is to harness the expertise of multidisciplinary family team conferences.[41] While the wisdom of these approaches is beyond question, it behooves practitioners and policy-makers to consider the pragmatics of implementation. This chapter, in summarizing the findings from an in-depth case study of one state highlights implications that are broadly applicable in all jurisdictions.

The West Virginia study emphasizes the importance of local institutional cultures. The professional literature on social work interventions focuses heavily on techniques and technologies. Yet effective responses to child abuse and neglect have an equally powerful cultural component. Different agents from a variety of agencies maintain a stake in child abuse and neglect cases. These responders are not unified by the normative framework of a single institutional culture. Indeed, we offer evidence to suggest that the responders are split across two dominant disciplinary frameworks. Effective multidisciplinary response models must recognize and accommodate the discrepancies between legal and practice-oriented responses.

Effective multidisciplinary teams are at once sensitive to institutional standpoints of its diverse members and anchored by policies that don't unwittingly privilege one profession over another. As the West Virginia case study suggests, MDT policies can undermine multidisciplinary participation. The title of this chapter drives this point home. If MDT practice routinely only involves two disciplines, referring to the gathering as multidisciplinary perpetuates a misnomer. Our data suggest that in the absence of policy that strongly encourages broad participation across the network for stakeholders in a family's situation, multidisciplinary teams quickly become bidisciplinary or even unidisciplinary. Such practice drifts far from the conceptual moorings of the MDT idea.

While it is necessary to establish clear policy guidelines emphasizing broad responsibility across the MDTs' constituent membership, these policies should also recognize the importance of local variation. That is, the best MDTs adapt to local conditions and resources. For instance, one jurisdiction in West Virginia draws upon a CAC to provide mediation and facilitation services. This innovation leveraged a unique set of local resources not available in all jurisdictions across the state. Accordingly, policy prescriptions must be sufficiently general to apply across all permutations of local conditions, allowing the locality to leverage its strengths.

Our study suggests that the best MDTs maximize broad participation by ensuring reciprocity across the membership. The best practices begin with specificity in the team's mission and clarity in assigned responsibilities. Each team member has a role which is valued by the collective whole. The influence and power within the MDT is balanced across the constituent sponsoring organizations so that one does not become dominant over the others. This allows the MDT to create mutually reinforcing accountability structures to ensure that each member is heard and has a proportional input to the team's deliberations.

Lastly, our study suggests that the best way to achieve true multidisciplinary treatment planning teams in child abuse and neglect cases is to draw upon the resources of a neutral facilitator. There are many appropriate strategies to implement such a model; West Virginia is currently experimenting with two. As long as this neutral facilitator is able to encourage broad participation and guarantee proportional influence, the facilitation model has achieved its objective. In this way, multidisciplinary teams can avoid the multidisciplinary misnomer.

NOTES

*Funding for the this research project was provided by the West Virginia Supreme Court of Appeals and the U.S. Department of Health and Human Services, Administration of Children and Families, under Court Improvement Program Matching Grants. The opinions presented in this chapter are the authors' and should not be attributed to any government agency.

1. Goldman, J., Salus, M. K., Wolcott, D., and Kennedy, K. Y. "A coordinated response to child abuse and neglect: The foundation for practice." Office on Child Abuse and Neglect (DHHS), Washington, DC (2003).

2. Goldman, Salus, Wolcott, and Kennedy. "A coordinated response to child abuse and neglect."

3. Kempe, C. H. "Foreword." In Schmitt, B. D., ed., *The Child Protection Team Handbook* (New York and London: Garland STPM Press, 1978).

4. Chadwick, D. L., and Bryson, D. B. "Private hospitals as an environment for child protection teams." In Bross, D. C., Krugman, R. D., Lenherr, M. R., Rosenberg, D. A., and Schmitt, B. D., eds., *The New Child Protection Team Handbook* (New York and London: Garland Publishing, Inc, 1988), 11–18.

5. Kaminer, B. B., Crowe, A. H., and Budde-Giltner, L. "The prevalence and characteristics of multidisciplinary teams for child abuse and neglect: A national survey." In *The new child protection handbook*, 548–67.

6. Kolbo J. R., and Strong E. "Multidisciplinary team approaches to the investigation and resolution of child abuse and neglect: A national survey." *Child Maltreatment* 2, no. 1 (1997): 61–72.

7. Kempe, "Foreword."

8. Bross, D. C., Krugman, R. D., Lenherr, M. R., Rosenberg, D. A., and Schmitt, B. D. "Foreword." In *The New Child Protection Team Handbook*.

9. Krugman, R. D. "University teaching hospital child protection team." In *The New Child Protection Team Handbook*, 3–10.

10. Chadwick, D. L. "Private hospitals as an environment for child protection teams." In *The New Child Protection Team Handbook*.

11. Krugman, "University teaching hospital child protection team."

12. Williamson, J. "The child protection team in a city." In *The New Child Protection Team Handbook*, 19–31.

13. Kolbo and Strong, "Multidisciplinary team approaches."

14. Lalayants, M., and Epstein, I. "Evaluating multidisciplinary child abuse and neglect teams: A research agenda." *Child Welfare* 84, no. 4 (2005): 433–58.

15. Lalayants and Epstein, "Evaluating multidisciplinary child abuse and neglect teams."

16. Newman, B. S., Dannenfelser, P. L., and Pendleton, D. "Child abuse investigations: Reasons for using child advocacy centers and suggestions for improvement." *Child and Adolescent Social Work Journal* 22, no. 2 (2005): 165–81.

17. Ells, M. "Forming a multidisciplinary team to investigate child abuse." Second Printing, ed. (Rockville: Office of Juvenile Justice and Delinquency Prevention, 2000).

18. Faller, K. C., and Henry, J. "Child sexual abuse: A case study in community collaboration." *Child Abuse & Neglect* 24, no. 9 (2000): 1215–25.

19. Jones, L. M., Cross, T. P., Walsh, W. A., and Simone, M. "Criminal investigations of child abuse: The research behind the 'best practices.'" *Trauma, Violence, & Abuse* 6, no. 3 (2005): 254–68.

20. Ells, M. "Forming a multidisciplinary team to investigate child abuse."

21. Lindsey, D. *The Welfare of Children* (New York: Oxford University Press, 1994).

22. Roth, R. A. "Multidisciplinary teams in child abuse and neglect programs." Washington, DC: National Center on Child Abuse and Neglect. U.S. Children's Bureau. Administration for Children, Youth and Families. Office of Human Development Services. U.S. Department of Health, Education, and Welfare, 1978.

23. Roth, "Multidisciplinary teams in child abuse and neglect programs."

24. Lalayants, "Evaluating multidisciplinary child abuse and neglect teams."

25. Munster, C. D. "Child maltreatment in West Virginia: The comprehensive state remediation model and the court improvement project." *West Virginia Lawyer* 18 (1998): 18–23.

26. "The child may participate in multidisciplinary treatment team meetings if such is deemed appropriate by the multidisciplinary treatment team."

27. There was no clear accessible sampling frame from which to properly draw random samples. Building such a sampling frame would have been prohibitively expensive. Accordingly, the statistical results reported in this chapter should be interpreted with caution. The questionnaire was designed to capture the perspective

and sentiments of *current* MDT participants (defined as someone who participated in an MDT at any point in the twelve months prior to receiving the questionnaire). Approximately 15 percent of those responding to the survey did not meet that criterion. This effectively dropped the number of cases available for statistical analysis (i.e., the N) from 432 to 361.

28. Colyer, C., and Plein, L. C. *Multidisciplinary teams in West Virginia: Final report* (Charleston: West Virginia Supreme Court of Appeals, 2008).

29. Colyer and Plein, *Multidisciplinary teams in West Virginia.*

30. Counsel is also provided to interveners who have a stake in the outcome of the process. Interveners include grandparents, foster parents seeking to adopt the child, siblings, etc.

31. Eisenstein, J., and Jacob, H. *Felony justice: An organizational analysis of criminal courts* (Boston: Little, Brown and Company, 1977).

32. Eisenstein and Jacob, *Felony justice.*

33. To be clear, this is not to say that court-oriented MDTs ignored treatment plans or progress. Rather, these concerns took subordinate position to concerns of the pending court hearing(s).

34. §49-6-12 of the West Virginia Code establishes that a court may grant respondents "improvement periods" to work on the deficiencies that led to a substantiated case of abuse or neglect. Most of the MDTs work with families who are in the midst of an improvement period.

35. Though, to be clear, there were exceptions to this pattern.

36. West Virginia Code: §49-6-5a(5).

37. McPherson, M., Smith-Lovin, L., and Cook, J. M. "Birds of a feather: Homophilly in social networks." *Annual Review of Sociology* 27 (2001): 415–44.

38. Kolbo and Strong, "Multidisciplinary team approaches."

39. Lalayants and Epstein, "Evaluating multidisciplinary child abuse and neglect teams."

40. Waldfogel, J. *The future of child protection* (Cambridge, MA: Harvard University Press, 1998).

41. Waldfogel, *The future of child protection.*

8

Identifying and Responding to the Needs of Children Residing in Domestic Violence Shelters: Results from the North Carolina Domestic Violence Shelter Screening Project

Yvonne Wasilewski, Robert A. Murphy, Leslie Starsoneck,
Margaret Samuels, Donna Potter, Audrey Foster,
and Lorrie Schmid

Every year in the United States up to 2.7 million children are exposed to violence against a parent.[1] Children who live with domestic violence not only endure the distress of being surrounded by violence, but are more likely to become victims of abuse themselves.[2] Studies place the percentage of concurrent maltreatment and domestic violence in the home upwards of 40 percent.[3] The effects on children of witnessing domestic violence are similar to those of direct abuse and can be severe and long-lasting.[4, 5, 6, 7] These effects can include depression, posttraumatic stress, and behavior problems that can manifest as: (1) chronic fearfulness, which can lead to aggression; (2) loss of trust and confidence that adult caregivers can provide physical safety and psychological security during times of distress; (3) feelings of isolation and shame that result from the confusion and secrecy surrounding domestic violence within and outside of the family; (4) assumption of inappropriate responsibility for protecting the adult victim; and (5) ambivalent feelings toward both the abusive and victimized parent.[8, 9, 10, 11] In North Carolina, as in the majority of the United States, the domestic violence community's standard approach to addressing the behavioral health needs of children has been to improve the well-being of the victimized parent as a way to restore the physical and emotional safety of her children. Although logical and consistent with the domestic violence community's philosophy of empowerment, this approach does not directly address the behavioral health needs of children[12] Also, domestic violence program staff does not routinely receive formal training on child development and the clinical effects of domestic violence on children; and domestic violence programs, including shelter programs, vary widely in capacity and quality.[13]

The North Carolina Domestic Violence Shelter Screening pilot project was undertaken to explore the feasibility of training domestic violence shelter staff to routinely screen, intervene, and refer children for services when they enter a shelter and also experience distress related to their exposure to violence and other adverse events. This pilot project took place for the full year of 2006; our time 1 and time 2 measures come from this period. A follow-up evaluation—to assess project sustainability—took place in 2007, which is when our time 3 measures were taken. The project was funded by the Z. Smith Reynolds Foundation and the Duke Endowment in collaboration with the Center for Child and Family Health, the Center for Child and Family Policy of Duke University, and domestic violence shelters in six North Carolina counties. That project is the focus of this chapter.

PART I PILOT STUDY

Methods

Sample

Domestic violence shelters were selected from across the one hundred counties in the state of North Carolina. The selection was based, in part, on the prevalence of county residents living at or below 200 percent of the poverty level, high child abuse rates, and high rates of teen pregnancy. Sites were also chosen to reflect urban and rural differences in location as well as differences in shelter organizational size and capacity.

Executive or shelter directors at each site completed agreement and consent forms confirming the participation of their sites in the project. Within each shelter site, all (N = 75) shelter staff were invited to participate, and those who accepted then completed informed consent procedures.

Overall, 61 percent of staff, including the six shelter directors (N = 46/75), agreed to participate in the training. Staff was predominantly female (95 percent), and the average age was forty-one years. Fifty-one percent of staff identified themselves as white, 41 percent as African American, 3 percent as Asian, and 2 percent as multiracial. With regard to education, 39 percent of staff had a high school diploma/GED, 47 percent a bachelor's degree, and 14 percent a master's degree. The average number of years of employment was 4.3, with a range from less than 1 year to 15 years.

Procedures

A collaborative learning approach was used to plan, implement, and evaluate the project over a twelve-month period.[14] The collaborative learning approach is modeled on the seminal work of the Institute of Health Care Improvement to improve health care processes and outcomes, and has been adapted for use by the National Child Traumatic Stress Network in its effort to address child traumatic stress.[15] The model applies principles of adult learning theory that emphasize an interactive learning process and skill-focused learning. Key components of this project included: (1) three-day-long training sessions conducted by project staff with extensive experience in evidence-based trauma treatment; (2) biweekly or monthly conference calls with consultation and feedback on the content of training sessions; (3) a half-day site visit with consultation and feedback; (4) a listserv to share resources and support sustained learning; and (5) a toolkit containing assessment, intervention, and collaboration resources. Each shelter received $1,000 for participating in the project ($500 upon signing the initial contract and $500 upon completion of the follow-up survey at the third training session). Each staff person received $50 for participating in the focus groups that took place one month after the training was completed.

During the three training sessions, shelter staff was trained to administer, score, and appropriately refer children to community resources using standardized screening tools. The tools were designed to assess child and adolescent posttraumatic stress, psychological symptoms, psychosocial functioning, and development concerns. Staff was also trained to coach parents to use behavioral management strategies to help their children overcome the deleterious effects of witnessing domestic violence, and finally, staff was assisted in identifying and strengthening their relationships with community partners to whom they could refer for child-focused services.

Instruments

Three measures were selected for training and screening: the UCLA Posttraumatic Stress Disorder Index (PSDI), an extensively used instrument available in caregiver and child self-report versions that assess posttraumatic symptomatology related to reexperiencing, arousal and avoidance symptom clusters,[16] the Strengths and Difficulties Questionnaire (SDQ),[17] a general screening of child symptomatology and functional impairment, and the Parents' Evaluation of Developmental Status (PEDS),[18] a measure widely used in pediatric settings to query parents about developmental and psychosocial problems in younger children.

A one-page screening form was developed to record screening activities of shelter staff during the course of the project.

A self-administered survey questionnaire was administered to staff before and after the trainings. In addition to assessing socio-demographic characteristics of staff, the survey used true/false questions to assess staff knowledge, attitudes, and beliefs about domestic violence and its effects on children, four-point Likert scale questions ranging from never to always to assess staff use of behavioral management strategies to help parents and children, and five-point Likert scale questions ranging from not at all confident to completely confident to measure staff self-confidence to assess, score, and make appropriate referrals to community agencies.

Data Analysis

Data from the pre- and posttest questionnaires were examined to assess changes in staff use of behavioral management strategies with children and parents, staff referral of parents and children to community services providers, and staff self-confidence to screen and refer children for behavioral health services. Mean scores for each variable were calculated within and across sites. Paired *t*-tests were used to assess differences in mean scores pre- and post-training.

Results

Staff Knowledge about the Effects on Children of Witnessing Domestic Violence

In the pre-test, shelter staff scored relatively high in their knowledge about the effects of witnessing of domestic violence on children (average of 78 percent correct). There were statistically significant changes from pre- to posttest on two items: (1) Children who have been chronically exposed to domestic violence from a young age are at risk for having a lower IQ than those who have not, $t(30) = 3.76, p < .001$; and (2) School age children who view their parents as scary are likely to take a controlling stance with peers, $t(30) = 2.13, p < .05$.

Staffs' Use of Behavioral Management Strategies with Children

There was one significant difference in staff use of behavioral management strategies with children: Shelter staff reported more frequent discussion with children about posttraumatic stress and its effects, $t(30) = 1.16, p < .05$.

Staff Teaching of Behavioral Management Strategies to Parents

There were statistically significant, positive changes from pre- to posttest on shelter staff teaching of two behavioral management strategies to parents residing in the shelter. These included teaching parents how to actively ignore, $t(30) = 4.71$, $p < .001$, and teaching parents to praise the opposite of misbehavior, $t(30) = 2.18$, $p < .05$.

Staffs Use of Behavioral Health Resources for Children

Staff reported more frequent referral to their local management entities (LMEs) from pre- to posttest, $t(30) = 2.21$, $p < .05$. (LMEs are agencies of local government who are responsible for managing, coordinating, facilitating, and monitoring the provision of mental health, developmental disabilities, and substance abuse services.) There were no other significant changes from pretest to posttest on frequency of referrals to other behavioral health facilities.

Staff Self-Confidence to Use Screening Measures

There were statistically significant, positive increases from pre- to posttest in staff self-confidence to correctly administer, $t(30) = 5.86$, $p < .0001$, score, $t(30) = 6.69$, $p < .0001$, and interpret results of, $t(30) = 7.19$, $p < .0001$, an instrument to measure PTSD in children. There were also statistically significant, positive increases from pre- to posttest in staff self-confidence to correctly administer, $t(30) = 4.66$, $p < .0001$, and interpret results of, $t(30) = 5.05$, $p < .0001$, an instrument that measures other symptoms of mental illness in children. In addition, staff reported increased self-confidence to recognize symptoms of mental illness in children due to exposure to domestic violence, $t(30) = 2.94$, $p < .001$.

Screening and Referral Results

Two hundred and seventy three children were eligible for assessment during the time that we monitored implementation of behavioral health measures by shelter staff. Eligibility was dependent on the measure used. For example, the eligibility criterion for the Strengths and Difficulties Questionnaire was that children fall between the ages of three and seventeen years; the eligibility criterion for the PTSDI was that children fall between the ages of seven and seventeen years; the eligibility criterion for the PEDS was that children fall between the ages of zero and eight years. This figure (278) represents 65 percent of the 423 children sheltered across the six pilot sites during the course of the pilot project. Fifty-six percent of the children were female and 44 percent were male. The average age of children assessed across shelters during the assessment period was 7.23 years (age range 0.6–17.5 years). Twenty-two percent were African American; 32 percent white; 12 percent Hispanic; 8.1 percent multiracial; 6.0 percent not reported. There were no statistically significant differences in gender, ethnicity, or age with regard to who was screened for behavioral health problems.

Of the 273 eligible children, 109 (39.9 percent) were assessed using any one of the three measures on which staff was trained. Forty-five percent of children who were assessed scored in a clinically elevated or at-risk range on at least one of the measures. However, only 47 percent of children who scored in this range were referred for follow-up services. In addition, there were considerable differences in referral rates by each shelter. The two shelters with the highest referral rates (80 percent and 75 percent respectively) had on-site therapeutic services, which may have contributed to their higher referral rates. These results are in table 8.1.

Table 8.1. Number of Children Who Scored Clinically Significantly or At-Risk on Any Screening Measure and Were Referred by Shelter

Shelter	Eligible Children		Assessed Children		Clinically Sig/At-risk Any Measure		Referred/ Assessed	
	n	%	n	%	n	%	n	%
Shelter A	64	23.4	36	56.3	18	50.0	12	66.7
Shelter B	91	33.3	16	17.6	10	62.5	8	80.0
Shelter C	20	7.3	7	35.0	5	71.4	0	0.0
Shelter D	44	16.1	29	65.9	8	27.6	0	0.0
Shelter E	17	6.2	12	70.6	4	33.3	0	0.0
Shelter F	37	13.6	9	24.3	4	44.4	3	75.0
TOTAL	273	100.0	109	39.9	49	45.0	23	46.9

PART II: FOLLOW-UP STUDY OF PROJECT SUSTAINABILITY

Methods

Sample

We contacted shelter pilot sites in January 2007 requesting their continued participation in the project in order to assess project sustainability six months after the pilot study ended. In June 2007 shelter directors and staff at all six sites were reconsented and administered a follow-up survey.

We also collected demographic data on children sheltered and measures administered between January 1 and June 30, 2007.

Nineteen (41 percent) of the original 46 shelter staff members and directors completed the project questionnaire at three time points—at pre-intervention (time 1), post-intervention (time 2), and six months after the post-intervention assessment (time 3).

Procedures

We defined project sustainability as the degree to which the project had been integrated into the shelter's daily functioning at the individual and site level in the absence of contact, consultation, or incentives from the project leaders.

At the individual level, we sought to determine the extent to which shelter staff continued to: demonstrate increased knowledge of the effects on children of witnessing domestic violence; use new behavioral management strategies with children; use new parenting strategies with parents; work with LMEs, in order to refer and respond to the service needs of children; remain confident in the ability to use the screening tools to assess, score, and appropriately refer children to services; and apply screening and referral measures in the shelter setting.

At the site level, we sought to determine the extent to which screening and referral had been integrated into the structure and functioning of the shelter, the extent to which screening and referral procedures had been modified over time, and to identify barriers and their solutions to the integration of screening and referral into the shelter's functioning.

Instruments

We used the pre-/posttest questionnaire to reassess staff use of behavioral management strategies with children and parents, staff referral of parents and children to community services providers, and staff self-efficacy to screen and refer children for services. We developed a scale based on Pluye and colleagues' model of program sustainability to assess the level of sustainability of screening and referral at the shelter level.[19] The scale examines four characteristics of "routinized activities" that promote sustainability: *memory, adaptation, values,* and *rules.* These four sustainability scales ask questions about the characteristics as they apply to the integration of screening and referral into the shelters' daily activities. We added a fifth subscale to measure the level of integration of *community partners* into the shelters' screening and referral activities, and a sixth subscale to measure the degree to which shelters have *Internet capability* (in order to gauge the potential for future use of the Internet as a shelter resource for screening and referral). All scales were tested for internal consistency using Cronbach's Alpha and had moderate to high scores ranging from 0.68 to 0.95.

For each item, shelter staff was asked "to circle the degree to which it was 'like' your shelter." The range was a four point scale (0 = Not at all; 1 = A little; 2 = Somewhat; and 3 = A lot). The results were calculated as means with standard deviations in parentheses below the mean for each subscale and for the total scale (table 8.2).

Data Management and Analysis

Mean scores for each variable were calculated within and across sites. ANOVA was used to assess differences in mean scores on survey items from pretest/baseline (time 1), to posttest (time 2) and six-month follow-up (time 3). To assess site level maintenance, we rated each shelter on each of six dimensions of sustainability drawn from the organizational literature and created a dimensional and total score for each shelter. To measure barriers and additional factors thought to promote sustainability, we analyzed open and closed questions also drawn from the organizational literature.

Results Individual-Level Sustainability

The findings reported below are drawn from the follow-up survey administered at time 3 and are based on reports from these nineteen individuals.

Shelter Staff Members' Knowledge of the Effects of Domestic Violence on Children

As in previous assessments, at the time of the follow-up survey, there was no significant change in the mean score on the index of staff knowledge of the effects of witnessing domestic violence on children. One item remained statistically significant at follow-up (time 3), as compared to time 1: Children who have been chronically exposed to DV from a young age are at risk for having a lower IQ than those who have not $F(2,54) = 6.35, p = .01$.

Staffs' Use of Behavioral Management Strategies with Children

An initial increase in staff application of behavior management strategies with children was not sustained during the follow-up period, perhaps due to the complexity of acquiring these new skills and because of the adult-focused practices within the shelters.

Staff Teaching of Behavioral Management Strategies to Parents

Shelter staff continued to use parenting support strategies that they learned as a result of training. They continued to report teaching parents how to actively ignore behavior, $F(2,54) = 9.23$, $p = < .05$, and teaching parents to praise the opposite of misbehavior, $F(2,54) = 5.66$, p = $< .05$. In addition, staff continued to report teaching parents about the effects of witnessing domestic violence on children, $F(2,54) = 6.46$, $p = < .01$, and teaching parents which behaviors to actively ignore, $F(2,54) = 5.66$, $p = .01$. One reason for the persistence of these skills may be that they fit best with the shelters' priority focus on acute stabilization and empowerment of mothers and other adult victims of domestic violence. Another reason may be that they are more readily incorporated into existing parenting classes that take place at the shelter pilot sites.

Staffs' Use of Behavioral Health Resources for Children

Despite some initial improvements, the shelters remained relatively isolated in terms of the partnerships with and referrals to other community resources. Increased referral to the LMEs was not sustained, $F(2,19) = .097$, $p = > .05$.

Staff Self-Confidence to Use Screening Measures

Staff members continued to report high degrees of self-confidence in their abilities to administer an instrument that measures posttraumatic stress in children, $F(2,54) = 8.49$, $p = < .01$, score an instrument that measures posttraumatic stress in children, $F(2,54) = 9.73$, $p = < .01$, interpret the results of the score to make a behavioral management decision, $F(2,54) = 14.53$, $p = < .01$, administer an instrument that measures other symptoms of mental illness in children, $F(2,54) = 3.86$, $p = < .05$, and correctly interpret the results of the score to make a behavioral management decision, $F(2,54) = 5.69$, p = $< .05$. This is encouraging because staff reported difficulty learning how to administer and score assessment instruments during the pilot phase. Finally, 70 percent of staff reported screening and referral to be a permanent activity at the shelter.

Screening and Referral Results

Staff from five of the six shelters reported that screening is still ongoing. However, despite frequent contact and encouragement, only two of the shelters submitted documentation to validate use of the screening measures. While we have no reason to doubt their reports, we have noted inconsistent documentation of programmatic activity across shelters that include screening, intake results, and other aspects of shelter care, and we lack the documentation to verify the reports of screening use in the other four shelters.

Results Site-Level Sustainability

Shelter Memory

Table 8.2 displays a summary of scores on each dimension of sustainability by shelter site. We defined shelter memory as the degree to which human, material, and financial resources (support and maintenance functions) are in effect at the shelters to conduct screening and referral. The items we developed to measure shelter memory are: (1) The budget includes separate funds to employ key personnel necessary to carry out screening and referral. (2) There is a permanent position designated for screening and referral. (3) We have more than one person trained to do the screening. (4) We have an interpreter to make sure screening can be implemented with non-English-speaking families. (5) There is a supervisor assigned to oversee administrative responsibilities for screening.

Four of the six shelters had mean memory scores above 2.0 on a scale of 0–3 indicating a fairly high degree of resources committed to continue screening and referral. Two key training objectives were reported by four of the six shelters at the time of the follow-up survey: (1) cross-training of multiple staff; and (2) a supervisor assigned to oversee administrative responsibilities for screening. Three of the shelters reported that a permanent position had been designated for screening and referral. However, only two shelters reported that a budget was somewhat in place that included separate funds to employ key personnel necessary to carry out screening.

Shelter Adaptation

We defined adaptation as the degree to which routine activities at the shelter have been modified to accommodate screening and referral activities. The items we developed to measure shelter adaptation are: (1) We have made changes in our intake procedures to incorporate screening into the shelter's daily functioning. (2) We have made changes in our client records to document screening results and referrals. (3) We have incorporated the results of screening into our annual report. (4) We have changed the staff's schedule in order to implement the screening procedures. (5) We have adapted the use of the screening tools to the comfort level of the staff. (6) We have identified ways to reduce the time it takes to screen children.

Shelters consistently scored lower on the degree to which routines were modified to integrate screening and referral into daily activities. Only one shelter had a mean score above 2.0 on this subscale. The only measure of adaptation that was reported by most of the shelters was client recordkeeping to document screening and referrals. Four of the six shelters reported modifying their shelter routine to integrate this practice. Three shelters made changes to intake procedures to incorporate screening into daily functioning and to adapt the use of the screening tools.

Shelter Value

We defined value as the degree to which screening and referral was positively and collectively valued at the shelter. The items we developed to measure value are: (1) The shelter director supports the use of the screening tools. (2) We have incentives or rewards that encourage our staff to carry out screening and referral. (3) We continue to implement screening in spite of cost in terms of time and effort on part of staff. (4) Our relationships with other agencies in the community have been enhanced as a result of screening and referral.

Four of the six shelters had mean scores above 2.0 on a scale of 0–3 indicating a fairly high collective value was placed on screening and referral. Staff across four of the six shelters reported high degrees of director support to use screening tools and staff commitment to continue to implement screening in spite of cost in terms of time and effort. Staff across all shelters reported few incentives to carry out screening and referral, which diminished the mean overall value score

Shelter Rules

We defined shelter rules as the written procedures governing decision-making and action that account for "the way things are done" at the shelter. We limited most of the rules questions to the use of the DVS toolkit that was provided to each shelter at the end of training. The items we developed to measure rules are: (1) The tool kit has been viewed by all staff at the shelter. (2) We use the tool kit to train all new shelter staff. (3) The tool kit is used as a reference resource by existing shelter staff. (4) We hold meetings periodically related to screening and referral. (5) A protocol has been written by our shelter that describes how screening should be conducted.

Three of the shelters had rules somewhat in place about the use of the toolkit. Among this group, the toolkit was routinely viewed by staff, routinely used to train new shelter staff, and routinely used as a resource for screening and referral.

Community Partners

The items we developed to measure routines related to use of community partners for follow-up after screening are: (1) Key community service providers are aware of the screening program. (2) We have met with key community service providers to discuss ways to work together to meet the needs of children. (3) Community service providers are supportive of our screening referral of children to their organizations. (4) We have or are developing targeted information for our key community service providers about screening and referral. (5) Children's Developmental Service Agencies (CDSAs) are among our key community service providers for children under three. (6) Child Service Coordinators in the Health Department are among our key service providers for children under five. (7) Mental health clinicians are among our key service providers for children. (8) LMEs are among our key service providers for children. (9) SS is one of our key service providers for children.

Shelters scored high on the degree to which they recognize key community partners as allies in their efforts to address the needs of children. All of the shelters reported that community service providers are supportive of screening and referral of children to their organizations. Four of the six shelters had met with key providers to discuss ways to work together to meet the needs of children. Four of the six shelters reported that CDSAs are among their key community service providers for children under three, and that Child Service Coordinators in the Health Department are among their key service providers for children under five. These findings are particularly significant because according to pretest data, prior to training, neither of these resources had been tapped by shelters to assist with children's mental heath needs. These findings do not, however, provide information on the extent to which these resources have been integrated into the shelters' daily routines.

Technology

We developed the following items to measure the extent to which technology is in place at the shelters to carry our future activities related to screening and referral: (1) Our supervisors have ready access to PCs with CD-ROMs, audio, and privacy. (2) Our supervisors have access to the Internet through a high speed, broadband connection. (3) Our supervisors have access to email. (4) Supervisors have taken computer-based training in the past for clinical, administrative, or compliance purposes.

All shelters had high sustainability scores on all technology items indicating that, at the supervisory level, capacity exists to engage in web-based training, and to conduct screening and referral over the Internet.

Overall Sustainability

We summed the scores of the six subscales by shelter in order to ascertain a mean sustainability score for each (table 8.2). Means scores above 2.0 indicate that shelters were somewhat engaged in routinized activities that enhanced screening and referral. Only two shelters scored above 2, while two scored only slightly lower than 2. Finally, two sites scored 1.07 and 1.04 respectively, indicating that they were not substantially engaged in activities that enhanced the sustainability of screening and referral. The mean sustainability score for all shelters was 1.79, indicating that shelter screening was only partially sustained.

Table 8.2. Mean Shelter Sustainability Score with Standard Deviations by Dimension of Sustainability at Time 3

Dimension	Shelter A	Shelter B	Shelter C	Shelter D	Shelter E	Shelter F
Memory	2.73	1.27	2.3	2.8	2.33	1.47
	(0.31)	0	(2.12)		(0.58)	(0.96)
Adaptation	1.05	0.52	2.5	1.14	1.62	0.71
	(0.79)	(0.46)	(0.51)		(0.22)	(1.01)
Values	233	1.67	2.75	2	2.25	1.08
	(0.14)	(0.38)	(0.35)		(0.43)	(0.95)
Rules	1.67	0.3	2.1	2.2	1.13	0.6
	(0.31)	(0.42)	(0.71)		(0.81)	(0.53)
Community Partners	2.3	1.22	2.89	2.22	2.15	1.37
	(0.67)	(0.33)	(0.16)		(0.13)	(1.2)
Technology	2.67	2.58	3	1.5	2.5	2.19
	(0.29)	(0.38)	0		(0.43)	(0.52)
Overall Sustainability	2.06	1.04	2.6	1.97	1.97	1.07
	(0.18)	(0.06)	(0.4)		(0.05)	(0.98)

Mean Sustainability Score All Shelters = 1.79

DISCUSSION

The primary purpose of this pilot project was to test the feasibility of recruiting and training domestic violence shelter staff to screen and refer children residing in shelters for behavioral health problems using evidence-based tools. This study was conducted in the context of using a collaborative learning approach that involved shelter directors and shelter staff in the planning, delivery, and evaluation of the project. The overall mission of this effort was to increase shelter staff awareness of the impact on children of witnessing domestic violence, to provide them with evidence-based screening tools to identify child behavioral health issues, and to connect staff with new and existing child behavioral health resources in the community.

Results from the pilot project indicated that trained domestic violence shelter staff can successfully and systematically evaluate children entering shelters using standardized screening tools addressing broad psychosocial functioning, developmental status, and traumatic stress symptoms. Quantitative results from participating shelter staff suggest that they acquired a sense of confidence in screening children for behavioral health problems during the pilot; that they screened at least 40 percent (range 18 to 71 percent) of eligible children; and that they were able to identify behavioral health concerns among sheltered children, as well as concerns related to developmental status. The assessments revealed significant levels of psychological distress, functional impairment, and developmental risk among a substantial number of child shelter residents. Almost half (45 percent) of children who received the screening scored in the clinically significant or at-risk range on at least one of the three screening measures.

Referrals to community behavioral health and other psychosocial resources for further evaluation following screening were more difficult to achieve. About half (47 percent) of children with an elevated score on at least one of these measures was referred for follow-up services. Staff attributed this to the timing of the administration of the tools, as well as the time necessary to administer, score, and interpret the results of the tools. For example, brief lengths of stay and the acute nature of shelter admissions tended to decrease the likelihood of both screening and/or referral. The outcome of referrals was not a focus of the current evaluation. As we discovered from pretest data and during the course of the intervention, partnerships between shelters and community agencies to which these referrals would most frequently be directed were largely nonexistent or very weak at the beginning of the project. Consequently, promoting these partnerships became a project objective, as well as identifying and removing real or perceived barriers to those partnerships.

Results of the study also indicated that staff members viewed the screening tools as a positive strategy for engaging, educating, and supporting parents. They were able to identify both risk and resiliency factors in children and apply newly learned skills in behavioral management when teaching parents and interacting with children. An explicit focus on providing developmentally informed and structured activities and care for children within domestic violence shelters represents a significant shift for shelters in terms of practice and philosophy. In addition, we found that shelter staff members had relatively high levels of preexisting awareness and knowledge about the effects of domestic violence on children. However, they were less familiar with specific strategies related to managing behavior, improving parenting skills, and identifying psychological or developmental needs and related community resources.

Results of the follow-up study indicated that shelter staff members' knowledge of the effects of domestic violence on children was comparable to that expressed at the outset of the project. This is attributed to the fact that staff knowledge about the effects on children of witnessing domestic violence was already fairly high to begin with and remained so over the course of this project. An initial increase in staff application of behavior management strategies (i.e., educating children about traumatic stress and confronting inappropriate verbal behavior) was not sustained during the follow-up period, perhaps due to the complexity of acquiring these new skills and the distinct nature of skills relative to the usual, adult-focused practices within the shelters. Shelter staff teaching of parenting strategies that they learned as a result of training was sustained at follow-up. They continued to report teaching parents about active ignoring of negative behavior, and appropriate use of praise. One reason for the persistence of these skills may be that they fit best with the shelters' priority focus on acute stabilization and empowerment of mothers and other adult victims of domestic violence. Another reason may be that they are more readily incorporated into existing parenting classes that take place at the shelter pilot sites.

There was no improvement in frequency of use of mental health resources among shelter staff. Despite the emphasis on the creation of new partnerships to address the behavioral needs of young children, shelters remained relatively isolated in terms of the partnerships with and referrals to other community resources. Even an increase in referral to LMEs was not sustained. This may have been due to a dramatic reduction in the size of staff at each of the shelters at the time of the follow-up study resulting in insufficient power to detect changes over time.

Staff members continued to report a high degree of self-confidence in their abilities to screen and refer children residing in shelters at follow-up. This is encouraging in light of the fact that staff reported difficulty learning how to administer and score assessment instruments during the pilot training year. Seventy percent of staff reported screening and referral to be a permanent activity at the shelter, though project staff was unable to document this.

Screening and referral of children was only partially sustained at the time of the follow-up evaluation. Shelters scored fairly high on the degree of resources allocated to continue screening and referral including assignment of a supervisor to oversee administrative responsibilities for screening, cross-training of multiple staff to conduct screening, and designation of a permanent position to conduct screening and referral. Shelters also scored high on the collective value placed on screening and referral. Shelters scored lower on the modification of rules and written procedures to accommodate screening and referral.

Limitations of the Project

Although the North Carolina Domestic Violence Shelter Screening Project is among relatively few to work directly with domestic violence shelter staff to identify and address the behavioral needs of sheltered children, it is not without limitations. First, use of multiple screening tools instead of one reduced the number of children who were ultimately screened. However, there was no one screening tool that was developmentally appropriate for all age groups. Second, this pilot project had no control group. Although it is clear that we have a biased sample of interested and motivated shelter directors and staff, pilot projects are designed to test the feasibility of ideas and typically begin with individuals and organizations that are most interested and willing to participate.

CONCLUSION

In conclusion, these results affirm that domestic violence agencies and shelters can and should effectively serve as an assessment and triage point for children and their parents who receive services. The use of standard approaches to assessment and service planning will facilitate more effective planning and collaboration within and across agencies and service systems. Affordable and accessible training made available to a broad range of professionals, including domestic violence program staff, who comprise the components of a de facto screening, intervention, and referral system would further this goal. Where appropriate and feasible, the training should be available online to enhance its accessibility to a broad range of participants. Policy-makers and -funders should actively promote this training as a means of quality improvement for domestic violence related programs; these efforts may include offsetting of training costs, assisting with recruitment, and as appropriate, setting requirements for funding related to domestic violence and children.

NOTES

1. UNICEF, "Behind Closed Doors: The Impact of Domestic Violence on Children," *UNICEF. Child Protection Section. Program Division*, 2006, www.violencestudy.org/IMG/pdf/SVITH_report.pdf (12 Aug. 2009).
2. Etienne G. Krug, Linda L. Dahlberg, James A. Mercy, Anthony B. Zwi, and Rafael Lozano, eds. "Summary," *World Report on Violence and Health, World Health*

Organization, 2002, www.who.int/violence_injury_prevention/violence/world_report/en/summary_en.pdf (12 Aug. 2009).

3. UNICEF, "Behind Closed Doors."

4. John Fantuzzo, Robert Boruch, Abdullahi Beriama, Marc Atkins, and Susan Marcus, "Domestic Violence and Children: Prevalence and Risk in Five Major U.S. Cities," *Journal of the American Academy of Child & Adolescent Psychiatry* 36, no. 1 (1997): 116–22.

5. Sandra J. Kaplan, David Pelcovitz, and Victor Labruna, "Child and Adolescent Abuse and Neglect Research: A Review of the Past 10 Years. Part I: Physical and Emotional Abuse and Neglect," *Journal of the American Academy of Child & Adolescent Psychiatry* 38, no. 10 (1999): 1214–22.

6. Katherine M. Kitzmann, Noni K. Gaylord, Aimee R. Holt, and Erin D. Kenny, "Child Witnesses to Domestic Violence: A Meta-Analytic Review," *Journal of Consulting and Clinical Psychology* 71, no. 2 (2003): 339–52.

7. Adrea D. Theodore, Jen J. Chang, Desmond K. Runyan, Wanda M. Hunter, Shrikant I. Bangdiwala, and Robert Agans, "Epidemiologic Features of the Physical and Sexual Maltreatment of Children in the Carolinas," *Pediatrics* 115, no. 3 (2005): e331–37.

8. Kitzmann, "Child Witnesses to Domestic Violence: A Meta-Analytic Review."

9. Jeffrey L. Edleson, "Children's Witnessing of Adult Domestic Violence," *Journal of Interpersonal Violence* 14, no. 8 (1999): 839–70.

10. John H. Grych, Ernest N. Jouriles, Paul R. Swank, Renee McDonald, and William D. Norwood, "Patterns of Adjustment among Children of Battered Women," *Journal of Consulting and Clinical Psychology* 68, no. 1 (2000): 84–94.

11. Marta Lundy and Susan F. Grossman, "The Mental Health and Service Needs of Young Children Exposed to Domestic Violence: Supportive Data," *Families in Society* 86, no. 1 (2005): 17–29.

12. Lundy, "The Mental Health and Service Needs," 331–37.

13. Lundy, "The Mental Health and Service Needs," 25.

14. Charles M. Kilo, "A Framework for Collaborative Improvement: Lessons from the Institute for Healthcare Improvement's Breakthrough Series," *Quality Management in Health Care* 6, no. 4 (1998): 1–13.

15. Institute for Healthcare Improvement, "The Breakthrough Series: IHI's Collaborative Model for Achieving Breakthrough Improvement," *Institute for Healthcare Improvement* (2003).

16. Robert Pynoos, Ned Rodriguez, and Alan M. Steinberg, *PTSD Index for DSM-IV* (Los Angeles: University of California, Los Angeles, 2000).

17. Robert Goodman, Robert Y. Herbert, and Veil Bailey, "The Strengths and Difficulties Questionnaire: A Pilot Study on the Validity of the Self-Report Version," *European Child & Adolescent Psychiatry* 7, no. 3 (1998): 125–30.

18. Kyle B. Brothers, "PEDS Developmental Milestones: A New Measure for Developmental Behavioral Surveillance and Screening," *Ambulatory Pediatric Association Newsletter* 43, no. 3 (2007): 21–22.

19. Pluye, L., J. Potvin, L. Denis, and J. Pelletier (2002), "Program sustainability: Focus on organizational routines," *Health Promotion International* 19, no. 4 (2004): 489–500.

9

African American Caregiver Age, Social Support, and the Well-Being of Children in Kinship Foster Care

Terry A. Solomon, James P. Gleeson, and Arden Handler

Many ethnic groups/cultures, particularly those of color, believe that the family, including extended family, has a moral and social responsibility to care for children. In some cultures, the child's primary caregiver is often a relative other than a parent, or, as sometimes defined in the United States, a "kinship" caregiver. According to the 2000 U.S. Census, nearly three million children live in families separate from their birth parents.[1] More than 2.1 million of these children live with relatives. Although the majority of these families have no involvement with the child welfare system, approximately 137,385 children are living with relatives under the custody of the child welfare system because of abuse, neglect, or abandonment by their birth parents. These arrangements are often referred to as kinship foster care, relative foster care, or home of relative care.[2] Children residing in kinship foster care represent approximately 25 percent of the children in the custody of the child welfare system. African American children are overrepresented in child welfare system caseloads as well as in kinship care. It is these children residing in kinship foster care, and their caregivers, that are the focus of this study.

KINSHIP CARE

A fundamental strength of kinship care is that it enables children to remain connected to their family and community.[3] However, kinship caregivers tend to be older and have fewer financial resources than unrelated foster parents.[4] The lower income and older age of relative caregivers raise questions about their ability to provide for the well-being of children placed in their care, particularly if the children are young and will require many years of care before they are grown.

KINSHIP CARE IN ILLINOIS

The increased reliance of the child welfare system on relative foster care-givers, particularly older grandparents, has generated interest by public policy-makers and child welfare professionals.[5] Concerns about this issue have been greater in states like Illinois, which historically have had large numbers of children in the custody of the child welfare system, with the majority of these children living with kin. In 1997, when the Illinois foster care caseload was at its peak, there were fifty-two thousand children in foster care, and 57 percent of these children were living with kin. The rising caseload and associated costs spurred a number of initiatives to reduce the number of children in foster care, partly by encouraging kinship caregivers to adopt or assume legal guardianship of the related children in their care, thereby providing legally permanent homes that would allow the child welfare system to discharge these children from the caseloads.[6]

CONTROVERSY IN ILLINOIS

These initiatives were very successful in reducing the size of the Illinois Department of Children and Family Services (DCFS) caseload to less than eighteen thousand by 2005.[7] However, concerns were raised about the rush to reduce the caseload and whether the resulting "permanent homes" adequately met the needs of children. It was at this time that the Illinois DCFS Office of the Inspector General released its *Kids and Older Caregivers* report (2005). The report expressed concerns about efforts to move children out of foster care and into permanent kinship placements by encouraging older caregivers to adopt or take guardianship of younger children. Moreover, concerns were raised about the well-being of these children and the ability of older caregivers to meet their needs. There were attempts to create policies that would prevent the child welfare system from placing young children with older caregivers and to prevent older caregivers from adopting or assuming legal guardianship of children for whom they were serving as kinship foster parents.

There was very little empirical evidence to inform the debate about the risks and benefits of placing children with older relatives or attempts to make these living arrangements permanent. No studies had systematically examined associations between the age of kinship foster parents and the well-being of children in their care. Researchers had focused on the burden, stress, and adaptation associated with caring for related foster children, but the effects of caregiver age on caregiver stress or burden were not a central focus.[8] Caregivers' stress was found to be associated with child behavioral problems, but again, there was no systematic examination of whether this child behavior–caregiver stress association varied by age.[9]

As the debate continued, many kinship care advocates argued that decisions about child placement and permanency planning could not be based solely on age of the caregiver; other factors had to be considered. Among these factors was the social support that the caregiver received. The argument was that social support might buffer or mediate any negative effects that increased caregiver age might have on the well-being of children. Social support—the access and ability to call on others for material and emotional assistance and for information and referrals—is an important aspect of caregiving.[10] Social support appears especially important in alleviating stressors on families potentially leading to more positive parent-child interaction. Mothers with more social support, for example, are more nurturing, more consistent in their interactions, and more positive and sensitive toward their children.[11] However to date, few studies have examined the social support provided to kin foster caregivers, particularly older caregivers, or the effects of caregiver social support on child well-being. The study described in this chapter attempts to address this gap in knowledge by examining the association between African American relative caregivers' age, social support, and the well-being of children in relative foster care. We focus on African American children because they are overrepresented on child welfare caseloads, and represent the overwhelming majority of kinship foster parents in Illinois.

This study examines whether: (1) the age of African American relative foster caregivers is associated with the well-being of children in kinship foster care; (2) the caregiver's social support is associated with child well-being; (3) the effect of caregiver's age is mediated by social support; and (4) the effect of caregiver's age is moderated by social support.

DESCRIPTION OF THE STUDY

This study analyzes cross-sectional secondary data from wave 2 of the Illinois Subsidized Guardianship (SG) Research Demonstration Evaluation, which was conducted from May 1997 to June 2002.[12] The demonstration was one of the initiatives undertaken in Illinois to assist children living with relatives in the custody of the Illinois child welfare system to achieve permanency through either subsidized guardianship[13] or adoption when reunification with parents was impossible. The study was conducted in three geographic areas in Illinois: Cook County, Peoria County, and East St. Louis. Children were eligible for the study if they had been in the custody of the state for a year or more and had lived with the same relative or foster parent for at least one year. The National Opinion Research Center designed a sampling plan to ensure representativeness. Caregivers and foster children were randomly assigned to either a control or experimental group. Those in the demonstration group were offered the option of subsidized guardianship if the child could not be reunified with birth parents and adoption was not a feasible permanent plan, while those in the control group were not given this option.

Research staff interviewed caregivers using computer-assisted, in-person, and telephone interviews.[14] Surveys were conducted at baseline (wave 1), a period spanning July 1998 through spring 1999, and at a two-year follow-up (wave 2) between June 2000 and February 2001. Wave 2 caregiver interviews are the data source used in this study. The wave 2 sample consisted of 2,869 caregivers. Each household was weighted, irrespective of assignment, prior to randomization and based on household characteristics. Research staff at the Children and Family Research Center of the School of Social Work at the University of Illinois at Champaign–Urbana assisted in identifying the appropriate weights for data analyses. This study focuses on all of the African American caregivers in relative foster care and children in both the demonstration and control groups in the Subsidized Guardian target areas of Cook Central region, East St. Louis subregion, and Peoria County ($n = 1,029$). Each caregiver provided information for one child, which resulted in an equal number of caregivers and children for the study.

Key Independent and Moderator/Mediator Variables

The key independent variable in this study is caregiver's age at the wave 2 interview. Caregiver age was examined both as a continuous and an ordinal variable [< forty years (younger), forty to fifty-nine years (middle age), and sixty+ years (older)] to facilitate interpretation. Potential mediators or moderators considered were emotional and instrumental social support. Emotional and instrumental support scales were constructed from caregiver ratings of the social support they received from family members, extended family members and fictive kin,[15] and church/faith-based members. The emotional support scale included six items of caregiver ratings of whether family members, extended family members, and fictive kin provide comfort when upset and talk with the caregiver about feelings. The mean emotional support scale score was 4.0, with a theoretical range = 0–6 and the standard deviation was 1.7. The instrumental support scale is a fifteen-item index constructed from ratings of whether family members, extended family members, and fictive kin provided child care, transportation, lent money, and helped with shopping or when someone is ill. The mean scale score was 8.4, the theoretical range = 0–15, and the standard deviation was 4.4. Internal consistency of the scales was determined using Cronbach's Alpha. An alpha of .7–.8 is considered acceptable.[16] Cronbach's Alphas of .70 and .90, respectively, indicate that the emotional support scale has adequate internal consistency reliability and the instrumental support scale has excellent internal consistency reliability.

Key Dependent Variables

Child well-being, was assessed using two indices: antisocial behavior and adverse emotional behavior. The antisocial behavior index included twelve items; each was assessed using a rating of never, sometimes, and often. Seven of these items assessed if the child had temper tantrums, physical fights with children, physical fights with adults, refused to do chores, ran away, destroyed property, or stole. Five reverse-scored items in the scale measured if the child got along well with friends, was funny, participated in family activities, helped around the house, or participated in recreational activities. When the total antisocial behavior index was scored, there was sufficient variance across children to justify further analysis. The mean antisocial behavior index score = 15.0, the theoretical range = 1–36, and the standard deviation (SD) = 2.7. Cronbach's Alpha was .70, indicating the antisocial behavior index has satisfactory internal consistency reliability.

The adverse emotional behavior index included seven items rated never, sometimes, often. Four items measured negative emotional behavior: if the child was sad/depressed, nervous/worried, moody, or hostile/aggressive. Three reverse-scored items measured whether the child displayed positive emotional behavior: loving, cheerful, or playful. As with the antisocial behavior index, the adverse emotional behavior index score also demonstrated sufficient variance across children to justify further analysis (mean = 8.2, theoretical range = 1–21, and standard deviation = 2.0). The Cronbach's Alpha for the adverse emotional behavior index was .73, indicating satisfactory internal consistency reliability.

Description of the Sample

Characteristics of African American Relative Foster Caregivers

Demographic information for the African American relative foster caregivers is provided in table 9.1. The mean age of the caregivers was fifty-three years; 68 percent were older than age fifty. Nearly all caregivers (97

Table 9.1.   African American Caregiver's and Child's Socio-demographic Characteristics

Characteristics	Responses	n^{ab}	%	M^b	S.D.^{b}
Caregiver's Characteristics (n = 1029)					
Relation	Great/Grandmother	589	57.6		
	Great/Grandfather	24	2.0		
	Great/Aunt	359	34.9		
	Great/Uncle	14	0.9		
	Great/Cousin	30	3.4		
	Sibling	11	1.0		
	Other relative	2	0.2		
Child's Characteristics (n = 1029)					
Child's Gender	Male	516	50.4		
	Female	513	49.6		
Child's Ethnicity	African American	1023	99.5		
	European American	3	0.3		
	Hispanic	1	0.1		
	Other	1	0.1		
Child's Age Group	0–2 years old	1	0.1	10.9	4.2
	3–5 years old	120	11.8		
	6–9 years old	280	26.1		
	10–12 years old	255	25.6		
	13–15 years old	216	21.9		
	16 years old or older	157	14.5		
Number of Times Child Moved	Not moved	917	89.7		
	Moved once	102	9.7		
	Moved twice	1	0.1		
	Moved 3 or more times	6	0.5		
Years Child Lived with Caregiver	0–5 years	326	31.7	6.2	2.6
	>5 years	703	68.3		
Permanency Exit Status	Relative foster care	244	24.1		
	Reunified	7	1.6		
	Adopted	609	59.6		
	Subsidized guardianship	169	14.8		

[a]Due to rounding, percents may not add to 100
[b]Based on weighted data

percent) were female; 57 percent did not graduate from high school; nearly three-fourths were single (73.9 percent); and, 60 percent were grandparents. While 28 percent were employed full-time and 10 percent part-time, 62 percent were not employed outside the home (either unemployed or retired). Slightly more than one-half (50.2 percent) reported a monthly government income of less than $1,000.[17]

Child Characteristics

The caregivers provided information for one child. Half the children were female (50.4 percent), and all but five were African American (99.5 percent).[18] Their mean age was eleven years. Nearly 90 percent had been with the same relative caregiver since the child welfare system intervened; 68 percent had lived with the caregiver for at least five years. At the time of wave 2 data collection, only seven children (1.6 percent) had reunited with a birth parent. All others remained with the relative caregiver: 24 percent were still in the custody of the child welfare system and in relative care, nearly 60 percent had been discharged from the system's custody because the relative adopted the child, and nearly 15 percent had been discharged because the relative assumed legal (subsidized) guardianship (table 9.1).

Data Analysis

Data were first analyzed at the univariate level to examine the characteristics of the sample and the distribution of independent, dependent, and mediator/moderator variables. Bivariate analyses were conducted to examine associations between caregiver age, child well-being, and social support. OLS (ordinary least squares) regression models were then generated to determine whether social support mediates or moderates the relationship between caregiver age and child well-being.

STUDY RESULTS

Age of the Relative Foster Caregivers and the Well-being of Children in Kinship Foster Care

Antisocial Behavior

Based on the reports of caregivers, most of the children appeared to be well adjusted. According to the caregivers, 80 percent of the children often got along well with friends; 52 percent never had temper tantrums; roughly two-thirds never had fights with other children; and 81 percent were often funny. When asked if the child participated in family activities, 87 percent reported that the child often did so; a little more than half (53.1 percent) reported that the child never refused to do chores; and, 61 percent reported that the child often helped around the house. Only 2 percent reported that the child sometimes ran away; 3 percent reported that the child sometimes had fights with adults; 8 percent reported that the child sometimes purposely destroyed property; and only 5 percent reported that the children sometimes stole or shoplifted.

Caregiver's age and child antisocial behavior in the past thirty days were significantly correlated (Pearson r = –0.10; p-value < 0.01). As caregiver age increased, child antisocial behavior decreased. In other words, older caregivers were more likely to take care of children who have lower antisocial behavior scores.

Adverse Emotional Behavior

Caregivers reported that the children largely were loving, playful, and cheerful. For example, 81 percent reported that the child had often been cheerful in the past month, while only 1 percent reported the child had never been cheerful. The two items that demonstrated greater differences were hostility and moodiness. Slightly more than one-third (35 percent) reported the child had never acted moody, while 47 percent reported that the child sometimes had acted moody, and 18 percent reported that the child often had acted moody. Similarly, 55 percent reported the child had never acted with hostility in the past month, while 36 percent reported that the child had sometimes acted so, and 9 percent reported that the child had often been hostile.

A statistically significant inverse association was observed between caregiver age and adverse emotional behavior (r = –0.17; p < 0.001). As caregiver age increases, child adverse emotional behavior scores decrease. Therefore, older caregivers are more likely to care for children who have lower adverse emotional behavior scores. In other words, children living with older caregivers tend to be functioning better, on average, compared to children living with younger caregivers.

Relative Caregiver's Social Support and Child Well-being

Social Support

Relative caregivers were asked if immediate family members (living in the same household), extended family, or church members were available to provide different types of emotional and instrumental support. Caregivers reported that extended family members and church members were more likely to provide emotional support than immediate family members, both in terms of comfort (immediate family = 43.9 percent; extended family = 88.1 percent; church members = 66.8 percent) and providing someone to talk to (immediate family = 42.6 percent; extended family = 86.4 percent; church members = 68.1 percent).

Caregivers were also more likely to receive instrumental support from extended family and church members than immediate family members. They were more likely to seek help with child care from extended family members (72.8 percent) and church members (51.3 percent) than from immediate family (43.4 percent). They were also more likely to seek help with transportation from extended family members (75.2 percent) and church members (55.7 percent) than from immediate family members (39.6 percent). They more frequently sought help for money issues from extended family members (72.0 percent) and church members (49.9 percent) than from immediate family (39 percent). For help with shopping, more caregivers turned to extended family members (73.8 percent) and church members (50.1 percent) than immediate family (39.6 percent); likewise, when someone was ill, more caregivers turned to extended family members (76.5 percent) and church members (57.2 percent) than immediate family members (40.7 percent).

Social Support and Antisocial Behavior

Caregiver emotional support and child antisocial behavior were not significantly correlated ($r = -0.04$, NS). In other words, emotional support did not affect child antisocial behavior scores. This was not true for the relationship between caregiver instrumental support and child antisocial behavior ($r = -0.09$; $p < 0.01$). There was an inverse relationship between caregiver instrumental support and child antisocial behavior. As caregiver instrumental support increased, child antisocial behavior decreased.

Social Support and Adverse Emotional Behavior

Caregiver emotional support and adverse emotional behavior were not highly correlated ($r = -0.03$, NS). In the case of caregiver instrumental support and adverse emotional behavior, again, there was a significant inverse relationship ($r = -0.09$; $p < 0.01$); caregivers with higher levels of instrumental support were more likely to care for children with lower adverse emotional behavior scores.

Does Social Support Mediate the Effect of Caregiver's Age on Child Well-being?

A mediator serves to explain the relationship between the independent and dependent variables. For a variable to be considered a mediator of the association between caregiver age and either of the dependent variables, all of the following conditions must be met: (1) change in caregiver age must significantly explain variation in the potential mediator variables of emotional support and instrumental social support; and (2) a change in the potential mediator variables of emotional and instrumental social support must be significantly related to change in the dependent variables of antisocial behavior and adverse emotional behavior; and (3) when in a model with caregiver age, emotional support and instrumental support are controlled, and the previously significant relationships between caregiver age and antisocial behavior and adverse emotional behavior no longer exist or are reduced.

Caregiver Age, Antisocial Behavior, and Social Support

Neither emotional nor instrumental support mediated the relationship between caregiver age and antisocial behavior. For emotional support, only one condition for mediation was met: caregiver age was significantly related to antisocial behavior; however, caregiver age was not significantly related to emotional support, nor was emotional support related to antisocial behavior. Also, the association between caregiver age and antisocial behavior was not significantly changed by the inclusion of emotional support in the model (table 9.2, model 2). For instrumental support, only two conditions were met: caregiver age and instrumental support were both significantly related to antisocial behavior. However, caregiver age was not associated with instrumental support and entering instrumental support into the model did not significantly change the association between age and antisocial behavior (table 9.2, model 2).

Caregiver Age, Adverse Emotional Behavior, and Social Support

Similar to findings for antisocial behavior, neither emotional support nor instrumental support mediated the relationship between caregiver age and adverse emotional behavior. For emotional support, only one condition for mediation was met: caregiver age was significantly related to adverse emotional behavior but no statistically significant relationships were detected between caregiver age and emotional support or between emotional support and adverse emotional behavior. When instrumental support was tested, only two conditions for mediation were met: caregiver age and instrumental support were both significantly related to adverse emotional behavior. Age was not related to instrumental support. Adding emotional or instrumental support to the models did not change the association between caregiver age and adverse emotional behavior (table 9.2, model 2).

Does Social Support Moderate the Effect of Caregiver's Age on Child Well-being?

Moderation (interaction) exists if the relationship between caregiver age and the antisocial behavior and emotional behavior indices differ based on the amount of emotional and instrumental support provided. Moderation of the relationship between caregiver age and child anti-

Table 9.2. Regression of Child Well-being (Antisocial and Adverse Emotional Behavior Indices) on Caregiver's Age, Social Support, and the Interaction of Caregiver Age and Social Support (Emotional and Instrumental Support Indices)

		Antisocial Behavior Index			Adverse Emotional Behavior Index		
Model		B	SE	t	B	SE	t
Emotional Support Index							
Model 1	Constant	16.18	0.41	39.72***	9.78	0.29	34.07***
	Caregiver's Age	−0.02	0.01	−2.98**	−0.03	0.01	−5.58***
Model 2	Constant	16.49	0.46	35.64***	9.97	0.33	30.47***
	Caregiver's Age	−0.02	0.01	−3.03**	−0.03	0.01	−5.63***
	Emotional Support	−0.08	0.05	−1.44	−0.05	0.04	−1.24
Model 3	Constant	16.15	1.02	15.82***	11.28	0.71	15.85**
	Caregiver's Age	−0.02	0.02	−0.88	−0.05	0.01	−4.20***
	Emotional Support	−0.02	0.25	0.07	−0.40	0.17	−2.29*
	Age × Emotional Support	−0.00	0.00	−0.38	0.01	0.00	2.08*
Instrumental Support Index							
Model 1	Constant	16.18	0.41	39.72***	9.78	0.29	34.07***
	Caregiver's Age	−0.02	0.01	−2.98**	−0.03	0.01	−5.58***
Model 2	Constant	16.63	0.44	38.06***	10.11	0.31	32.83***
	Caregiver's Age	−0.02	0.01	−2.96**	−0.03	0.01	−5.58***
	Instrumental Support	−0.06	0.02	−2.79	−0.04	0.01	−2.94**
Model 3	Constant	16.11	0.83	19.52***	10.65	0.58	18.50***
	Caregiver's Age	−0.01	0.02	−0.78	−0.04	0.01	−3.70***
	Instrumental Support	−0.01	0.90	−0.11	−0.11	0.06	−1.74
	Age × Instrumental Support	−0.001	0.00	−0.75	0.00	0.00	1.10

Significant at:
*$p \leq 0.05$
**$p \leq 0.01$
***$p \leq 0.001$

social behavior by emotional and instrumental support were examined by first assessing the relationship between caregiver age and child antisocial behavior (table 9.2, model 1); then caregiver age and antisocial behavior including emotional (or instrumental) support in the model (table 9.2, model 2); finally, caregiver age was included in a model with the emotional (or instrumental) support scale and the interaction term of "Age ×

Emotional (or Instrumental) Support" (table 9.2, model 3), with antisocial behavior as the dependent variable.

Caregiver Age and Antisocial Behavior Scale

When caregiver age was entered in the simple model (table 9.2, model 1), an unstandardized beta of -0.02 ($t = -2.98$, $p < 0.01$) was obtained (table 9.2). There was a significant inverse relationship between caregiver age and child antisocial behavior; caregivers who were older reported more children with lower antisocial behavior. When emotional support was added into the equation (table 9.2, model 2), there was no change in the relationship between caregiver age and child antisocial behavior. Model 3 included the interaction term of "Age $\times$ Emotional Support," which was not significant. Emotional support did not buffer the effects of caregiver age on child antisocial behavior. Similar results were obtained for instrumental support. The final model (table 9.2, model 3) included the interaction term, which was not significant; instrumental support did not moderate or buffer the effects of caregiver age on child antisocial behavior.

Caregiver Age and Adverse Emotional Behavior

Moderation of the relationship between caregiver age and child adverse emotional behavior and emotional support was examined in the same manner. When caregiver age was entered in the simple model (table 9.2, model 1), an unstandardized beta of -0.03 ($t = -5.58$, $p < 0.001$) was obtained, demonstrating a significant inverse relationship between caregiver age and child adverse emotional behavior. The addition of emotional support (model 2) did not result in a change in the relationship between caregiver age and child adverse emotional behavior. Model 3, the final model, included the interaction term of "Age $\times$ Emotional Support Scale," which resulted in an unstandardized beta of 0.01, which was significant ($t = 2.08$; $p < 0.05$). Overall, younger caregivers were more likely than older caregivers to care for children with higher levels of adverse emotional behavior. However, emotional support does appear to moderate the effects of caregiver age on adverse emotional behavior. While younger caregivers of children with the highest scores on the adverse emotional behavior scale reported lower levels of emotional support compared to those caring for children with relatively lower adverse emotional behavior scores, the opposite was true for older caregivers. Older caregivers of children with higher scores on the adverse emotional behavior scale reported higher levels of emotional support compared to older caregivers of children with lower adverse emotional behavior scores. This is represented graphically in figure 9.1.

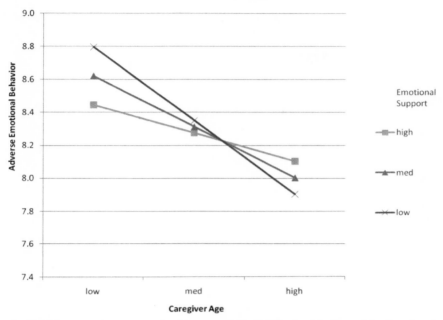

Figure 9.1. Caregiver Age and Adverse Emotional Behavior Moderated by Emotional Support

Moderation of the relationship between caregiver age and adverse emotional behavior by instrumental support was examined using similar models. Instrumental support did not moderate the relationship between caregiver age and adverse emotional behavior.

IMPLICATIONS OF STUDY RESULTS

The child welfare system was created to ensure the safety and well-being of children who are abused or neglected by their birth parents. When parents are unable to care for their children, child welfare agencies in many states rely on relatives to open their doors and hearts to provide shelter, food, clothing, and medical care. This is particularly true for African American children, who are overrepresented on child welfare caseloads and among children living in kinship foster care. It should not be surprising that African American extended families have demonstrated their willingness to care for children. An enduring strength and legacy of African Americans is their ability to rely on extended families, fictive kin, or church members for social support, including emotional and instrumental support. The extended family structure of African Americans is rooted in African tradition and was institutionalized as a support and coping mechanism for African Americans as a result of slavery.[19] While many laud the strengths of extended family support and shared caregiving particularly among African Americans, others have expressed concerns about the ability of kinship caregivers, particularly those who are older, single, and low-income, to adequately provide for the basic human needs of related children in their care.[20]

Since the late 1980s, there has been an increase in the average age of kinship foster caregivers.[21] Kinship foster caregivers tend to be older than non-kin foster caregivers.[22] Many child welfare advocates, scholars, and public policy-makers have expressed concerns about the ability of older caregivers to care for children. Several states have responded to this concern by implementing policies restricting the number of children and the age of children placed with relative caregivers. Results of this study suggest that there is little need for concern, and restricting older relatives from becoming kinship foster parents may actually prevent African American children from benefiting from a valuable resource. Based upon caregiver ratings, children living with older caregivers appeared to display lower levels of antisocial and adverse emotional behavior compared to children living with younger relative caregivers. Since the data analyzed in this study is cross-sectional, it is not possible to determine whether there is something about older caregivers that contributes to healthier functioning and greater child well-being or if child welfare caseworkers and extended families are careful to place children with greater behavioral problems with younger caregivers and to not place these children with older caregivers. Future research is needed that addresses this question. Regardless, results of this study suggest that decisions to place children with older caregivers should not be based only on caregiver age.

Although not presented in this paper, other analyses indicate that the relationship between caregiver age and adverse emotional behavior holds when controlling for the age of the child and a number of other covariates. The relationship between caregiver age and antisocial behavior is not significant in models that include the same covariates, but in no analysis is age positively associated with higher levels of behavior problems (Solomon 2006).[23] It seems that age alone does not contribute significantly to negative child behavioral functioning and it may be that older caregivers have a positive impact on children's functioning. Most likely, there are a number of factors in addition to age that contribute to child well-being. It seems likely that the emotional and instrumental support received by older caregivers is among these factors.

Emotional support for relative foster caregivers in this study affected the caregiver age and child adverse emotional behavior relationship. While younger caregivers in this study were more likely to care for children with higher levels of behavior problems, those caring for the children with the highest levels of behavior problems received less emotional support than their similarly aged peers who were caring for children with somewhat lower levels of behavior problems. This is somewhat concerning, since it is likely that the greater the level of child behavior problems, the greater the need for caregiver emotional support. This was the case for older caregivers. Although overall, older caregivers were caring for children with lower levels of behavior problems, those caring for children with relatively greater problems received more emotional support than their similarly aged peers who were raising children with fewer problems. Perhaps our concerns are misplaced—perhaps we should more closely examine the needs of younger caregivers who are raising children with the most serious adverse emotional behaviors. Likewise, maybe we should also be concerned about whether the needs of these caregivers are being met and what types of support they may need to successfully care for these children.

Results of this study indicate that caregivers received most of their social support from extended family and church members. Research is needed to determine whether child welfare professionals' efforts to assess and strengthen both emotional and instrumental support have positive effects on caregivers and children. In particular, research is needed to determine if child welfare casework interventions to engage both informal and formal sources of support affect the burden and stress experienced by caregivers of children with the highest levels of behavior problems, and if this contributes to positive outcomes for children.

It makes good sense to empirically test the effectiveness of extending opportunities for relative foster caregivers to invite extended family members and church members to participate in family meetings, administrative case reviews, and support groups in addressing child adverse emotional behavior. Including informal network members in such activities may be one way to help them understand the social and emotional needs of the child as well as the crisis and stressors related to caregiving, both of which may spur them to provide greater support to the caregivers and perhaps to share some of the burden of caring for the child. Research is needed to determine if such interventions would contribute to positive outcomes for caregivers and the related children they are raising.

Policy and Programmatic Implications

The findings of this study support the need to provide instrumental support to relative foster caregivers to contribute to improved child well-being. Instrumental support, which in this study included child care, transportation, money, assistance with shopping, and help when someone was ill, was associated with lower levels of child antisocial behavior and adverse emotional behavior. Although the caregivers relied on extended family and church members to provide such support, this should not be their only source of support, particularly when federal dollars are used to reimburse states for the same services for children living with nonrelated foster parents. Financial support and services for children living with relative caregivers vary by state and may depend on whether the caregiver is licensed as foster parents. Those who are not able to meet licensing standards very often are allowed to continue to care for related children but receive considerably lower levels of financial support.

CONCLUDING REMARKS

Results of this study reveal an inverse relationship between kinship caregiver age and adverse emotional behavior and antisocial behavior of children in their care. Older caregivers tended to report lower levels of adverse emotional behavior and antisocial behavior than younger caregivers. While emotional support had no direct effect on antisocial behavior or adverse emotional behavior, emotional support did moderate the relationship between caregiver age and adverse emotional behavior. In addition, although the data are cross-sectional and causality cannot be determined, higher levels of instrumental support across caregiver age groups were associated with lower levels of adverse emotional behavior and antisocial behavior. Additional research is needed to determine the degree to which level of financial support and the provision of other needed services may impact the functioning and overall well-being of children living in kinship foster care. Social policies that determine who receives what services and supports should be shaped by empirical evidence of the effect these resources have on children and the persons they depend on for their ongoing care.

NOTES

1. U.S. Census Bureau, "Table C2 Household Relationship and Living Arrangements of Children Under 18 Years/1, by Age, Sex, Race, Hispanic Origin/2, and Metropolitan Residence: March 2000," 2001, www.census.gov/population/socdemo/ hh-fam/p20-537/2000/ tabC2.pdf (22 Jan. 2004).
2. U.S. Department of Health and Human Services, "The AFCARS Report: Interim FY 2000 Estimates As of August 2002 (7), 2002, Health and Human Services," www.acf.hhs.gov/programs/cb/publications/afcars/report7.pdf (24 Jan. 2004).
3. Joseph Crumbley and Robert L. Little, "Federal and State Policy and Program Issues," in *Relatives Raising Children* (Washington, DC: Child Welfare League of America, 1997), 93–111; Beverly Davidson, "Service Needs of Relative Caregivers: A Qualitative Analysis," *Families in Society* 78, no. 5 (1977): 502–10.

4. Jennifer Ehrle and Rob Geen, "Kin and Non-Kin Foster Care—Findings from a National Survey," *Children & Youth Services Review* 24, no. 1/2 (January–February 2002): 15–35; Rob Geen, "Foster Children Placed with Relatives Often Receive Less Government Help." The Urban Institute, 2003, www.urban.org/Uploaded-PDF/310774_A-59.pdf. (20 Oct. 2004).

5. Jill Duerr Berrick, Richard P. Barth, and Barbara Needell, "A Comparison of Kinship Foster Homes and Foster Family Homes: Implications for Kinship Foster Care as Family Preservation," *Children & Youth Services Review* 16, no. 1/2 (1994): 33–64; Howard Dubowitz, Susan Feigelman, and Susan Zuravin, "A Profile of Kinship Care," *Child Welfare* 72, no. 2 (March–April 1993): 153–69.

6. James P. Gleeson, "Kinship Care as a Child Welfare Service: Emerging Policy Issues and Trends," in *Kinship Foster Care: Policy, Practice, and Research*, ed. Rebecca L. Hegar and Maria Scannapieco (New York: Oxford University Press, 1999), 28–53.

7. Illinois Department of Children and Family Services, "Children in Substitute Care, FY 1985–Present," Illinois Department of Children and Family Services, www.state.il.us/dcfs/foster/index.shtml (20 Feb. 09).

8. Rocca A Cimmarusti, "Caregiver Burden in Kinship Foster Care," in *Kinship Care: Improving Practice through Research*, ed. Creasie Finney Hairston and James P. Gleeson (Washington, DC: Child Welfare League of America, 1999), 257–78; Ehrle and Geen, *Kin and Non-Kin Foster*, 15; Rob Geen, "Foster Children Placed with Relatives Often Receive Less Government Help," The Urban Institute, 2003, www.urban.org/UploadedPDF/310774_A-59.pdf (20 Oct. 2004); Donna Petras, "The Effect of Caregiver Preparation and Sense of Control on Adaptation of Kinship Caregivers," in *Kinship Care: Improving Practice through Research*, ed. Creasie Finney Hairston and James P. Gleeson (Washington, DC: Child Welfare League of America, 1999), 233–55.

9. Cimmarusti, "Caregiver Burden," 257.

10. James Garbrino and Deborah Sherman, "High-Risk Neighborhoods and High-Risk Families: The Human Ecology of Child Maltreatment," *Child Development* 51, no. 1 (March 1980): 188–98; Marsha Weinraub and Barbara Wolf, "Effects of Stress and Social Support on Mother-Child Interactions in Single- and Two-Parent Families," *Child Development* 54, no. 5 (October 1983): 1297–1311.

11. Keith A. Crnic and Mark T. Greenberg, "Minor Parenting Stresses with Young Children," *Society for Research in Child Development, Inc.* 61, no. 5 (October 1990): 1628–37.

12. Mark F. Testa, Leslie Cohen, and Grace Smith, "Illinois Subsidized Guardianship Waiver Demonstration," Children and Family Research Center, University of Illinois at Urbana–Champaign School of Social Work, 2003, cfrcwww.social.uiuc.edu/pubs/Pdf.files/sgfinalreport.pdf (18 Nov. 2005).

13. Subsidized guardianship provides financial support that is equivalent to the foster care payment provided while children are in the custody of the child welfare system. This type of subsidy is normally available to foster parents who adopt children with special needs, supported with a combination of state and federal matching funds. Federal policies did not allow federal matching funds to foster parents who were not willing to adopt children but were willing to assume legal guardianship. The demonstration project tested whether allowing states to provide the same

subsidy for guardianship or adoption increased the likelihood of permanency for the child, thereby reducing the number of children on child welfare caseloads.

14. Testa, Cohen, Smith, and Westat, "Illinois Subsidized Guardianship," 2003.

15. Fictive kin is defined as individuals unrelated by blood or marriage, extended family networks, and godparents that provide resources and social support to families. The interrelatedness of the roles is based on mutual support, cultural beliefs, and caregiving based on family roles.

16. Joseph H. Abramson and Z. H. Abramson, *Survey Methods in Community Medicine: Epidemiological Research: Programme Evaluation, Clinical Trials* (New York: Churchill Livingstone, 1999).

17. Government income is defined as the amount of government money per month that the caregiver receives to care for the child, which includes adoption or guardianship subsidy, foster care boarding payment, day care assistance from DCFS, day care assistance from the welfare department, welfare or TANF checks, child support payments, SSI (Supplementary Security Income), and Social Security Survivor Benefits.

18. The focus of this study are the African American caregivers and the children in their care. African American caregivers who meet the study's criteria were included in the study, regardless of the ethnicity of the child.

19. Robert B. Hill, *The Strengths of African American Families: Twenty-Five Years Later* (Washington, DC.: R&B, 1997); Jillian Jimenez, "The History of Grandmothers in the African American Community," *Social Service Review* 76, no. 4 (December 2002): 523–51; Harriette Pipes McAdoo, *Black Families* (Thousand Oaks, CA: Sage, 1997).

20. Berrick, Barth, and Needell, "A Comparison of Kinship," 33; Cynthia Andrews Scarcella, Jennifer Ehrle, and Rob Geen, "Identifying and Addressing the Needs of Children in Grandparent Care," The Urban Institute, 2003, www.urban.org/Uploaded PDF/310842_B-55.pdf (18 Aug. 2004).

21. Maria Scannapieco and Rebecca L. Hegar, "Kinship Care in the Public Child Welfare System," in *Kinship Foster Care: Policy, Practice, and Research*, ed. Maria Scannapieco and Rebecca Hegar (New York: Oxford University Press, 1999), 141–54.

22. Berrick, Barth, and Needell, "A Comparison of Kinship," 33.

23. Terry A. Solomon, "African American Caregivers' Age, Social Support, and the Well-Being of Children in Kinship Care," unpublished doctoral dissertation (University of Illinois at Chicago: Illinois 2006).

10

Examining "Emerging Adulthood" in the Context of the Justice System

Anne Dannerbeck Janku

Youth, the time of life between childhood and adult maturity, is often equated with adolescence. Our notions of maturity are evolving as social conditions change as well as our understanding of brain development and associated cognitive capabilities. Jeffrey Arnett[1] has identified a new developmental stage between adolescence and adulthood, "emerging adulthood," which is between the ages of eighteen to twenty-five. This stage of life is of particular relevance to youth involved with the criminal justice system because this age group tends to have worse outcomes than older individuals, yet criminal justice systems have not typically focused attention on them as a distinct group situated within a discrete life-cycle stage of development.

In this chapter I examine this stage—emerging adulthood—in the context of the justice system. The status of this age group is compared to younger and older age groups of offenders in Missouri. The age range is expanded to include seventeen-year-olds because they straddle the youth and adult court systems; system-involved youth of this age also tend to have the same characteristics as eighteen- and twenty-five-year-olds (not in school, little parental control, heavily influenced by peers).

A CASE EXAMPLE OF EMERGING ADULTHOOD

Consider John's (fictitious name) story: he is a twenty-one-year-old high school dropout and a parent who has been living on his own since he was sixteen. He participated in a court-ordered drug treatment program although apparently not for serious drug abuse. His counselor told him that he has an addiction to a lifestyle involving fast, easy money obtained through drug sales. He spends the money on himself and to support his extended family. He likely learned this lifestyle by observing family members as he was growing up and then copying them.

> You grow up seeing your older cousins and brothers doing this (drug sales). You like what you see. They have good clothes, shoes, game systems . . . just trying to live the good life without having to do nothing for real. It is just somebody putting the money in your hand real quick and easy like that.

John has no idea what he wants to be to do with his life. After spending thirteen months in a specialized drug court program focused on offenders who were reentering society after "shock treatment" in prison (so named for the "shock value" that a brief stint in prison might have on an individual), he was terminated from the program. He had entered the program as a low-risk offender, with just one conviction (for drug trafficking) and no history of violence. John did have a history of family and financial problems and little experience with employment. Between his release from prison and program termination, he moved four times, at one point living with his girlfriend, who is the mother of his child. While in the program he had eight technical violations and one arrest. Within three months of his termination from the program, he returned to prison on a violation of probation.

TRENDS AMONG JUVENILE OFFENDERS AND POLICY RESPONSES

John is, in many ways, typical of a high proportion of all offenders involved with the justice system. In the correctional population, younger offenders have shorter time spans to rearrest.[2] In John's home state of Missouri, younger offenders, seventeen- to twenty-five-year-olds, in the Department of Corrections had the highest risk scores for recidivism, and 75 percent of them returned to prison within three years of being released.[3]

National studies report that the same pattern holds for drug court participants like John. Younger participants tend to have higher rates of recidivism[4] and a shorter time period to rearrest.[5] In Missouri, in any given year almost half of all adult drug court participants fall in the seventeen- to twenty-five-year-old age group. They are a group of particular concern because their success rate in the program is lower than that of older adults. In the three-year period from 2005 to 2007, 42 percent of seventeen- to twenty-five-year-olds graduated compared to 61 percent of those twenty-six and older.

This age group is also a concern for the juvenile justice system. In Missouri, as in other states, the juvenile court can maintain custody of individuals until they are twenty-one if they were sixteen or younger at the time of their offense. By the time juveniles are seventeen, if they have had much court involvement, the juvenile system has already used a full range of interventions and programs with them and may have no alternative ways to treat them. In 2008 the Missouri Legislature passed and the governor signed HB 1550, a bill expanding juvenile court jurisdiction to include youth up to age seventeen who committed status offenses. Because they are older, these youth may require a different constellation of programs and services than younger youth.

In the justice system this age group is treated the same as either younger juveniles or older adults. Do emerging adults involved in the justice system have different treatment needs than other age groups? The differential patterns of outcomes cited above suggest that their needs and risk factors may not be the same as other age groups. If so, how do we distinguish significant differences between them and other age groups, differences that may impact justice system outcomes? Many states are using actuarial assessment tools to discern the needs of individuals in the justice system. Do the assessments adequately distinguish the distinct needs of this developmental life stage? Using assessment information from three statewide databases (a statewide juvenile risk and needs assessment, a treatment court reporting system, and a Department of Corrections offender criminal history and assessment), this study compares seventeen- to twenty-five-year-olds with those of other age groups from the same system to determine whether and how they may differ and to determine if the assessment instruments adequately identify the relevant factors for this life stage. Social control theory and life course development research inform the analysis and interpretation.

LIFE COURSE DEVELOPMENT RESEARCH ON EMERGING ADULTHOOD

The life course development perspective addresses the role of chronological age on human behavior changes. Some changes in life are ordered and typically tied to discrete age groups. The factors leading to behavioral changes are referred to as "normative age-graded influences," such as the start of primary school or the age of retirement.[6] They are reflected in age-differentiated patterns of behavior and influences on those behaviors.[7] This perspective accounts for the impacts of social factors that may affect behavior. Recognition of social factors and distinct behavioral patterns has led scholars to identify this new stage of life previously discussed, emerging adulthood. This perspective helps to identify factors that may be important for individuals aged seventeen to twenty-five who have particularly high rates of offending behaviors.

Emerging adulthood is a period of extended exploration before one settles into stable adult roles and responsibilities.[8] This stage of life is characterized by instability and stress, the absence of social controls, a tendency to associate with peers who engage in similar behaviors, and experimentation with lifestyle choices. Just as adolescence became recognized as a discrete life stage because of changes in social conditions at the turn of the last century, emerging adulthood is an outgrowth of the current social environment, namely delayed family formation and continued economic dependence, key markers of adulthood. Many young adults consider family formation, namely marriage and parenthood, as perils to avoid in their early twenties.[9]

Economic independence, a key indicator of adulthood, is often delayed as individuals in their late teens and twenties pursue education rather than employment. Among twenty- to twenty-one-year-olds, 57 percent have had some college education,[10] but labor market conditions make it more difficult for young people to become independent. Finding a job that provides a living wage is difficult. Recent statistics from the U.S. Census Bureau show that among this age group, 55 percent of men and 46 percent of women were living with their parents[11] at the time of the survey.

While these social conditions impact achievement of adult milestones, science has also played a part in the identification of this new life stage. New brain research techniques allow brain activity to be observed via sensory images such as magnetic resonance imaging. Observations of brain activity lead scientists to conclude that the capacity for new and complex forms of thinking develop during not only childhood but also emerging adulthood. Results indicate that those in emerging adulthood are not able tap into this capacity until they can gain adequate experience to apply them.[12] One's cognitive capacities and brain maturity impact the ability to function as an adult. To make adult decisions requires making connections between emotions and logic, a task that is difficult for an immature brain.[13]

Transitioning to Adulthood

Transitioning from emerging adulthood to young adult status occurs when an individual has adopted a conventional lifestyle which may involve employment and family formation, two factors which impose social control on individuals and keep them away from negative peer influence.[14] To transition to adulthood, individuals need support from family, a sense of purpose about the future, and freedom to explore options in various domains of life.[15]

The transition to adulthood has become more difficult for many young people. Emerging adults are increasingly dependent on their families of origin for assistance with the transition.[16] The majority of youth who successfully transition into adulthood continue to receive substantial assistance from family or other support systems well into their twenties or even their thirties. In addition to financial help, this assistance can include emotional resources like encouragement, educational resources such as information about going to college, or occupational assistance, including career advice. This assistance helps to engage emerging adults and lead them to invest in positive activities like employment and education.[17]

The transition to adulthood may be prolonged for those involved with the justice system. Especially for individuals who are incarcerated, key markers of the transition to adulthood may be delayed: independent living, marriage, employment, and earnings. Spending time restrained by the justice system reduces one's ability to accumulate work experience, to gain status, and to increase earnings. Less work and lower earnings inhibit one's ability to find adequate housing and support a family. People in such a situation may have more difficulty in finding a stable intimate relationship. Those who have served time are also hindered from even being considered for certain jobs because of restrictions on who qualifies for specific employment.[18]

Drug Use and Emerging Adults

For most offenders involved with the justice system, drugs play a direct or indirect role in their criminal behavior. Even if they were not arrested and charged with possession or trafficking, many were under the influence of drugs while committing a crime or else the crime (burglary, fraud) provided a means to acquire drugs. The emerging adult group has the highest prevalence rates for most types of drug use.[19] The use of so-called gateway drugs is particularly prevalent in this age group.[20] Alcohol and marijuana are called gateway drugs because they can lead to hardcore drug use in later life.[21, 22] For youth, gateway drugs tend to be more easily accessible and to have less stigma attached to them than hardcore drugs.[23]

Arnett[24] has posited several explanations for the high prevalence of drug use in this age group. His explanations are grounded in the characteristics of this developmental stage. First, this is a time of identity exploration, which can involve pursuing a wide range of experiences including experimentation with drugs. Some individuals may find this period of uncertainty regarding identity as stressful and turn to drugs to cope with the stress.

As noted, emerging adulthood is also a period of great instability. Individuals make frequent changes in many aspects of their lives ranging from romantic partners to living arrangements and status as a student or worker. Individuals are required to make many decisions about their life choices but may not have the experience and knowledge to make well-informed decisions. The instability, uncertainty, and inexperience may create anxiety and stress. Drugs may provide a way to cope with the stressors typically experienced at this time of life.

Finally, social norms of acceptable behavior often vary by age. Experimentation with alcohol and drugs among young people is more accepted than among full-fledged adults. Emerging adults may feel less social pressure to "behave like adults" who are supposed to avoid recreational drug use. Arnett's research[25] indicates that most people in the eighteen- to twenty-five-year-old group do not fully identify as adults, so they have little motivation to behave as such.

SOCIAL CONTROLS

Hirschi's widely recognized control theory[26] posits that social conditions exert external control over behavior, especially the consequences of that behavior. His theory provides an explanation for the prevalence of offending behaviors among emerging adults as well as the relatively low responsiveness to interventions. It also provides some direction in how to distinguish significant differences between this age group and others. Without adequate social controls, one may perceive that the consequences of deviant behavior are minimal or even somehow beneficial. One characteristic of this age group that makes them especially vulnerable to drug use and criminal behavior is the lack of social controls.

Hirschi identifies four types of social control, the first of which is attachments linked to relationships with family, peers, and school. An attachment is a process of forming an emotional bond with another person. As a result of that bond, an individual will care about the opinions of the other person, including views about appropriate behavior. Through this process of attachment, individuals can be influenced to behave in a manner that is condoned by those to whom one shares an attachment. For emerging adults these attachments may be especially weak because they typically no longer live with parents and tend to associate with like-minded peers. If they do not attend school, they also miss opportunities to form attachments in this social setting. Most emerging adults move out of the family home around age eighteen or nineteen. They are less likely than other age groups to have enduring social networks or stable relationships with people who can offer support and guidance. They tend to be surrounded by age mates who are experiencing the same instability and uncertainty.

A second type of social control derives from a commitment to succeed through legitimate means. Individuals will assess the opportunities available to succeed through law-abiding behaviors to determine how feasible is such a commitment. Social control is derived from weighing the costs and benefits of their actions to determine if they can succeed through legitimate behavior. Many emerging adults remain dependent on others for support and may feel their opportunities to succeed through legitimate channels of education and employment are limited. They may aspire to earn money to support themselves and a family but may not feel they can achieve that goal without resorting to illegal means of earning an income. Many of those in the justice system have not experienced much success in school so they may feel that educational attainment is outside their reach. Inadequate educational achievement may further constrain their employment opportunities and prompt them to look at illegal means of earning an income.

A third form of social control is involvement in legitimate activities including school and employment as well as marriage/partnership and family formation. The more involved individuals are in these activities, the more likely they are to behave in a manner that allows them to continue to engage in these activities. Today, emerging adults tend to delay involvement in some legitimate activities like marriage/partnership and family formation. Those in the justice system often cannot find adequate employment and typically are not in school. This is a time when many in this age group are exploring work and career options, and some emerging adults may not be fully engaged in this form of social control. Instead, they may be focused on figuring out "who they are," or experimenting with illegitimate activities like drugs or a criminal lifestyle.

Finally, social control can be derived from a belief in conventional morality and respect for authority. Most social interactions in this age group are with like-minded friends who share the same interests and values, and these beliefs may not mirror convention. Those who use illicit substances, for instance, are likely to associate with others who do the same and to avoid individuals who might counter drug use behavior. Thus it may be that emerging adults who do not have the employment opportunities, community attachments, and family supports needed to succeed in conventional society have little motivation to engage in a law-abiding lifestyle. They may perceive few rewards, thus they may have more motivation to continue to engage in deviant behavior than to cease such behavior. The transition from informal and formal social controls imposed by family, peers, and school to that imposed by marriage/partnership, family formation, and employment often takes place after this life stage, leaving the emerging adult open to involvement in illicit activities like substance abuse.

Hirschi's theory provides a guide to identify which factors in the lives of emerging adults are related to social controls. Using relevant information from three assessments, these factors are compared between emerging adults and younger and older individuals in the justice system to determine if significant differences exist. In addition, although the literature on emerging adulthood does not provide much guidance on how gender may mediate the experiences of emerging adults, extensive literature exists on how gender impacts delinquent and criminal behavior in general. Thus, the specific purpose of this study is to compare indicators of well-being among a correctional sample, between different age and gender groups to determine if those in emerging adulthood differ from those in other age groups. Identification of such differences will help justice system professionals determine if emerging adults should be treated differently, and if so, what type of treatment can best respond to their needs.

METHODS

Data

The data for this study come from administrative databases maintained by the Office of State Courts Administrator[27, 28] and the Missouri Department of Corrections.[29] In Missouri, adjudicated youth in juvenile court as well as all individuals under correctional supervision undergo an assessment of their risk for recidivism and their psychosocial needs. In drug court, individuals are assessed on how well the program impacts individual and family well-being. Details about these assessments can be found in references at the end of this publication (see notes 27–29). While the three sets of assessments vary in information collected, this study pulls together some common indicators of social control that are relevant in emerging adulthood to compare differences between the seventeen- to twenty-five-year-old group and younger and older age groups across systems. Items are taken from each assessment that measure substance abuse, education/employment, and social relationships.

The juvenile group includes 4,461 females aged ten to sixteen years old, 1,235 females aged seventeen to nineteen years old, 8,868 males aged ten to sixteen years old, and 2,479 males aged seventeen to nineteen. All the included youth had received a risk and a needs assessment in juvenile court in 2007. Any youth who had incomplete or missing data was excluded from analyses. What will be referenced as the adult DOC (Department of Corrections) group includes individuals who were sentenced to 120-day shock treatment in a correctional institution because of a drug offense. The group includes 48 females aged seventeen to twenty-five, 141 females aged twenty-six to sixty, 292 males aged seventeen to twenty-five, and 702 males aged twenty-six to sixty-three; data is from 2006 to 2008. All individuals participated in the evaluation of a treatment program for drug offenders, and the data was readily available. The group referred to as adult DC (drug court) group includes all individuals who exited an adult drug court in the state between 2005 and 2007. The group includes 412 females aged seventeen to twenty-five, 570 females aged twenty-six to fifty-nine, 1,232 males aged seventeen to twenty-five, and 1,192 males aged twenty-six to seventy.

For the juvenile group, two instruments were used to assess individuals who were being adjudicated in court for their offense. The assessment is used to identify an appropriate level of supervision and services. For this study, variables are included which indicate whether or not the juveniles have a substance abuse problem, whether or not they are failing school, whether or not they are employed (if they dropped out of school), and whether their social support system provides positive or negative support, and whether or not they are influenced by negative peers. Juvenile court staff conduct a face-to-face interview with the youth and a guardian; they may crosscheck some of the material with official records.

Individuals under the jurisdiction of the DOC are assessed when they exit prison and then by their probation officer during a monthly meeting while they are under community supervision. This study used the assessment information collected after they exited prison and had been in the community at least three months. For the drug abuse indicator, we compare them on whether or not they continue to have a drug abuse problem (as indicated by urinalysis tests) after they are released from prison, whether they are employed (there is no education indicator), and for social relationships, whether they live alone, with family, or in a halfway house.

DC staff complete an entry and exit form for each drug court participant. The information is extrapolated from the participant files and from a face-to-face meeting with the participant. For the DC group, having a drug abuse problem is a requirement for program entry. The original dataset contains a checklist of drugs, and respondents are to indicate which ones they use regularly. For this study if a participant used just marijuana and/or alcohol, the drug of choice was coded as gateway drugs. All other drugs were included in one category of "other." For education they are compared on whether or not they at least completed high school or its equivalent. They are compared on the proportion unemployed between age groups, and for social relationships they are compared on whether they live with family or friends, own or rent a home, or are homeless.

Analytic Plan

Because the variables are categorical, chi-square analysis is used to determine if significant differences exist on each variable between male and female emerging adults and either juveniles or adults.

FINDINGS

Drug Use

Drug abuse is a significant issue throughout the justice system. Results indicate some distinct patterns of drug use in the emerging adult groups. Referring to table 10.1, a significantly larger proportion (39 percent) of

Table 10.1. Comparison of Social Control Indicators for Emerging Adults and Other Age Groups, by Gender

	Drug Abuse Problems			
	Juvenile Females*		Juvenile Males*	
	10–16	17+	10–16	17+
	n = 4461	n = 1235	n = 8868	n = 2479
Percent with drug abuse problem	25%	39%	24%	44%
	Adult DOC Females		Adult DOC Males	
	26+	17–25	26+	17–25
	n = 141	n = 48	n = 702	n = 292
Percent with continued problem	33%	27%	27%	30%
	Adult DC Females*		Adult DC Males*	
	26+	17–25	26+	17–25
	n = 570	n = 412	n = 1192	n = 1232
Percent using gateway drugs	20%	50%	48%	60%
	Low Educational Achievement			
	Juvenile Females		Juvenile Males*	
	10–16	17+	10–16	17+
Failing School	13%	11%	16%	24%
	Adult DC Females*		Adult DC Males*	
	26+	17–25	26+	17–25
No high school diploma or GED	37%	50%	31%	53%
	Employment Status			
	Juvenile Females*		Juvenile Males*	
	10–16	17+	10–16	17+
Unemployed	18%	24%	18%	29%

	Adult DOC Females		Adult DOC Males*	
	26+	17–25	26+	17–25
Unemployed	73%	69%	70%	77%

	Adult DC Females*		Adult DC Males*	
	26+	17–25	26+	17–25
Unemployed	51%	59%	31%	53%

Living Arrangements

	Adult DOC Females*		Adult DOC Males*	
	26+	17–25	26+	17–25
Live with friend or halfway house	27%	18%	18%	9%
Live with Family	55%	64%	70%	83%
Live Alone	18%	18%	12%	8%

	Adult DC Females*		Adult DC Males*	
	26+	17–25	26+	17–25
Live with family or friends	39%	67%	35%	73%
Own a home	17%	2%	22%	3%
Rent	42%	30%	41%	23%

Peer Relationships

	Juvenile Females*		Juvenile Males	
	10–16	17+	10–16	17+
Negative peer influence	59%	68%	60%	63%

Source: Missouri Judicial Information System Annual Data Extraction 2007; Missouri Treatment Court Reporting System, 2005–2007; Missouri Department of Corrections, 2006–2008, select counties
DOC = Department of Corrections dataset
DC = Drug Court dataset
*Statistically significant at p = .05

emerging adult juvenile females have drug abuse problems compared to their younger counterparts (25 percent). For males, the same pattern exists in the juvenile system; a significantly larger proportion (44 percent vs. 24 percent) in the emerging adult group have drug abuse problems. Within the adult offender group, no significant differences appear between the two age demographics regarding continuing drug use after they are released from prison. This group of offenders received some drug treatment while incarcerated, but the treatment did not seem to have a differential impact by age group or gender.

In keeping with a behavior pattern of experimentation and a lifestyle typified by instability, emerging adults may use marijuana and alcohol experimentally, as a coping mechanism, or in an addictive manner. Compared to older adults, a greater proportion (50 percent females, 60 percent males) of emerging adult drug court participants identify the gateway drugs as their drugs of choice. For the other drugs, the older group reports using them more often (80 percent females, 52 percent males). In the female emerging adult group half are using other drugs beyond just the gateway drugs.

Educational Achievement and Employment Status

Next, educational achievement patterns were compared for two of the offender groups, and emerging adults had lower levels of achievement. Among youth in the juvenile system who are in school, a higher proportion of the emerging adults than juveniles were failing. Among drug court participants, a significantly higher proportion of both male (53 percent) and female (50 percent) emerging adults had no high school diploma or equivalency certificate compared to older participants (31 percent males, 37 percent females.)

Among juveniles who should be employed because they are out of school, a significantly larger proportion of the emerging adult females (24 percent) were unemployed compared to younger youth (18 percent). Among juvenile males the same pattern holds with 29 percent of the emerging adult males unemployed compared to 18 percent of the younger males. Among the adult corrections population, a smaller proportion of the emerging adult females (69 percent vs. 73 percent of older group) are unemployed when they begin the program. For males, a significantly larger proportion of the emerging adult group (77 percent vs. 70 percent of older group) is unemployed. For the drug court participants, emerging adult females are more likely to be unemployed (59 percent vs. 51 percent of older group) and emerging adult males are also more likely to be unemployed (53 percent) compared to older offenders (31 percent).

Social and Family Support

Family support and guidance have a complex relationship with the transition to adulthood. Too much, too little, or inappropriate support can hinder development. Neither the drug court nor the corrections assessments include a direct indicator of social support. Both do have indicators of living arrangements which indirectly suggest the availability of support from family, friends, or others. Within the DOC adult groups, significantly larger proportions of emerging adults—both females (64 percent vs. 55 percent older group) and males (83 percent vs. 70 percent)—live with their extended families and/or immediate families. Among drug court participants, emerging adult females (67 percent) and males (73 percent) are much more likely to live with family or friends. Most older individuals live in a home they own or rent (59 percent females, 63 percent males).

An indicator is available in the juvenile system regarding the nature of family and social support, but no significant differences exist by age group, so the results are not reported. Peer influence can have a profound influence on the behavior of youth. In the juvenile system a significantly greater proportion of emerging adult females (68 percent vs. 59 percent younger group) were negatively influenced by their peers. The differences for males were not significant although the proportions influenced are substantial—63 percent of the emerging adult group and 60 percent of the younger group.

DISCUSSION OF FINDINGS

This study provides a preliminary look at emerging adults across the justice system using assessment information from three populations: juvenile offenders, drug court participants, and correctional drug offenders. Variables were selected for the study based on their relevance to the emerging adult life-cycle stage and to social control theory. The analysis indicates that for all of the indicators for which there are significant differences, emerging adult groups have larger proportions reporting the area of concern. The comparison also examined gender differences and found differing patterns of distinction by gender and age group. Using the available data, this analysis shows that emerging adults differ from their counterparts in their drug abuse behavior, educational achievement, employment status, and the nature of relationships with family and friends. These differences support the idea that emerging adults may lack adequate social controls to successfully transition to adulthood.

Previous research on emerging adulthood and gender has focused on identity and intimacy, two factors not generally linked to offending behaviors. Even within that narrow focus, research has shown more similarities than differences in the status of men and women relative to these two factors.[30, 31] This analysis on offender populations also indicates that while the emerging adult men and women differ from other age groups, for the most part, the patterns of difference are similar for men and women.

Juvenile drug problems are worse for emerging adults; both males and females have higher proportions of serious drug abuse problems. For the adult DOC population, no significant differences exist for the indicator of continuing drug abuse problems, suggesting that either the indicator does not adequately assess an underlying construct of relevance or that gender and age are not appropriate groups to differentiate drug use problems in the correctional population. The drug court assessment takes a different perspective with an indicator for type of drug used. Male and female emerging adults were more likely to use the so-called gateway drugs—alcohol and marijuana. These are drugs which other studies have shown to be more prevalent in younger populations. To understand better why individuals of any age are using drugs, assessments should evaluate whether the individual is addicted, exposed to risk factors that can lead to an addiction, or a recreational drug user. Abuse prevention strategies may be more effective than addiction treatment, depending on the assessment results. As in the example of John, recreational drug use may reflect a lifestyle.

The lifestyle of emerging adults is often not conducive to having conventional social controls that can influence behavior. The emerging adult groups tend to lack social control mechanisms associated with education and employment. In the juvenile population, the emerging adult females are doing about the same in school as their younger counterparts, and the juvenile emerging adult males are doing somewhat worse than the younger ones. A pattern of low educational achievement is particularly noteworthy in the drug court population. Over half the emerging adult groups have not completed high school, indicating that educational enrichment and engagement programs might help them as well as the juveniles who are failing. Interventions which focus on educational achievement can help this age group not only acquire this important marker of educational achievement, but also provide a link to education as a mechanism of social control. Those who are still in school or have completed high school may benefit from encouragement and reinforcement of the idea that schooling is important.

Employment provides a mechanism to promote pro-social development and transition successfully into adulthood. The emerging adult group in the juvenile population is less likely than youth to be employed (among those who have dropped out of school). In the drug court population and among males in the correctional system, a higher proportion of the emerging adult groups are unemployed than is true of the older groups. Offenders are often required to find employment as part of their rehabilitation and may receive some basic job preparation. For the emerging adult group a more effective strategy may be to focus more on training and educational achievement, building tangible skills that prepare them for employment and that give them a means to commit to a conventional lifestyle to pursue their goals.

Individuals not connected to formal social controls through education or employment can still rely on ties to informal social controls in the form of support from family and friends to desist from crime.[32] Appropriate support can positively impact emerging adults, and research shows that many individuals in this age group depend on such support from family. Of the three assessment systems, only the juvenile one has an indicator for social support, and no differences were found by age group in level of support. Negative peer influence seems to have a greater impact among the older juveniles. Given this age group's tendency to spend more time with peers, they may benefit from interventions that provide interactions with more positive peers or interventions that help them distinguish positive and negative influences on their behavior.

For the drug court and correctional populations, living arrangements served as a proxy for social support, albeit an imprecise one. Those who live with family, or even with friends, may have support readily available. At the same time, too much dependence on family at this time of life may indicate an individual who is not equipped to function independently; moreover, relying too much on a family that is not functioning well can impede development. Those who live alone may be socially isolated and not be getting enough support, or they may be functioning well and have transitioned to independent adulthood. Without a more straightforward indicator of social support, its role in the lives of emerging adults cannot be readily assessed.

Emerging adulthood is a transition period between youth and adulthood. Assessments tend to focus on current status and past experiences. For the emerging adult group, a better focus may be on the direction in which individuals are headed. Typically assessments, such as those presented in this study, do not provide adequate detail to evaluate an individual's ability to transition to adulthood and identify needed skills to make that transition. For instance, one can consider the drug abuse assessments in the context of readiness to transition to adulthood. The three systems demonstrate different approaches to assessment, yet they all reflect current status of drug use: by current use and severity of use, by continued use after some treatment, and by drug of choice. None of these indicators address whether the behavior is addictive or indicative of a lifestyle or experimentation. Instead of treating all offenders who use drugs as addicts, prevention interventions that address alternative methods to cope with stress or alternative lifestyles may be more effective in helping this age group transition to adulthood.

Emerging adults may also be receptive to interventions that help them consider lifestyle alternatives which would facilitate their transition to adulthood. To refine indicators of education and employment, assessments may need to cover whether the individual has experience in the formal labor market or what skills are needed to gain that experience. If the individual is working, some assessment of the adequacy of the individual's income would indicate whether the individual is on a pathway toward financial independence.

Recognizing that social support plays an integral role in the transition to adulthood, assessment indicators for emerging adults could be refined to examine the nature of social support. Besides often receiving financial support from family, many individuals in this age group need encouragement, information about acquiring new knowledge and skills through college or training, and career advice. Many emerging adults who are involved in the justice system do not receive such support from their family. This is a group who would likely be receptive to interventions that focused on providing these types of support.

One key question not answered by this study concerns the nature and extent of differences between emerging adults in the justice system and those not involved with it. Most prior research on emerging adults has been based on studies of college students. Much of what is known reflects the college student experience, and because they tend to be from middle-class backgrounds, the cultural context of their experience may be different from other groups of emerging adults.[33] One of the ways they differ from emerging adults in this study is that they are engaged in the educational system. Most prior research has found that emerging adults no longer live with their families; as college students they may live on campus or in student-oriented housing off-campus. In the justice system populations, a high proportion of emerging adults than older adults still live with family. The college student population typically has ties to the labor economy, either through work or with a goal of preparing for work through education. The offender population, on the other hand, is building a history that may lower their chances of finding employment given the reluctance of many to hire individuals with a criminal history.

In considering this life stage of emerging adulthood, one must also recognize that all individuals aged seventeen to twenty-five are not emerging adults nor are all individuals older than twenty-five considered to have reached adulthood.[34] Individual situations determine adult status, especially financial independence and family formation. Assessments and interventions targeting this period of life can be useful for younger and older individuals as well. In particular, individuals who have been abusing drugs and incarcerated may not have had the opportunities to transition to adulthood. Their transition may be delayed indefinitely, and an assessment that focuses on what they need to make the transition may help them achieve status as mature adults.

CONCLUSION

While emerging adulthood represents a time of great challenges for those in the justice system, it also offers opportunities. Many youth experience turning points at this stage of life that lead them away from a life of crime.[35] The justice system has the opportunity to intervene with this age group to create turning points. A first step is to better identify the particular risks and needs of this group and create interventions to prepare them to transition to adult status as individuals who have adopted a conventional lifestyle typically involving employment and family formation.

NOTES

1. J. Arnett, "Emerging Adulthood: A Theory of Development from the Late Teens through the Twenties," *American Psychologist* 55 (2000): 469–80.

2. J. Hepburn and C. Albonetti, "Recidivism among Drug Offenders: A Survival Analysis of the Effects of Offender Characteristics, Type of Offense, and Two Types of Interventions," *Journal of Quantitative Criminology* 10, no. 2 (1994): 159–79.

3. Missouri Department of Corrections, internal memo, Jefferson City, MO (2004).

4. J. Roman, W. Townsend, and A. Bhati, *Recidivism Rates for Drug Court Graduates: Nationally Based Estimates* (Washington, DC: U.S. Dept. of Justice, 2003).

5. R. Peters, A. Haas, and M. Murrin, "Predictors of Retention and Arrest in Drug Court," *National Drug Court Institute Review* 11, no. 1 (1999): 33–60.

6. J. Ashford, C. LeCroy, and K. Lortie, *Human Behavior in the Social Environment* (Belmont, CA: Thompson Brooks/Cole, 2006), 37.

7. U. Bronfenbrenner, "Toward an Experimental Ecology of Human Development," *American Psychologist* 32 (1977): 513–31.

8. G. I. Roisman, A. S. Masten, J. D. Coatsworth, and A. Tellegen, "Salient and Emerging Developmental Tasks in the Transition to Adulthood," *Child Development* 75 (2004): 123–33.

9. J. Arnett, *Emerging Adulthood: The Winding Road from the Late Teens to Early Twenties* (Oxford: Oxford University Press, 2005).

10. M. Lopez and B. Elrod, "College Attendance and Civic Engagement among 18 to 25 Year Olds," Center for Information and Research on Civic Learning and Engagement, 2006, www.civicyouth.org/PopUps/FactSheets/FS_Non-college_corrected.pdf (29 Jun. 2009).

11. "Growing Up Is Taking Longer," *Christian Science Monitor*, 14 January 2004, 16.

12. G. Labouvie-Vief, "Emerging Structures of Adult Thought," in *Emerging Adults in America: Coming of Age in the 21st Century*, ed. J. Arnett and J. Tanner (Washington, DC: American Psychological Association, 2006), 60–84.

13. A. Baird and C. Bennett, "Anatomical Changes in the Emerging Adult Brain," *Human Brain Mapping* 27, no. 9 (2005): 766–77.

14. R. Mischkowitz, "Desistance from a delinquent way of life?" in *Cross-National Longitudinal Research on Human Development and Criminal Behavior*, ed. E. Weitekamp and H. Kerner (Dordrecht, The Netherlands: Kluwer ,1994).

15. Arnett (2000), "Emerging Adulthood: A Theory of Development."

16. R. Setterson, F. Furstenberg, and R. Rumbaut, *On the Frontier of Adulthood: Theory, Research, and Public Policy* (Chicago: University of Chicago Press, 2005).

17. J. Laub, D. Nagin, and R. Sampson, "Trajectories of Change in Criminal Offending: Good Marriages and the Desistance Process," *American Sociological Review* 63 (1998): 225–38.

18. S. Raphael, "Early Incarceration Spells and Transition to Adulthood," *Policy Brief Network on Transition to Adulthood* (Philadelphia: MacArthur Foundation, 2006).

19. Substance Abuse and Mental Health Administration, *Results from the 2005 National Survey on Drug Use and Health* (Rockville, MD: Office of Applied Studies, 2007), oas.samhsa.gov/NSDUH/2k5NSDUH/2k5results.htm.

20. D. Lee, "Residential Mobility and Gateway Drug Use among Hispanic Adolescents in the U.S.: Evidence from a National Survey," *The American Journal of Drug and Alcohol Abuse* 33 (2007): 799–806.

21. J. Lessem, C. Hopfer, B. Haberstick, D. Timberlake, M. Ehringer, A. Smolen, and J. Hewitt, "Relationship between Adolescent Marijuana Use and Young Adult Illicit Drug Use," *Behavioral Genetics* 36, no. 4 (2006): 498–506.

22. L. Midanik, T. Tam, and C. Weisner, "Concurrent and Simultaneous Drug and Alcohol Use: Results of the 2000 National Alcohol Survey," *Journal of Drug and Alcohol Dependency* 90, no. 1 (2007): 72–80.

23. A. Beal, J. Ausiello, and J. Perrin, "Social Influences on Health-Risk Behaviors among Minority Middle School Students," *Journal of Adolescent Health* 28, no.6 (2001): 474–80.

24. J. Arnett, "The Developmental Context of Substance Use in Emerging Adulthood," *Journal of Drug Issues* (Spring 2002): 235–53.

25. Arnett (2005), *Emerging Adulthood: The Winding Road.*

26. T. Hirschi, *Causes of Delinquency* (Berkley: University of California Press, 1969).

27. "Juvenile Offender Classification System Missouri" (Jefferson City, MO: Office of State Courts Administrator, 2000), www.courts.mo.gov/page.asp?id=1200 (5 June 2009).

28. "Treatment Court Reporting Forms" (Jefferson City: Missouri Office of State Courts Administrator, 2008).

29. "Monthly Supervision Report Board of Probation and Parole" (Jefferson City: Missouri Department of Corrections).

30. J. Durell, E. Brady, R. McNair, D. Congdon, J. Niznik, and S. Anderson, "Identity as a Moderator of Gender Differences in the Emotional Closeness of Emerging Adults' Same-and-Cross-Sex Friendships," *Adolescence* 42, no. 165 (2007): 1–23.

31. K. Radmacher and M. Azmitia, "Are There Gendered Pathways to Intimacy in Early Adolescents' and Emerging Adults' Friendships?" *Journal of Adolescent Research* 21, no. 4 (2006): 415–48.

32. A. Piquero, R. Brame, P. Mazerolle, and R. Haapanen, "Crime in Emerging Adulthood," *Criminology* 40, no. 1 (2001): 137–68.

33. Arnett (2005), *Emerging Adulthood: The Winding Road.*

34. L. Blinn-Pike, S. Worthy, J. Jonkman, and G. R. Smith, "Emerging Adult versus Adult Status among College Students: Examination of Explanatory Variables," *Adolescence* 43, no. 171 (2008): 577–91.

35. Laub, Nagin, and Sampson (1998), "Trajectories of Change."

FAMILY SUPPORT:
POLICIES AND PROGRAMS

11

The Effect of Paternal Incarceration on Early Child Development

Terry-Ann L. Craigie

By 2001, approximately 2.7 percent of adults living in the United States had served time in prison, a 50 percent increase since the previous decade. More interesting is the fact that six out of ten inmates from 1996 to 2002 were racial/ethnic minorities: 40 percent were black and 19 percent were Hispanic. What could account for this trend among minorities? Over 50 percent of all inmates grew up in a single-parent household, and 46 percent had a family member who had been previously incarcerated. This means that not only are minorities at risk per se, but also that their children have an increased probability of being incarcerated as well. This study will subsequently attempt to isolate the effect of paternal incarceration on child development among at-risk or fragile families.

The main problem associated with answering this research question is the difficulty in distinguishing between the impact paternal incarceration has on child outcomes and the impact of unobserved factors (also associated with incarceration). For instance, if a criminal offender lived in unfavorable circumstances *ex ante* (before incarceration), incarceration may not be the "cause" of the child's poor outcomes *ex post* (after incarceration), but just a continuation of the preexisting conditions.

Extensive literature has already found evidence that father absence has a negative effect on child outcomes.[1, 2, 3, 4] As such, it is believed that paternal incarceration should have adverse impacts as well. However, it has been shown that paternal absence may not always have a negative effect on child development. A father may do more harm than good when he exhibits anti-social, abusive, or violent behavior.[5, 6, 7, 8] Hence, paternal incarceration may possibly induce an improved family situation due to the timely removal of an anti-social presence from the household.

Other studies argue that it is the instability of paternal presence (or absence) that engenders negative effects on child development.[9, 10, 11, 12] These studies spark the question of whether incarceration is more detrimental because of the circumstances under which the father became absent. Therefore, this study will test whether early child development is negatively affected by paternal incarceration during the child's life, or whether the effect is driven by preexisting conditions associated with incarceration.

The study finds that a father's incarceration does indeed have significant adverse effects on the early child developmental outcomes. While the adverse incarceration effect on the child's cognitive ability is only marginally significant, robust effects are found for early child aggression and oppositional defiant disorder (ODD).

PREVIOUS RESEARCH ON FATHER ABSENCE

The incarceration literature has focused mainly on the consequences of incarceration on economic outcomes. Incarceration not only inhibits the growth of human capital but often erodes it as well, reducing employment and earnings opportunities *ex post*.[13, 14, 15] Further, the institutional stigma of incarceration creates barriers to entry into the workforce and society in general.[16, 17, 18] This gives rise to financial hardships for children of incarcerated fathers, eventually resulting in stymied child development.[19, 20]

A generally unexplored effect of parental incarceration is its effect on the parent-child relationship. Incarceration disrupts the attachment mechanism between the incarcerated parent and the child, especially at early ages. This subsequently could have short-term and long-term effects on child well-being. Elicker, Englund, and Sroufe (1992) postulate that attachment of the child to the parent, particularly during infancy, increases social competence among peers. Incarceration is expected to negatively affect (however inadvertently) child development due to its inherently disruptive nature. Previous works have also found that family instability produces negative childhood outcomes.[21, 22, 23, 24] Wildeman (2008) also finds that disruption from paternal incarceration engenders an adverse effect on child behavioral problems.

The most apparent effect of parental incarceration is the strain on economic resources in the household. It is worth noting that strain caused by incarceration does not only refer to economic capital, but social capital, or connections between social networks, as well. The structure and quality of family relationships is unavoidably disrupted by incarceration. Non-custodial parents are able to maintain frequent contact with children (if they so choose and are permitted to do so) even though the relationship cannot be upheld within a residence. In the event of incarceration, however, children are more at a disadvantage since the avenue for frequent contact is physically obstructed.[25]

Conversely, the incarcerated parent may have been a serious drain on family resources. Incarceration is often enforced on parents who disrupt the stable and supportive environment of the household (e.g., due to violence, abuse, or negligence). Consequently, the parent's removal from the household may in fact yield positive effects.[26, 27, 28, 29, 30]

Criminal offenders and men predisposed to incarceration already possess traits that frustrate family cohesiveness. Weak attachment to the family could have occurred even if incarceration did not. Therefore, the factors and influences that predate paternal incarceration could potentially engender incarceration. Children of criminal offenders are exposed to unobserved factors, which not only increase the probability of parental incarceration, but persist to adversely affect child well-being.[31, 32] On the other hand, children whose parents have never been incarcerated are arguably unexposed to these factors. An attempt to simply compare children of incarcerated parents to children whose parents have never been incarcerated (but have similar background characteristics) will yield a *biased* or imprecise incarceration effect. The purpose of this study was to find the direction and magnitude of the effect of a father's incarceration on early child cognition and behaviors. In addition, the main characteristics that typify children and families of incarcerated men are identified.

METHODS

The data for this analysis came from the Fragile Families and Child Well-being Study (FFCWS). The study follows a sample of approximately five thousand children born between 1998 and 2000, with follow-up interviews occurring at around ages one and three thereafter. The data are representative of non-marital births in large cities in the United States, with about 75 percent of the sample being comprised of unmarried couples. The age distribution in the FFCWS is not statistically different from that of the United States in general. Racial/ethnic minority groups are oversampled in the FFCWS, with 69 percent of blacks, 19 percent of Hispanics, and 8 percent of whites making up the sample.[33] This creates a diverse and policy-relevant sample for the study of this research problem.

Data are gathered on not only the child's developmental outcomes and characteristics, but also on family relationships, demographics, and environmental factors that impact the parents and focal child. Because both parents are interviewed on these issues, the role of both parents and particularly the father can be more readily examined. There is a large sample of incarcerated fathers with about 40 percent of all fathers in the sample having been incarcerated at some point in their lives. The FFCWS includes reports from both parents on the father's past and current incarceration. There is also a wide array of child developmental outcomes in the FFCWS, but for the purposes of this study, I examined cognitive development as measured by the Peabody Picture Vocabulary Test—Revised (PPVT-R) and behavioral problems displayed in the forms of aggression and oppositional defiant disorder (ODD).

Variables of Interest

Peabody Picture Vocabulary Test—Revised (PPVT-R)

The Peabody Picture Vocabulary Test—Revised (PPVT-R) is administered to children over the age of two and a half years old to measure verbal ability and English language proficiency. Children must state the noun or verb which best describes the image given on the picture plate.[34] PPVT-R is commonly used as a measure of academic readiness among preschoolers and is reliable even for children with mental and language impediments. For children living in households where English is not predominantly spoken, it is not reliable. Standardized PPVT-R scores are used to adjust for the child's mental-age score.

Aggressive Behavior Disorder

Aggressive behavior disorders in a child involve acts undeniably intended to hurt or frighten another person.[35, 36, 37] The Third-Year In-Home Longitudinal Study measures thirteen aggressive acts such as hitting others, not showing guilt, and starting fights (see appendix at the end of this chapter). Intentionality is quite difficult to determine, and aggressive acts by preschool-aged children do not necessarily imply that the child suffers from a conduct disorder. Nevertheless, parental incarceration and criminal propensities may be closely linked to child aggressive behaviors and, hence, they are still relevant to examine.[38] All thirteen acts of aggression were averaged to create a measure of aggression, which ranged from 0 to about 2,[39] where 0 indicates the least aggression.

Oppositional Defiant Disorder (ODD)

Oppositional defiant disorder can be described as recurrent disobedient, defiant, and aggressive acts, particularly towards those in authority.[40] The

Third-Year In-Home Longitudinal Study provides six symptoms of ODD (see appendix) that are imperative for the diagnosis of this type of conduct disorder. These symptoms were averaged to create an ODD index for each child, which ranged from 0 to 2 with 2 indicating the highest level of defiance.

The Incarceration Measure

The father's incarceration status was reported by both parents in the FF-CWS. Mothers were asked about the fathers' current and historical experiences with incarceration. Fathers were asked about their current incarceration status and also about their most recent incarceration and release. It is important to note that mother and father interviews were conducted at different times, and hence, if the reports were conflicting, this does not necessarily mean that either report was false. For instance, if the mother reports that the father is currently in jail in her interview but the father reports otherwise in his own interview (occurring later), these reports are still consistent if the father had been jailed and released prior to his report. *Ex post* incarceration, or incarceration post-childbirth, was therefore categorized as such if either parent reported that the father was currently jailed or if the father's most recent incarceration year was after the year of the child's birth.

Summary Statistics of the Sample

The general summary statistics for all the dependent outcomes and independent variables are presented in table 11.1. With scores ranging from 40 to 137, the average PPVT-R standardized score for children in the analysis sample is approximately 86 points. The child's aggression measure is an average of thirteen acts of violent and defiant behavior. On a scale of 0 to about 2—with 1.92 being the most aggressive—the average of the aggression scale is 0.58. Similarly, the ODD index ranges from 0 to 2 with 2 being the most defiant. The average of the ODD index is 0.63. These averages indicate that in general, the children in the analysis sample do not exhibit very aggressive and defiant behavior.

Blacks comprise almost 50 percent of the analysis sample for both parents while Hispanics constitute approximately 25 percent. Mothers are on average twenty-five years old at the time of the child's birth while fathers are on average about twenty-eight. For the fathers of the children in the analysis sample, 38 percent of them had been incarcerated at some point in their lives; 10 percent had been incarcerated *ex post*.

Another important pattern displayed by the data is that parents exhibit characteristics associated with a high-risk environment. Table 11.1 illustrates that most parents had a high school degree or less and annual household income was a little over $32,000; the average household income per

Table 11.1. Summary Statistics of Sample

Variables	Obs.	Mean	SD	Min	Max
PPVT-R (standardized)	1617	86.18	17.14	40	137
Aggression Index	2085	0.58	0.34	0	1.92
ODD Index	2096	0.63	0.43	0	2
Incarcerated *Ex Post*	2909	0.10	0.30	0	1
Ever-Incarcerated	2909	0.38	0.48	0	1
Mother Black	2909	0.48	0.50	0	1
Mother Hispanic	2909	0.24	0.43	0	1
Mother White	2909	0.33	0.47	0	1
Father Black	2909	0.49	0.50	0	1
Father Hispanic	2909	0.24	0.43	0	1
Other	2909	0.27	0.44	0	1
Birth Order	2902	2.13	1.30	1	13
ADHD Symptoms	1686	0.91	0.47	0	2
Male	2909	0.52	0.50	0	1
Mother's Age at Child's Birth	2909	25.41	6.14	14	46
Father's Age at Child's Birth	2888	27.93	7.21	16	80
DDI Scale	2909	3.01	0.67	1	4
Mother is High School Dropout	2909	0.27	0.44	0	1
Mother has High School Degree	2909	0.31	0.46	0	1
Mother has less than College Degree	2909	0.23	0.42	0	1
Mother has College Degree	2909	0.13	0.34	0	1
Father is High School Dropout	2909	0.24	0.43	0	1
Father has High School Degree	2909	0.35	0.48	0	1
Father has less than College Degree	2909	0.18	0.38	0	1
Father has College Degree	2909	0.12	0.32	0	1
Household Income	2502	32279.44	49190.59	0	999,999
Household Income per Person	2493	8338.92	13871.99	0	333,333

Source: Fragile Families and Child Wellbeing Study (FFCWS)

person is also about $8,000. With low parental education and household income, the children in the FFCWS are at a greater disadvantage.

Table 11.2 presents comparisons of variable means by father's incarceration status. A child whose father has been incarcerated *ex post*, scores about six points lower on the PPVT-R, compared to a child whose father has never been incarcerated. Similarly, children whose fathers have been incarcerated also display more aggressive and defiant tendencies. Conversely, children of non-incarcerated fathers tend to have parents who are more educated. Households with non-incarcerated fathers have higher incomes by over $25,000 in general and have almost $7,000 higher incomes per person compared to households with fathers incarcerated *ex post*. The data also show that black fathers are more likely to be incarcerated and black mothers are more likely to have mates or spouses who are incarcerated relative to their white counterparts.

Table 11.2. Summary Statistics by Incarceration History

	Incarcerated Ex Post			Never Incarcerated		
	Obs.	Mean	SD	Obs.	Mean	SD
PPVT-R (standardized)	194	82.18	15.08	905	88.22	17.48
Aggression Index	222	0.67	0.40	1248	0.54	0.31
ODD Index	223	0.70	0.46	1251	0.60	0.41
Mother Black	291	0.73	0.45	1814	0.41	0.49
Mother Hispanic	291	0.13	0.34	1814	0.26	0.44
Mother White	291	0.14	0.37	1814	0.34	0.47
Father Black	291	0.74	0.44	1814	0.42	0.49
Father Hispanic	291	0.14	0.35	1814	0.26	0.44
Other	291	0.12	0.32	1814	0.33	0.47
Birth Order	290	2.42	1.50	1811	2.03	1.18
ADHD Symptoms	162	0.89	0.45	1071	0.92	0.48
Male	291	0.49	0.50	1814	0.53	0.50
Mother's Age at Child's Birth	291	22.65	4.89	1814	26.57	6.26
Father's Age at Child's Birth	290	25.44	6.99	1801	28.89	7.26
DDI Scale	291	2.65	0.78	1814	3.12	0.61
Mother is High School Dropout	291	0.44	0.50	1814	0.21	0.41
Mother has High School Degree	291	0.34	0.47	1814	0.28	0.45
Mother has less than College Degree	291	0.13	0.34	1814	0.26	0.44
Mother has College Degree	291	0.02	0.13	1814	0.20	0.40
Father is High School Dropout	291	0.45	0.50	1814	0.18	0.38
Father has High School Degree	291	0.37	0.48	1814	0.31	0.46
Father has less than College Degree	291	0.06	0.24	1814	0.22	0.41
Father has College Degree	291	0.00	0.06	1814	0.18	0.39
Household Income	243	13122.18	17304.11	1563	40423.55	57843.17
Household Income per Person	240	3664.72	5299.76	1561	10438.34	16460.30

Source: FFCWS

Econometric Issues and Analysis

Omitted Variable Bias

The statistical model employed in this study takes into account unobserved factors that could simultaneously influence child development and the probability of paternal incarceration. Some of these factors include:

paternal innate ability, deviant tendencies, values, and preferences. This is called *omitted variable bias*. By leaving this bias unaddressed, the estimated effect of paternal incarceration on the early child developmental outcomes would be imprecise. A method must be used to eliminate this bias and ensure correct estimates of the incarceration effect.

Measurement Error

Paternal incarceration is expected to be underreported by both parents in the FFCWS.[41, 42] In prior studies, it has been concluded that convicted criminals tend to underreport their crimes by about 35 percent.[43, 44] We can therefore assume that fathers in the FFCWS also significantly underreport their criminal activity as well as their jail sentences. In addition, it would be erroneous to assume that the mother's account of the father's incarceration status is more accurate. Even if she truthfully reports what she knows about the father's criminal past, she may not be fully informed about what happened before she met him. The true indicator of paternal incarceration is equal to 1 when the father was incarcerated, despite mother or father reports that may deny this. To measure observed incarceration, the indicator is set equal to 1 only if the father was reported as incarcerated and 0 otherwise. This constitutes measurement error in the incarceration data and may be typified as *nonclassical measurement error*. Nonclassical measurement error, put simply, could either overestimate or underestimate the incarceration effect.[45] Therefore, it must be addressed in order to get a more precise estimate of the incarceration effect on child developmental outcomes.

The Instrumental Variables (IV) or Two-Stage Least Squares Estimation Method

A method that can be used to address both omitted variable bias and the measurement error problem is instrumental variables (IV) or two-stage least squares estimation. This technique is used when the independent variable of interest (in this case, father's incarceration) is correlated with the error term of the statistical model. The challenge is finding a valid instrument (i.e., a variable that explains incarceration but not the child developmental outcomes or the unobserved characteristics in the error term).

One such variable comes from Dickman's Dysfunctional Impulsivity (DDI) index.[46] Dickman identifies two different types of impulsivity— functional and dysfunctional. Functional impulsivity can be described as responses that reflect enthusiasm, adventuresomeness, or any response in which quick thinking is optimal. Dysfunctional impulsivity, on the other hand, is "the tendency to deliberate less than most people of equal ability before taking action."[47] This diagnosis insinuates that if we hold ability constant, dysfunctional impulsive individuals tend to act with less fore-thought or self-control when this is not the optimal response (e.g., drinking or gambling). It is in this way that dysfunctional impulsivity explains criminal behavior since the capacity for self-control is a key determinant of crime.[48] It is also uncorrelated with ability and other omitted variables while concurrently not affecting the child outcomes other than through incarceration. The FFCWS includes six items from the original twenty-three-item DDI scale; the items are then averaged to create the impulsivity index. The alpha for these questions using the FFCWS father sample is 0.84, indicating that this subset is representative of the full scale (see appendix for list of items).

Nevertheless, if the DDI index is correlated with unobservables in the error term, this would render it an invalid instrument. This said, dysfunctional impulsivity is a heritable trait, and may influence the child development other than through incarceration. Impulsivity in humans is linked to serotonin levels in the brain, which is in part genetically determined.[49] If the heritable component of impulsivity can be controlled for in some way, the case can then be made that dysfunctional impulsivity is uncorrelated with the error term and is a valid instrument for incarceration. I made the argument that impulsivity in the child, genetically inherited from the father, would be evidenced in symptoms of attention deficit and hyperactivity disorder (ADHD) in the child.

To be diagnosed with ADHD, the child has to display prolonged levels of hyperactiveness, inattentiveness, and impulsiveness.[50, 51, 52] Children with ADHD have difficulty paying attention, staying in one place, and being patient. As a result, they are oftentimes mischaracterized as mischievous and demanding when in fact their educational and psychosocial challenges are directly associated with this disorder.[53, 54] Students with ADHD symptoms, particularly with inattentiveness, do worse in the classroom than their counterparts on average.[55] This measure is hence important as a control in this study due to its implications for cognitive performance and behavioral problems of young children.

There are six symptoms that must persist over a six-month period for ADHD to be diagnosed,[56] and the Third-Year In-Home Longitudinal Study aptly covers six key symptoms of ADHD (see appendix for list of items). I averaged these to create a measure that captures the heritable component of dysfunctional impulsivity. Its inclusion in the model should subsequently net out any impulsivity the child may have inherited from the father, rendering the DDI index a valid instrument. This should hopefully correct biases from omitted variables and nonclassical measurement error, yielding an unbiased or more precise estimate of the impact of paternal incarceration on each child developmental outcome.

DISCUSSION OF RESULTS

The ordinary least squares (OLS) and IV regression models are exploited to make causal arguments about the impact of paternal incarceration on the child outcome measures. Both models also control for *exogenous* variables or time-invariant characteristics that explain the child outcomes.[57] These variables include race, age, gender, birth order, parents' geographical region of birth, and year of the interview. Table 11.3 presents findings on the impact a father's incarceration *ex post* has on early child development. The outcome measures are in logarithm form, and therefore both OLS and IV estimates should be interpreted as percentages.

OLS estimates of the effect of paternal incarceration on the child developmental outcomes are presented in the left-hand column under each outcome measure. The incarceration effects are not statistically significant for PPVT-R scores or ODD symptoms. However, paternal incarceration *ex post* increases aggression by about 4 percent, and this is significant at the 5 percent level. It is important to note that OLS does not account for omitted variable bias and measurement error from the incarceration variable; however, IV estimation addresses both of these issues.

The IV estimates are given in the right-hand column under each outcome measure in table 11.3. Paternal incarceration *ex post* reduces child PPVT-R scores by approximately 21 percent, but this estimate is only marginally significant. Paternal incarceration *ex post* increases early child aggressive behaviors by nearly 34 percent, and this is statistically significant at the 1 percent level. Similarly, ODD symptoms increase by about 50 percent when a father is incarcerated *ex post*, and this estimate is statistically significant at the 1 percent level. Therefore, aggressive behaviors and ODD symptoms of the child are heightened by paternal incarceration *ex post*, and these findings are all statistically meaningful.

LIMITATIONS AND REQUIREMENTS

The consistency or precision of these results rests with the validity of the DDI index as an instrument for paternal incarceration. An instrument is valid if it explains the endogenous variable of interest while not being correlated with unobserved variables in the error term of the model. It is important to caution that the DDI index may not meet the requirements of a valid instrument, thus rendering incorrect estimates of the incarceration effect on early child outcomes.

For instance, if ADHD symptoms are poorly measured or the genetic link associated with impulsivity is not sufficiently captured by ADHD, then the

Table 11.3. OLS and IV Estimates of the Effect of Paternal Incarceration *Ex Post* on PPVT-R Scores, Aggression, and ODD Symptoms

	PPVT-R		AGGRESSION		ODD	
	OLS β (SE)	IV β (SE)	OLS β (SE)	IV β (SE)	OLS β (SE)	IV β (SE)
Incarcerated *Ex Post*	-0.020 (0.016)	-0.205 (0.114)	0.037** (0.017)	0.336* (0.116)	0.029 (0.020)	0.496* (0.147)
Mother Black	-0.064* (0.021)	-0.055** (0.023)	-0.026 (0.020)	-0.046** (0.023)	-0.099* (0.026)	-0.130* (0.031)
Mother Hispanic	-0.065* (0.020)	-0.067* (0.021)	0.009 (0.019)	0.007 (0.020)	-0.025 (0.024)	-0.027 (0.026)
Father Black	-0.054** (0.023)	-0.046 (0.025)	0.044** (0.020)	0.037 (0.022)	0.055** (0.026)	0.041 (0.030)
Father Hispanic	-0.041 (0.022)	-0.041 (0.022)	0.009 (0.020)	0.013 (0.021)	-0.005 (0.025)	-0.003 (0.027)
Birth Order	-0.022* (0.005)	-0.017* (0.006)	0.011* (0.004)	0.005 (0.005)	0.005 (0.005)	-0.005 (0.006)
ADHD Symptoms	0.011 (0.016)	0.008 (0.016)	-0.006 (0.013)	-0.002 (0.014)	-0.035** (0.016)	-0.029 (0.018)
ADHD (Missing)	0.012 (0.018)	0.010 (0.018)	0.002 (0.015)	0.006 (0.016)	-0.032 (0.019)	-0.027 (0.021)

(continued)

Table 11.3. *(continued)*

	PPVT-R		AGGRESSION		ODD	
	OLS β (SE)	IV β (SE)	OLS β (SE)	IV β (SE)	OLS β (SE)	IV β (SE)
Male	-0.032* (0.011)	-0.033* (0.011)	0.024* (0.009)	0.027* (0.010)	0.026** (0.011)	0.030** (0.013)
Mother's Age	0.005* (0.002)	0.004** (0.002)	-0.003* (0.001)	-0.001 (0.002)	-0.002 (0.002)	0.001 (0.002)
Father's Age	-0.001 (0.001)	-0.001 (0.001)	-0.001 (0.001)	-0.001 (0.001)	-0.001 (0.001)	-0.001 (0.001)
First-Stage Regression						
DDI Index	-0.07* (0.01)	-0.07* (0.01)	-0.07* (0.01)			
F-Statistic	56.44*	56.44*	56.44*			
R-Squared	0.11	—	0.04	—	0.05	—
Observations	1599	1599	2064	2064	2075	2075

Source: FFCWS

The table presents the incarceration estimates and standard errors for the child's PPVT-R scores, aggression, and ODD indices. All standard errors (in parentheses) are robust to heteroskedasticity. The PPVT-R scores, aggression, and ODD indices are also in logarithm form, and therefore estimates should be interpreted as percentages. All regressions include interview-year dummies and parent's geographical region-of-birth dummies.

*indicates statistical significance at the 1% level; ** indicates statistical significance at the 5% level use of the child's ADHD symptoms to measure the latent heritable component of dysfunctional impulsivity will not help correct the bias in the model. Further, not only does dysfunctional impulsivity have to be uncorrelated with unobserved factors affecting both incarceration and child development, it also has to be a strong correlate of incarceration. An easy way to test this is to use the first-stage F-statistic and the Stock and Watson "rule of thumb." According to this rule, the F-statistic on the DDI index in the first stage of the IV regression (i.e., regressing the DDI index on paternal incarceration) must exceed 10 in order to prevent bias resulting from a weak instrument.[58] A weak instrument, or a variable that is not a "strong explainer" of incarceration, may exacerbate the preexisting biases from omitted variables and measurement error, making the IV estimates essentially worse than the OLS estimates.[59] In table 11.3, the DDI index as an instrument for endogenous paternal incarceration yields a first-stage F-statistic of 56.44. This largely exceeds the Stock and Watson simple "rule of thumb" that the first-stage F-statistic should be at least equal to 10.

CONCLUSION

This study sought to isolate the effect of a father's incarceration on early child development while addressing serious concerns associated with omitted variable bias and nonclassical measurement error. By using instrumental variables (IV) estimation, it can be concluded that paternal incarceration indeed has substantial effects on early child development. Paternal incarceration *ex post* marginally reduces test scores of preschool-aged children, but amplifies their aggressive and defiant behaviors at the 1 percent level of significance. These results confirm Wildeman's (2008) findings that there is a statistically significant and positive relationship between father incarceration and child aggressive behaviors. It is salient to note that conduct disorders in young children tend to continue into adolescence[60] and a parent's criminal stigma may also reproduce criminogenic or deviant traits in children. If this rings true, increased conduct disorders in affected preschoolers may herald the imminence of their troubled future.[61]

These results therefore champion the importance of attending to children of incarcerated parents and particularly during their early developmental years. Based on the strength of the findings—that children display more aggressive and violent behaviors when a father becomes incarcerated—mental health care providers and school systems should screen for incarceration.[62] The proclivity of these children towards aggressive and violent behavior strengthens the need for services that address the mental health of young children.[63] Further, families and schools should be advised about these types of consequences inextricably linked to paternal incarceration. It may even be useful for the government to fund after-school programs and private counseling in schools and community-based organizations to assist in the behavioral challenges children of incarcerated fathers face. The implementation of programs that support children of incarcerated fathers will help ensure that these tendencies are not proliferated into adolescence and later adulthood.

APPENDIX

Scales Documentation

Aggression	ODD	ADHD	DDI—Father's Impulsivity
Can't wait turn	Defiant	Can't concentrate	I often say whatever comes into my head without thinking
Demanding	Disobedient	Can't sit still	Often I don't think enough before I act
Destroys others' things	Angry moods	Quickly shifts actions	I often say/do things without considering the consequences
Easily frustrated	Temper tantrums	Demanding	My plans fail because I fail to think them through first
Gets in fights	Uncooperative	Gets into everything	I often make up my mind w/o considering the situation
No guilt after misbehaving	Stubborn/irritable	Can't wait turn	I get into trouble because I don't think before I act
Hits others			
Hurts animals/people unintentionally			
Attacks people			
Punishment doesn't change behavior			
Screams a lot			
Selfish/won't share			
Wants a lot of attention			
Likert Scale:			
0 = Not True	0 = Not True	0 = Not True	1 = Strongly Agree
—	—	—	—
2 = Very True	2 = Very True	2 = Very True	4 = Strongly Disagree
Alpha on Full Sample:			
0.88	0.77	0.72	0.84

Notes: The items are averaged to create each scale.

NOTES

1. Antecol, Heather, and Kelly Bedard. 2007. "Does single parenthood increase the probability of teenage promiscuity, substance use, and crime?" *Journal of Population Economics* 20: 55–71.

2. Corak, Miles. 2001. "Death and divorce: the long-term consequences of parental loss on adolescence." *Journal of Labor Economics* 19(3): 682–715.

3. Lang, Kevin, and Jay Zagorsky. 2001. "Does growing up with a parent absent really hurt?" *The Journal of Human Resources* 36(2): 253–73.

4. Painter, Gary, and David Levine. 2000. "Family structure and youths' outcomes: Which correlations are causal?" *The Journal of Human Resources* 35(3): 524–49.

5. Jaffee, Sara, et al. 2003. "With (or without) father: The benefits of living with two parents depend on the father's antisocial behavior." *Child Development* 74(1): 109–26.

6. Murray, Joseph, and David Farrington. 2008. "Effects of parental imprisonment on children." *Crime and Justice* 37: 133–206.

7. Western, Bruce, and Christopher Wildeman. 2009. "The black family and mass incarceration." *Annals of the American Academy of Social and Political Science* 621: 221–42.

8. Wildeman, Christopher. 2008. "Paternal incarceration and children's aggressive behaviors: Evidence from the Fragile Families and Child Wellbeing Study." *Center for Research on Child Well-being Working Paper Series* 2008-02-FF.

9. Cavanagh, Shannon, and Aletha Huston. 2006. "Family instability and children's early problem behavior." *Social Forces* 85(1): 551–81.

10. Craigie, Terry-Ann. 2008. "Effects of paternal presence and family instability on child cognitive performance." *Center for Research on Child Well-being Working Paper Series* 2008-03-FF.

11. Fomby, Paula, and Andrew Cherlin. 2007. "Family instability and child well-being." *American Sociological Review* 72(April): 181–204.

12. Osborne, Cynthia, and Sara McLanahan. 2007. "Partnership instability and child well-being." *Journal of Marriage and Family* 69 (November): 1065–83.

13. Becker, Gary. 1968. "Crime and punishment: An economic approach." *The Journal of Political Economy* 76: 169–217.

14. Geller, Amanda, Irwin Garfinkel, and Bruce Western. 2006. "The effects of incarceration on employment and wages: An analysis of the Fragile Families Survey." *Center for Research on Child Well-being Working Paper Series* 2006-01-FF.

15. Grogger, Jeffrey. 1995. "The effect of arrests on the employment and earnings of young men." *The Quarterly Journal of Economics* 110(1): 51–71.

16. Amanda Geller, Irwin Garfinkel, Carey Cooper, and Ronald Mincy. "Parental incarceration and child wellbeing: Implications for urban families." *Social Forces*, forthcoming.

17. Hairston, Creasie Finney. 2007. *Focus on children with incarcerated parents.* Annie E. Casey Foundation.

18. Western, Bruce. 2006. *Punishment and inequality in America.* New York: Russell Sage Foundation.

19. Geller et al., "Parental incarceration."

20. Hairston, *Focus on children.*

21. Cavanagh and Huston, "Family instability."

22. Craigie, "Effects of paternal presence."

23. Fomby and Cherlin, "Family instability."

24. Osborne and McLanahan, "Partnership instability."

25. Parke, Ross, and Clarke-Stewart, K. Alison. 2002. *Effects of Parental Incarceration on Young Children.* U.S. Department of Health and Human Services. The Urban Institute.

26. Jaffee et al., "With (or without) father."

27. Murray and Farrington, "Effects of parental imprisonment."

28. Parke, Clarke-Stewart, and Alison, "Effects of parental incarceration."

29. Western and Wildeman, "The black family."

30. Wildeman, "Paternal incarceration."

31. Western, *Punishment.*

32. Wildeman, "Paternal incarceration."

33. Reichman, Nancy, Julien Teitler, and Sara McLanahan. 2001. "Fragile families: Sample and design." *Children and Youth Services Review* 23(4/5): 303–26.

34. Jeruchimowicz, Rita, Joan Costello, and Susana Bagur. 1971. "Knowledge and action and object words: A comparison of lower and middle-class Negro preschoolers." *Child Development* 42(2): 455–64.

35. Grusec, Joan, and Hugh Lytton. 1988. *Social development.* New York: Springer-Verlag.

36. Maccoby, Eleanor. 1980. *Social development.* New York: Harcourt Brace.

37. Shaw, Daniel S., Miles Gilliom, and Joyce Giovannelli. 2000. "Aggressive behavior disorders." In *Handbook of Infant Mental Health,* ed. C. H. Zeanah, second edition, 397–411. New York: Guilford Press.

38. Wildeman, "Paternal incarceration."

39. Note here that each individual measure ranged from 0 to 2, but averaging all measures created a maximum of 1.92.

40. Greene, Ross, et al. 2002. "Psychiatric comorbidity, family dysfunction, and social impairment in referred youth with oppositional defiant disorder." *The American Journal of Psychiatry* 159: 1214–24.

41. Geller et al., "The effects of incarceration."

42. Wildeman, "Paternal incarceration."

43. Locander, William, Seymour Sudman, and Norman Bradburn. 1976. "An investigation of interview method, threat, and response distortion." *Journal of the American Statistical Association* 71: 269–75.

44. Witte, Ann Dryden. 1980. "Estimating the economic model of crime with individual data." *The Quarterly Journal of Economics* 94(1): 57–84.

45. Haider, Steven, and Gary Solon. 2006. "Life-cycle variation in the association between current and lifetime earnings." *American Economic Review* 96(4): 1308–20.

46. Dickman, Scott. 1990. "Functional and dysfunctional impulsivity: Personality and cognitive correlates." *Journal of Personality and Social Psychology* 58(1): 95–102.

47. Dickman, "Dysfunctional impulsivity," 95.

48. Farrington, David. 1998. "Predictors, causes and correlates of male youth violence." *Crime and Justice* 24: 421–75.

49. Hodges, Gayle. 2006. *The role of impulsive aggression in a cohort of suicide attempters*. PhD diss., The University of Texas Southwestern Medical Center at Dallas.

50. Alloway, Tracy, et al. 2009. "The diagnostic utility of behavioral checklists in identifying children with ADHD and children with working memory deficits." *Child Psychiatry Human Development* 40: 353–66.

51. American Psychiatric Association. 2004. *Diagnostic and Statistical Manual of Mental Disorders, fourth ed.* American Psychiatric Association, Washington DC.

52. Winkler, Mary. 2006. "ADHD symptoms ADHD diagnosis—diagnosis criteria of ADHD." Web4Health. web4health.info/en/answers/adhd-diagn-dsm.htm

53. Alloway, "The diagnostic utility of behavioral checklists."

54. Biederman, Joseph. 2005. "Attention-deficit/hyperactivity disorder: A selective overview." *Biological Psychiatry* 57: 1215–20.

55. Nussbaum, Nancy L., Mitzie L. Grant, Mary J. Roman, John H. Poole, and Erin D. Bigler. 1990. "Attention deficit disorder and the mediating effect of age on academic and behavioral variables." *Journal of Developmental and Behavioral Pediatrics* 11: 22–26.

56. Winkler, "ADHD symptoms."

57. It is imperative to exclude potentially endogenous variables (i.e., independent variables correlated with the error term) such as education and income from the regression since the estimated incarceration effect would be incorrect.

58. Wooldridge, Jeffrey. 2002. *Econometric analysis of cross-section and panel data.* Cambridge, MA: MIT Press, 90–92.

59. Staiger, Douglas, and James H. Stock. 1997. "Instrumental variables regression with weak instruments." *Econometrica* 65(3): 557–86.

60. Shaw, Gilliam, and Giovannelli, "Aggressive behavior disorders."

61. Wildeman, "Paternal incarceration."

62. Wilbur, MaryAnn B., et al. 2007. "Socio-emotional effects of fathers' incarceration on low-income, urban, school-aged children." *Pediatrics* 120 (3): 678–85.

63. Geller et al., "Parental incarceration."

12

The "State" of Paid Family Leave: Insights from the 2006 and 2007 Legislative Sessions

Melissa Brown

Over the past twenty-five years, there has been a growing interest in the work-family interface among researchers, workplace practitioners, and policy-makers. As many employees with family responsibilities report challenges in meeting both work and family demands,[1] more recent research in this area has explored if employees, families, and/or employers benefit when employees have access to workplace resources that assist them in managing work and family responsibilities.[2] While many "family-friendly" resources are offered at the discretion of individual employers, the Family and Medical Leave Act (FMLA) is one resource that is mandated by the federal government. The FMLA provides eligible employees up to twelve weeks of unpaid leave per year to care for a newborn or newly adopted child, a family member (child, spouse, or parent) with a serious medical issue, or to recover from their own serious medical issue.[3, 4]

While the FMLA was hailed as a victory for working families, many have acknowledged that the legislation has several significant limitations.[5] A number of states have since proposed legislation to address these limitations,[6] yet these most recent efforts of states to do so have been largely overlooked by researchers.[7] This chapter begins to address this gap by presenting the findings of a research study exploring states' efforts to enact legislation that would provide payment to employees utilizing FMLA. The basic theoretical framework that informs the methodology of the study is discussed first, followed by a review of the limitations of the FMLA and the actions some states have taken to address these limitations. Following this, the methodology and research findings are presented. The chapter closes with some final thoughts on the future of paid family leave legislation.

THEORETICAL PERSPECTIVES
ON SOCIAL POLICY DEVELOPMENT

The passage of the FMLA in 1993 ended the United States' notorious distinction of being the only industrialized country without a universal medical leave policy for workers.[8] Research investigating the legislative life of the FMLA has attributed its successful passage to one or more of the following factors: structural changes of society, the political institutions in power, and interest group mobilization.[9] Each of these factors represents a major theoretical perspective of social policy development.

Perspective 1: Structural Changes

One theoretical perspective of social policy development posits that social policies result from structural changes in society.[10] These fundamental shifts in our economic and social lives necessitate new social policies to reflect this new reality. In the case of the FMLA, there have certainly been massive changes over the past fifty years in how families manage work and family responsibilities. In the decades preceding the passage of the FMLA, the percentage of women in the workforce rapidly increased, as did the number of dual earner and single parent families.[11] Research on the development and passage of the FMLA has recognized the role structural forces played in these processes: "The emergence of mandated family leave is largely a result of unprecedented changes in the composition of the workforce and the nature of worker's family responsibilities."[12] These changes ushered in a new reality, one where the traditional family model of a male breadwinner and stay-at-home mother was no longer representative of the vast majority of families. A universal family leave policy was born from these unprecedented changes, established to assist families in meeting both work and family responsibilities.[13]

Perspective 2: Political Institutions

A second theoretical perspective of social policy development argues that political institutions shape social policies. Accordingly, social policies are a function of politics, the passage of the bill a reflection of the ideological perspectives of the party in power within the political institutions.[14] The long legislative process involved in enacting the FMLA has been cited as support for the perspective that political institutions drive the development of social policy.[15] Initially introduced in 1985, the bill languished in Congress for eight years and was twice vetoed by then President George H. W. Bush. However, when the 1992 elections changed the balance of control in both the House and Senate and in the White House, the bill was reborn. The bill quickly moved through Congress and became one of the first pieces of legislation signed into law by President Bill Clinton.[16]

Perspective 3: Special Interest Groups

A third theoretical perspective—the mobilization of interest groups—has also been cited as a driving force for social policies such as the FMLA.[17] Interest groups exert a great deal of pressure on legislators by bringing an issue to the public's attention and engaging members to participate in grassroots organizing campaigns. This strategy can be particularly effective when multiple interest groups form into a coalition, as was the case with the FMLA. Research on the FMLA has acknowledged that the coalition advocating for the FMLA was instrumental in securing the passage of this legislation: "Although socioeconomic changes exerted pressures on citizens, that pressure could not be translated into policy enactment without the mobilization of interest groups and politicians in an effective issue network."[18] While the demonstrable need for the FMLA was important for getting it on the agenda, the mobilization of interest groups was necessary to secure its passage.

LIMITATIONS OF FMLA

FMLA provides a narrow definition of "family," and it is unpaid, thus, the FMLA is perceived by many as an inadequate piece of legislation.[19] One of the major limitations of the FMLA is lack of coverage. Because certain employees are exempted, as are employers with less than fifty employees, approximately 60 percent of the workforce qualifies for the FMLA,[20] hardly constituting a "universal" leave policy. A second limitation of the legislation is the lack of payment. Research has revealed that many of those who qualify for FMLA cannot utilize it, despite having a need to, because they cannot afford the loss of income that would result.[21] Given that workers who have been able to utilize the FMLA report positive effects for doing so—both themselves and their family members—the lack of universal access is concerning.[22] Ultimately, employees who are not eligible or who cannot afford to take the FMLA may find themselves and their loved ones forced into an increasingly precarious and disadvantaged situation.

The narrow purview of how a family member is legally defined is a third limitation of this legislation. Under federal guidelines, eligible employees may only take leave to care for the serious medical condition of a child,[23] spouse, or parent These restrictions deny employees with caregiving responsibilities that extend beyond their immediate family: employees cannot take leave to care for a parent-in-law, nor are grandchildren eligible to take leave to care for a grandparent (or vice versa). With the population rapidly aging and the number of workers with elder care responsibilities increasing,[24] providing additional family members with access to the FMLA in order to care for their older relatives may be essential to meeting the caregiving needs of an aging society.

In addition, the legislation discriminates against same-sex couples, even in the few states that provide same-sex couples the legal right to marry one another (currently Connecticut, Iowa, Massachusetts, Maine, New Hampshire, and Vermont), or recognize same-sex marriages from other states (New York and Rhode Island) and the District of Columbia.[25] In states where same-sex marriage is not a legal right, individuals in a same-sex relationship are deprived of the opportunity to take FMLA to care for their partner by default. Yet even married same-sex couples are not necessarily guaranteed the right to take FMLA to care for a spouse with a serious illness or injury. For the purposes of all federal legislation, the Defense of Marriage Act (1996) explicitly defines marriage as a legal union of one man and one woman.[26]

As a result of these limitations, millions of workers do not have access to a "family-friendly" resource that guarantees them time off from work to address the urgent medical needs of a family member (or to care for a new child).[27] These workers remain at risk of facing a "family care crisis," wherein they cannot take time off from work to meet the medical needs of a family member or to provide care for a new child.

FAMILY MEDICAL LEAVE AT THE STATE LEVEL

Several individual states, however, have enacted legislation related to one or more of these shortcomings. Six states (Maine, Minnesota, Oregon, Rhode Island, Vermont, and Washington) and the District of Columbia have expanded FMLA to cover employers with fewer than fifty employees, providing more employees access to this resource.[28] In addition, nine states (California, Connecticut, Hawaii, Maine, New Jersey, Oregon, Rhode Island, Vermont, and Wisconsin) and the District of Columbia have modified the law to allow workers to take leave to care for family members in addition to those defined at the federal level.[29] Finally, California, New Jersey, and Washington have enacted legislation providing some form of paid leave. Given the fact that over thirty states had already established medical leave policies prior to the enactment of FMLA,[30] it is not surprising that progress on this issue continues to come primarily from state governments.

Despite their success in expanding the access and scope of the legislation, states have generally had less success in their attempts to pass legislation to provide some form of payment for those taking leave under FMLA. Since its inception, more than two dozen states have proposed some form of paid leave; only three have been successful. One of the major stumbling blocks for states has been the difficulty in establishing a funding mechanism to pay for the proposed benefits.[31] When the Clinton administration proposed regulations that enabled states to tap unemployment insurance to provide paid leave to parents after the birth or adoption of a child in 1999, a flurry of activity followed. By 2000, thirteen states had proposed some form of paid family leave, and by 2003 this number had nearly doubled.[32]

Despite these efforts, California was the only state successful in getting paid family leave legislation passed before 2007. Analogous to the FMLA, California's success has been attributed to interest group mobilization as well as to structural and political factors. From a structural perspective, there was a clear need for this legislation. The inadequacies of the FMLA necessitated legislation to support employees not covered under the FMLA, as well as those who could not afford an unpaid leave. Political forces also pushed the bill forward as the underlying ideology of the bill was reflective of the ideology of those in power. When the bill was signed into law in 2002, there was a Democrat majority in both Houses as well as a Democrat as governor. The mobilization of interest groups was also an important force in pushing paid family leave forward in California, as a strong, active coalition helped secure the passage of this legislation. Finally, the presence of a relatively healthy state economy is cited as another important factor in the passage of paid family leave.[33]

CALIFORNIA'S PAID FAMILY LEAVE PROGRAM

California's Paid Family Leave Program covers approximately 80 percent of the workforce, and provides eligible workers up to six weeks of paid leave. The leave can be used to care for a newborn baby, an adopted or foster child, or a seriously ill parent, child, spouse, or registered domestic partner.[34] In covering a larger percentage of the workforce, providing paid leave, and recognizing domestic partners as family members, California's Paid Family Leave Program is seen as a model for other states, and possibly even the federal government.

California had an advantage, however, that most states, and the federal government, lack: Temporary Disability Insurance (TDI). Established in California in 1946, TDI provides workers with a partial wage replacement for a temporary illness or injury (including pregnancy) not related to work. There are four other states with similar programs: Hawaii, New Jersey,

New York, and Rhode Island. In essence, Temporary Disability Insurance (TDI) provides eligible workers in these states with paid FMLA leave for their own illness or injury. California's passage of Paid Family Leave was essentially an expansion of their existing TDI program, enabling workers to take leave not just for themselves, but also for the family members covered under FMLA (as well as domestic partners). A major reason California was able to establish Paid Family Leave was because their existing TDI program provided a funding mechanism for the legislation. Lack of a TDI program is one of the largest challenges many other states have faced in passing similar legislation.[35]

RECENT ACTIVITY

Any progress toward providing more comprehensive coverage has been limited by regulations imposed during the George W. Bush administration in 2003 that prohibit states from using unemployment insurance as a funding mechanism for workers to care for a newborn or newly adopted child. With this funding mechanism no longer available, far fewer states have considered paid family leave legislation since 2003. As an alternative, many states have focused on legislation that would allow workers to use their paid sick days (typically up to fourteen days a year) for the illness or injury of a family member.[36] While a step in the right direction, this legislation ignores the reality that nearly half of the workforce does not have access to paid sick days[37] and fails to address the needs of workers who have to take an extended leave to care for a loved one.

Not all states have stepped back their efforts to establish paid family leave. Ten states have proposed paid family leave legislation since 2004 (Arizona, Connecticut, Illinois, Pennsylvania, Massachusetts, Minnesota, New Jersey, New York, Oregon, and Washington), and two have successfully enacted such legislation. In 2007, Washington passed a bill providing workers up to five weeks of paid leave to care for a newborn or newly adopted child. In 2008, New Jersey, a state with a TDI program, passed a bill providing workers up to six weeks of paid leave to care for a child, parent, spouse, or domestic partner with a serious illness or injury. Despite this activity, researchers have largely overlooked the efforts of states to pass paid family leave legislation.[38]

This study was conducted in order to address this gap by exploring the experiences of legislators who introduce paid family leave legislation. The following research questions were proposed: (1) What influences a legislator's decision to introduce paid family leave legislation? (2) What strategies do legislators and key stakeholders engage in to get paid family leave legislation passed? (3) What internal and external factors influence the legislative process for paid family leave legislation?

METHODS

Using the bill-tracking feature that is offered by LexisNexis, I identified seven states (Arizona, Illinois, Massachusetts, Oregon, New Jersey, New York, and Washington) that introduced paid family leave during the 2006–2007 legislative session. For the purposes of this project, paid family leave legislation was defined as a bill that would provide at least four weeks of paid leave to care for a family member with a serious medical condition and/or bond with a new child. In addition, the bill had to provide coverage to at least those workers eligible for the FMLA, though many covered a much larger percentage of the workforce (table 12.1 provides detailed information on each bill). I contacted each of the legislators who had sponsored paid family leave legislation to ask if they (or a legislative aide, if they were unavailable) would be willing to participate in a study about paid family leave legislation. In two of the interviews, a key participant in the process (a leader from an advocacy organization) was named. These key participants were also solicited to participate in the study.

After obtaining informed consent from each individual who agreed to participate, phone interviews were conducted at a time convenient for the participant. Each interview was conducted using a semi-structured interview guide, which covered four substantive areas of inquiry: recognizing paid family leave as a policy issue, drafting the legislation, the legislative life of the bill, and their thoughts on the future of paid family leave legislation. Following the interviews, which lasted between thirty to forty minutes, the interviews were transcribed. A total of nine interviews were conducted: six with legislators who had sponsored paid family leave legislation, two with leaders of advocacy organizations lobbying for the bill, and one with the aide of a legislator who sponsored paid family leave. Data analysis followed a process of content analysis and constant comparison[39] to identify reoccurring themes both within and between interviews.

GETTING PAID FAMILY LEAVE ON THE AGENDA

Certainly, the first part of the process is getting paid family leave on the agenda. Like any piece of legislation, paid family leave gets on the agenda when a legislator decides to sponsor it. But what motivates legislators to sponsor this type of legislation? From the interviews with legislators and

Table 12.1. Paid Family Leave Legislation Proposed in 2006–2007

State	Proposed Bill	Funding Mechanism	Outcome
AZ	Five weeks ($250 a week for FTEs, pro-rated for PTEs) to care for self, spouse or domestic partner, child, or parent with a serious medical condition (or bond with new child)	Employer tax of .02/hr per employee (up to forty hrs/wk), can have employees pay half	Never had a hearing
IL	Four weeks (67% of weekly wages up to $380 a week for FTEs, pro-rated for PTEs) to care for self, spouse, child, parent, parent-in law, or person residing in the same house for 6+ months with a serious medical condition (or bond with new child)	Employee tax of .75 a week for FTEs, pro-rated for PTEs; employer match	Never had a hearing
MA	Twelve weeks (80% of wages up to $750 a week, pro-rated PTEs) to care for self, spouse, child, or parent (or bond with new child)	Employee tax, amount not specified	Voted favorably from committee; no further action taken

NJ*	Twelve weeks (67% of average weekly wage, up to $524) to care for spouse, domestic partner, child, or parent with a serious medical condition (or bond with new child)	Tax on employees of 0.1% of wages up to an amount equal to the Social Security tax base	Bill providing six weeks of leave signed in May 2008
NY*	Twelve weeks (50% of average weekly wage, up to $170 a week) to care for spouse or domestic partner, child, parent, parent-law, or grandchild with a serious medical condition (or bond with a new child)	Tax on employees of up to .60 a week	Passed Assembly on June 22, 2007; no action by Senate
OR	Six weeks ($250 a week) to care for self, child, spouse, or parent with a serious medical condition (or bond with new child)	Tax on employees of .01 per hour worked, up to .40 a week	Passed House with amendments; failed to pass Senate
WA	Five weeks ($250 a week) to care for self, spouse, or domestic partner, child, or parent (or bond with new child)	TBD	Bill providing five weeks "new child" leave signed in May 2007

*Note: State with Temporary Disability Insurance (TDI)

key stakeholders, two themes related to getting paid family leave on the agenda emerged: perceiving the need and having external support.

Perceiving the Need

Legislators were motivated to sponsor paid family leave legislation because they perceived that there was a real need for it, consistent with the structural perspective in social policy development. Many noted that the overall structural changes that have occurred in society necessitate this legislation. As voiced by one legislator:

> Wage rates are stagnant, health care costs are going up, People are working more hours . . . there more women are in the workforce . . . the outcome of all of that is that families are really put to the test when they (have) any kind of medical crisis or a new baby joins the family so it's incumbent to do everything to make families healthier.

Having an awareness of general macro-economic trends is one way that legislators perceived the need for this legislation; hearing from constituents is another.

Legislators also perceived the need for this legislation on a more personal level, with many sharing a heart-wrenching story of a constituent who had endured a family care crisis:

> A constituent, who was pregnant, was working for a small nonprofit organization. She had saved her two weeks of vacation to use after the birth of the baby. Well, the baby was born premature and had to be transferred to an intensive care unit in a hospital up-state. She had to make a Hobbesian choice of whether to be with her newborn son, or go back to work and use her paid leave when he got out of the hospital instead. So she gave birth on a Thursday night and was back to work on Monday morning.

Legislators who introduced this legislation recognized it as a critical resource for workers with family responsibilities, including those they represented.

Having External Support

Having external support—from both constituents and interest groups—was also a significant factor in motivating legislators to introduce this legislation. The need for constituent support was reiterated throughout the interviews. One legislator succinctly stated how constituent support for an issue can catalyze legislators to introduce legislation: "We have to make an effort by introducing items that are important to our communities. That's why we are there." In addition to the external support from constituents, external support from interest groups—notably advocacy organizations and organized labor groups—also plays a role in influencing legislators to sponsor paid family leave legislation.

One legislator shared how an advocacy organization lobbied her to introduce paid family leave legislation:

> An [advocacy] organization came to me about prospects for passing legislation to create paid family and medical leave. . . . I value the work this organization has done. I knew then as I do now even many years later that they are on the cut of cutting issues and what's going on all over the country.

Ultimately, the opportunity to work with an external interest group on an issue they recognized as a priority and that the majority of their constituents supported was a winning combination in motivating legislators to place paid family leave on their state's political agenda.

GETTING PAID FAMILY LEAVE PASSED

In addition to playing a key role in getting paid family leave on the agenda, external support from constituents and interest groups is instrumental to getting paid family leave passed. Other themes that emerged as influencing the process included: building off existing legislation, political institutions, the right "timing," the state's familiarity with the legislation, and compromise.

Interest Group Mobilization and Constituent Support

Interest group mobilization is cited as an essential component in establishing paid family leave, particularly so in states without a TDI program. Having a strong, active coalition is acknowledged as one of the major reasons for Washington's success. As described by a leader of the organization that spearheaded this coalition:

> We have quite a large coalition of organizations—women's groups, senior groups, children's advocacy groups, faith based organizations, labor unions, some employers, some health based organizations—a whole variety of different kinds of organizations that have come together and seen this as a high policy priority so we've worked to both build that coalition and to provide coalition members with the materials they need to education their own membership to educate policymakers on the issue and that kind of thing.

This large, diverse, action-oriented coalition was instrumental in establishing paid family leave in Washington. A coalition that formed in New Jersey was also a large and diverse group, and certainly played a key role in securing passage of paid family leave in that state as well. Conversely, the absence of a strong coalition was offered as one of the reasons why other states were unsuccessful in establishing paid family leave.

The constituent pressure on legislators that can result from effective interest group mobilization is also an integral part of the process. Effective coalitions are able to build a movement around an issue, mobilizing constituents across the state to lobby their legislators through grassroots organizing campaigns. It is this constituent pressure that helps motivate legislators into action.[40] As exemplified by one legislator: "A very big component of state policy is constituent interest and constituent pressure. . . . When there is a demand made on us from our constituents we pay attention. . . . Significant issues that emerge and that rise to the surface are those that have the most effective grassroots campaign behind them." These sentiments lend support to the theoretical perspective that interest groups influence social policy development, as it is evident that interest group mobilization is a critical component to establishing paid family leave.

Building Off Existing Frameworks

Some researchers have argued that it is "highly unlikely" for states without a TDI program to establish paid family leave.[41] At the very least, the opportunity to build off existing legislation—namely a TDI program—is a tremendous advantage for states attempting to establish paid family leave, and one well recognized by legislators, as evidenced by the following comments of one legislator:

> In California's case, they were adding to a long established program that everyone was familiar with. I think that is one of keys to California's success. . . . Sometimes through accidents of history we benefit later on in being able to build on some existing policies. It's much easier to add something if it's already in place, it's a pretty big lift for a state that doesn't have any existing program to build on, to basically start from scratch.

The challenge of creating a brand-new program is not exclusive to paid family leave; it is a defining feature of the legislative process. As one legislator explained, the legislative process is typically one of incremental change: "That's just the nature of legislation, once you get a law on the books that creates a program then any amendment to change some of the parameters of that program is really much easier to achieve than to create a brand new program . . . it's always easier to tweak something, amend something."

Yet the state of Washington has shown that while creating a paid family leave program may be a formidable task, it is not an impossible one. It is reasonable to assume, however, that the bill that passed—leave for a new-born or newly adopted child—was such a stripped down version of the original bill (which included leave for the serious illness of the worker, their child, parent, spouse, or domestic partner) for precisely this reason. But with a paid leave program—albeit a minimal one—established, it will be much easier to expand this program to include other family members. In fact, there are already plans to do so once the program is up and running. It is possible for other states without TDI programs to follow a similar trajectory.

Political Institutions

The FMLA, and the paid family leave programs in California, New Jersey, and Washington, were all passed during legislative sessions in which Democrats held the majority in both Chambers, as well as the presidency or governorship. In addition, all of the legislators who introduced paid family leave legislation during the 2006–2007 session were Democrats. These facts lend support to the perspective that political institutions shape social policy. The legislators interviewed, however, did not necessarily perceive paid family leave as a completely partisan issue: "I don't see this necessarily as a partisan issue. This is a people issue—it's to help people keep the quality or improve the quality of the life that they have." In addition, legislators did not necessarily vote along party lines. One legislator shared that in his state "the deciding vote (in committee) was left up to a Republican legislator, and he voted yes."

Nonetheless, it was acknowledged that politics did play a role in the process and there was a general consensus that a Democratic majority was an important component in getting a paid family leave passed by any legislature. As noted by one legislator: "The issue of paid family and medical leave is not going to get a hearing or a fair shot of becoming law in this state if it has to follow the legislative process. You would have to have a little more than a majority of Democrats in both Houses (in order to pass the bill)." As with the FMLA, Democrat control of the legislative and executive branches appears to be a determining factor in the success of paid family leave legislation. While individual legislators may cross the aisle, that paid family leave legislation is generally voted on a partisan basis supports the theoretical perspective that political institutions matter.

A related theme emerged that might extend the explanatory power of the 'political institutions' perspective: individual politicians within these political institutions matter too, particularly those in leadership roles. Leadership can control the legislative life of a bill and exert pressure on other legislators to support the bill. An aide to a legislator who had sponsored paid family leave offered the following:

> Leadership has a big hand in what actually gets passed, so they have a strong influence with other members. If you can get them to support a bill sometimes that can help sway other members who were sitting on the fence. . . . They have a lot of power over what bills actually make it out of committee and onto the floor for a vote.

While having the support of the political party in power is important, the bill must also have the support of the individuals controlling the political process.

The Right "Time"

Another theme that emerged in the interviews was the issue of "timing." Efforts to establish paid family leave legislation may be stymied when the timing is not right. For example, if the legislature is facing a pressing issue or if the economy is not strong, the timing may not be right for establishing this type of legislation. When the legislature is preoccupied with a major piece of legislation or crisis, as was the case in two of the states, the timing for paid family leave legislation is not right. As shared by a legislator from a state that recently enacted major health care reform:

> Honestly, with all this other stuff going on, there hasn't been a major discussion in terms of what leadership's position on this (bill) is. We recently implemented the healthcare reform law so the timing of this (bill) has to be careful. . . .I think that the health care reform needs to play itself out a little bit longer. . . . Once it plays out . . . there can be more discussion about paid family and medical leave.

When a legislature is still engrossed in working out the details of a major reform, other pieces of legislation will likely remain on the back burner. Other issues can also arise that divert attention from this legislation; many times these issues may be difficult or impossible to predict ahead of time as highlighted by a legislator from another state: "We had a very unusual session. . . . I've been working 24/7 on a completely different issue." When the legislature is preoccupied with another issue, issues that are not immediate priorities will likely not be considered.

The timing must also be right from an economic standpoint. An advocate for paid family leave legislation in Washington explained: "We ran (the bill) in 2001 and the recession hit, the state budget was in a recession, everyone was scrambling to retain existing programs, so it wasn't time to advocate for a big new program when everyone was sort of dashing around to try to prevent things from falling apart." Economic downturns create a particularly unfavorable environment for expanding programs or establishing new ones. With the vast majority of states facing budget shortfalls in 2009 and many projecting that their fiscal problems will continue into 2010 as well,[42] states will be hard-pressed to pass paid family leave until economic conditions improve. As one legislator stated succinctly, "When you have economic problems, anxiety sets in and very little happens."

Familiarity with the Legislation

Familiarity with the legislation—both within the legislature and among constituents—was another theme that emerged as influencing the legislative life of paid family leave legislation. The legislative process involved in establishing new social policies is generally a lengthy one, occurring over multiple legislative sessions and many years. As the bill is reintroduced over multiple sessions, the legislature and the public become more familiar with it, and ideally, the bill garners additional support and makes further progress in the legislative process. As described by one legislator:

> I've learned this process works slowly, particularly for more complicated and more novel legislation. It takes awhile to build a coalition strong enough, and very often it takes several years to do it . . . [The] legislators here, most of them aren't focusing on this bill, they're focusing on their district issues, bills they've signed on, or their constituents have raised. . . . It takes a long time to build support . . . and for people to understand it and to feel more comfortable about creating a whole new structure. . . . A lot of it is education and meeting with people and negotiation and making some changes, and going back and just working it through.

Because it takes time to familiarize legislators and constituents with new legislation, the process of establishing paid family leave occurs incrementally, particularly in states where it is necessary to create a brand-new program in order to do so.

In fact, legislation creating a new social policy is often not even brought to a vote the first time it is introduced. According to one legislator, "We think of legislation as a multiyear kind of experience. [It is] still useful for educational purposes to put it in the hopper even if we are not actually going to call it for a vote." In some cases, paid family leave is introduced as part of a longer-term strategy to get it passed in the future, not as an attempt to get it passed that particular session. It takes time for legislators and constituents to become comfortable with paid family leave legislation, though the successes of California, New Jersey, and Washington may expedite this process in other states. It is much easier for states to pass legislation already tested in another state than to create and pass completely novel legislation, just as it is easier to build off an existing program rather than create a new one.

Along with familiarizing legislators and constituents with the legislation, introducing the bill can catalyze interest group mobilization. With a specific piece of legislation to rally around, interest groups can form coalitions and engage in grassroots organizing campaigns to raise public awareness and garner support for the legislation. When the support is there, the bill is reintroduced:

> This [bill] has been tried before. So it's not like it's a brand new piece of legislation, they've been trying to do it for quite a few years and they felt like this is good time now. The unions have a bigger voice now, there's a lot more union legislators and union elected officials so they figured this would be a pretty good time to do it.

Establishing paid family leave legislation occurs after years of familiarizing legislators and constituents and garnering enough external and internal support.

Compromise

Making compromises is a defining feature of the legislative process,[43] and the process involved in establishing paid family leave legislation is no exception. In order to pass the FMLA as well as the paid family leave legislation in California, New Jersey, and Washington, significant concessions were made. An interviewee from New Jersey engaged in this process of compromise noted: "We started out with twelve weeks [of leave] and we are down to ten right now, and it will probably go down even more than that." The final version of the bill that passed provided six weeks of paid—half of what was first proposed.

Even more substantial concessions were also necessary in order to get the legislation passed in Washington. The legislation that was first introduced provided paid family leave for the serious medical needs of employees, their spouse or domestic partner, child, or parent, as well as to bond with a new child. The bill that was signed into law only provides paid leave to bond with a new child. As explained by one interviewee from Washington:

> The bill that was originally introduced in Washington and the law that was actually passed here is pretty far from the ideal . . . but on the other hand I think that we all thought that what we got was still a very significant victory. That it was important, even though with all the compromise and even though it was far from what we wanted, actually getting a program started and achieving something that we could build on was something we couldn't pass up.

While compromise is a fundamental part of the process in establishing paid family leave, it is also a very precarious period in the legislative life of a bill. In making concessions to appease the opposition, it is possible to alienate key supporters of the bill, as revealed by one legislator:

> Once the bill was scoped down, groups that were really cut out [from] the coverage were disappointed and in many ways sort of stood down from the fight at that point because they really thought they had been left behind. So it was difficult to get passed because we did lose some support by that amendment. . . . In fact, it was very difficult to get a final bill passed. . . . At one point we almost lost the bill in the Senate because it was too small.

Ultimately they were able to get the bill passed, though states finding themselves in a similar position may not have the same outcome.

However, interviewees did not suggest that other states without TDI programs should propose less ambitious legislation in an attempt to avoid this potentiality. Legislation with a broader scope more effectively facilitates the development of a large broad-based coalition, which is critical to the success of this type of legislation.[44] For example, the proposed paid family leave bill in the state of Washington was able to attract the attention and garner the support of a large number of organizations and a diversity of organization(s) because it initially included leave for the serious illness of the worker, their child, parent, spouse, or domestic partner. Having such a broad and expansive bill enabled such a large, diverse, and powerful coalition to form. If Washington had initially proposed a bill providing paid leave only for families with a newborn or newly adopted child, the coalition would have been much smaller, more homogeneous, and ultimately, less powerful. While significant compromises were made, the bill that was passed establishes a framework that can be expanded with future legislation.

CONCLUSION

The findings of this research lend support to each of the three major theoretical perspectives on social policy development. It is clear that structural forces, political institutions, and interest group mobilization all play critical roles in the process of getting paid family leave legislation enacted. Other themes that emerged from the interviews introduce some complexity into these perspectives. For example, while overall structural changes in society may influence decisions to place the legislation on the agenda, additional structural forces, notably the health of a state's economy, influence whether or not it will be passed. Similarly, while political institutions matter, gaining the support of the individuals who control the process is equally important.

Interestingly, one interviewee proposed that having favorable political institutions was not essential to establishing paid family leave. While conceding that paid family leave could never be legislated in an unfavorable political environment, an alternative method to establishing this legislation was suggested:

> The issue of paid family and medical leave is not going to get a fair shot of becoming law in (state) if it has to follow the legislative process. Rather if the labor community wants to have the family and medical leave become a reality then they have to do a ballot initiative . . . they have to bring it to the voters.

A ballot initiative could possibly be an effective strategy to get paid family leave passed, provided that the timing was right and public support for the issue was strong. While paid family leave has never been a ballot initiative, other ballot initiatives have been successful. For example, voters in Arizona, Colorado, Missouri, Montana, Nevada, and Ohio used the ballot initiative to raise the minimum wage in 2006.[45]

The opportunity to build off existing frameworks is another theme providing additional insight into the process of establishing paid family leave legislation. Prior to 2003, many states introduced legislation providing paid leave for workers to care for a newborn or newly adopted child, using unemployment insurance as a funding mechanism. When it became prohibitive to use this existing framework for this purpose in 2003, fewer states attempted to establish any type of paid family leave legislation. While it is possible that the Obama administration will lift this regulation, thus providing a possible funding mechanism for states without a TDI program, it is unlikely in the current economic climate. Furthermore, it is likely the "timing" will not be right until states recover from the current economic crisis.

However, while having an existing framework to build off of is certainly advantageous, the state of Washington has shown that it is not essential, though serious compromises may need to be made. One final theme that emerged in the study as influencing the process was familiarity with the legislation. It is possible that the recent successes of Washington and New Jersey may expedite the "familiarization process" in other states. If enough states can succeed in establishing paid family leave programs, legislatively or otherwise, the federal government may follow suit. This would ensure that more workers have access to a "family-friendly" resource that is critical to managing a family care crisis.

NOTES

1. James Bond, Cindy Thompson, Ellen Galinsky, and David Prottas, "Highlights of the National Study of the Changing Workforce." New York: Families and Work Institute. (2002).

2. One recent example: James A. Breaugh and Kathleen N. Frye, "Work-Family Conflict: The Importance of Family-Friendly Employment Practices and Family-Supportive Supervisors," *Journal of Business Psychology* 22 (2008): 345–53.

3. U.S. Department of Labor, "Family and Medical Leave Act Overview," www .dol.gov/esa/whd/fmla/ (29 June 2009).

4. Recently, the FMLA has been expanded to include employees who have a spouse, parent, or child who is on or has been called to active duty and experience a "qualifying exigency." Additionally, employees who are the spouse, parent, child, or next of kin of a service member who incurred a serious injury or illness on active duty in the Armed Forces may take up to twenty-six weeks of leave to care for the injured service member in a twelve-month period.

5. Steven K. Wisensale, "Two Steps Forward, One Step Back: The Family and Medical Leave Act as Retrenchment Policy," *The Review of Policy Research* 21, no. 1 (2003): 135–51.

6. National Partnership for Women and Families, "State Family and Medical Leave Laws That Are More Expansive Than the Federal FMLA," www.nationalpartner ship.org/site/DocServer/StatesandunpaidFMLLaws.pdf?docID=968 (4 Jan. 2009).

7. For an exception, see Richard Haygood and Robert Hensley, "Beyond the FMLA: A Survey of State Laws and Legislation Mandating Paid Family Leave," *Employment Relations Today* 34, no. 3 (1997): 63–75.

8. Janet Shibley Hyde et al., "Parental Leave: Policy and Research," *Journal of Social Issues* 52, no. 3 (1996): 91–109.

9. See Anya Bernstein, "Inside or Outside? The Politics of the Family and Medical Leave," *Policy Studies Journal* 21, no. 1 (1997): 87–99; Sonja K. Elison, "Policy Innovation in a Cold Climate: The Family and Medical Leave Act of 1993," *Journal of Family Issues* 18, no. 1 (Jan. 1997): 30–54; and Michelle R. Marks, "Party Politics and Family Policy: The Case of the Family and Medical Leave Act," *Journal of Family Issues* 18, no. 1 (Jan. 1997): 55–71.

10. Elison, "Policy Innovation in a Cold Climate," 30–55.

11. Andrew E. Scharlach and Blanche Grosswald, "The Family and Medical Leave Act of 1993," *Social Service Review* 71, no. 3 (1997): 335–59.

12. Scharlach and Grosswald, "The Family and Medical Leave Act of 1993," 355.

13. Scharlach and Grosswald, "The Family and Medical Leave Act of 1993," 355–59.

14. Marks, "Party Politics and Family Policy," 55–71.

15. Marks, "Party Politics and Family Policy," 55–71.

16. Wisensale, "Two Steps Forward, One Step Back," 135–51.

17. Elison, "Policy Innovation in a Cold Climate," 30–55.

18. Elison, "Policy Innovation in a Cold Climate," 30.

19. Robert B. Hudson and Judith G. Gonyea, "Time Not Yet Money: The Politics and Promise of the Family Medical Leave Act," *Journal of Aging and Social Policy* 11, no. 2/3 (2000): 189–200.

20. Steven K. Wisensale, "Commentary: What Role for the Family and Medical Leave Act in Long-Term Care Policy?" *Family and Aging Policy* 18, no. 3/4 (2006): 79–92.

21. Naomi Gerstel and Katherine McGonagle, "Job Leaves and the Limits of the Family and Medical Leave Act," *Work and Occupations* 26, no. 4 (1999): 510–34.

22. Jane Waldfogel, "Family and Medical Leave: Evidence from the 2000 Surveys," *Monthly Labor Review* 124, no. 9 (2001): 17–23.

23. "Son or daughter" is broadly defined to include biological children, adopted or foster children, stepchildren, legal wards, or children of a "parent" if those persons are either under eighteen years of age or are incapable of self-care because of a disability.

24. Jennifer E. Swanberg, Terri Kanatzar, Marta Mendiondo, and Margaret McCoskey, "Caring for Our Elders: A Contemporary Conundrum for Working People," *Families in Society* 87, no. 3 (2006): 417–26.

25. National Conference of State Legislatures, "Same Sex Marriage, Civil Unions, and Domestic Partnerships," www.ncsl.org/IssuesResearch/HumanServices/SameSexMarriage/tabid/16430/Default.aspx (28 June 2009).

26. Public Law No. 104-199, 110 Stat. 2419.

27. Gerstel and McGonagle, "Job Leaves and the Limits of the Family and Medical Leave Act," 510–34.

28. National Partnership for Women and Families, "State Family and Medical Leave Laws That Are More Expansive Than the Federal FMLA," www.nationalpartnership.org/site/DocServer/StatesandunpaidFMLLaws.pdf?docID=968 (4 Jan. 2009).

29. National Partnership for Women and Families, "State Family and Medical Leave Laws."

30. Wisensale, "Commentary," 79–92.

31. Wisensale, "Two Steps Forward, One Step Back," 135–51.

32. Wisensale, "Commentary," 79–92.

33. Steven K. Wisensale, "California's Paid Leave Law: A Model for Other States?" *Families and Social Policy: National and International Perspectives* 39, no. 1/2 (2006): 177–95.

34. California Employment Development Department, "Paid Family Leave: About the Paid Family Leave Insurance Program," www.edd.ca.gov/Disability/Paid_Family_Leave.htm (29 June 2009).

35. Wisensale, "California's Paid Leave Law," 177–95.

36. Wisensale, "Commentary," 79–92.

37. Vicky Lovell, "No Time to Be Sick: Why Everyone Suffers When Workers Don't Have Paid Sick Leave 2004," *Institute for Women's Policy Research*, www.iwpr.org/pdf/B242.pdf (29 June 2009).

38. For an exception, see Haygood and Hensley, 2007.

39. Barney Glaser and Anselm Strauss, *The Discovery of Grounded Theory* (Chicago: Aldine, 1967).

40. Elison, "Policy Innovation in a Cold Climate," 30–55.

41. Wisensale, "California's Paid Leave Law," 177–95.

42. Elizabeth McNichol and Iris J. Lav, "State Budget Troubles Worsen," *Center on Budget and Policy Priorities* 2009, www.cbpp.org/9-8-08sfp.htm (17 Jan. 2009).

43. Elison, "Policy Innovation in a Cold Climate," 30–55.

44. Wisensale, "Two Steps Forward, One Step Back," 135–51.

45. Ana Campoy, "Voters in Six States Decide to Raise Minimum Wages," *Markettimer*, 8 November 2006, www.marketwatch.com/story/voters-in-six-states-decide-to-raise-the-minimum-wage (28 June 2009).

13

New Parents Taking Time Off: A Look at California Paid Family Leave

Stacy Ann Hawkins, Sherylle J. Tan, and Diane F. Halpern

The number of women and men in the American workforce is nearly equal, and few families can afford to live off a single paycheck.[1, 2] From 1970 to 2000, the percentage of married couples with both spouses in the workforce rose from 41 percent to 70 percent.[3] According to the U.S. Bureau of Labor Statistics, approximately half of working Americans have no paid sick or vacation days, so if they miss a day of work, they miss a day of pay.[4] For many men and women, the lack of paid leave can make negotiating work and family obligations extremely challenging. New parents, in particular, struggle to balance time for both work and a newborn, and inadequate leave options can make this balance even more difficult to achieve. Family leave policies, such as California Paid Family Leave (CPFL), legislate maternity and paternity leave, providing working parents with additional time to spend with their newborns. This chapter will discuss family leave policies, with particular attention to CPFL, and present the results of an empirical study examining parents' awareness of the program, attitudes toward it, and intentions to use it to extend their parental leave.

PARENTAL LEAVE

For working mothers, the postpartum weeks filled with excitement, happiness, and stress also hold a difficult decision: if and when to return to work. The vast majority of women work during their pregnancy,[5] and most of these mothers take some maternity leave. The average length of maternity leave is eight to ten weeks, and 85 percent of new mothers return to work within sixteen weeks.[6, 7] For many working mothers, however, this leave does not come with pay; in one sample, 40 percent of mothers taking maternity leave took unpaid leave.[8] Working mothers taking unpaid leave must often return to work soon after the birth of their infant, and may miss out on the benefits that maternity leave affords. Studies find that a shorter maternity leave places new mothers at greater risk for anxiety and depression.[9, 10] Shorter maternity leaves are also associated with poorer mental health outcomes for mothers at nine and twelve months postpartum.[11] In fact, as maternity leave increases from six weeks to twelve weeks, there is a significant decrease in mothers' anxiety levels.[12] Improved mental health is also tied to increased maternal affect and sensitivity toward one's newborn.[13] Clearly, maternity leave is important to the health and well-being of new mothers.

Not only are there benefits of maternity leave to the well-being of the mother, but newborns also benefit from a mother's maternity leave. For example, breast-feeding is optimal for infants and has been found to protect against childhood infections and diseases; however, mothers who took less than six weeks of maternity leave were four times less likely to breast-feed their babies.[14, 15, 16] Women who do not return to work or who return to work part-time are more likely to initiate breast-feeding in comparison to women who plan to return to work full-time.[17] Maternity leave was especially important for full-time working mothers in nonmanagerial positions who lack job flexibility or experience psychosocial distress.

Few studies have explored the benefits of paternity leave for infants and working fathers. Not surprisingly, fathers are less likely to utilize parental leave, and even when they do take leave, fathers take far less time off than mothers. Fathers in the United States, on average, take about one week of paternity leave.[18, 19, 20] Regardless of the short length of leave, paternity leave is still beneficial to fathers and their families. Fathers who utilize family-friendly work policies reported less work-family conflict.[21] Also, fathers taking longer leaves are generally more attached to their infants, and are more likely to be involved in the daily activities of their babies than fathers taking shorter leaves.[22, 23, 24, 25] Fathers' involvement and their positive interactions with infants have been linked to cognitive outcomes for infants. Fathers interact with infants in different ways from mothers, and these unique father-infant interactions may stimulate cognitive and language development in ways that mothers' interactions with infants do not. One study on fathers in Ireland found that fathers who soothed their infants when they cried, fed their infants, sang to their babies, and changed their diapers at one month were more likely to continue to be involved fathers at one year.[26]

Furthermore, fathers' involvement in early infancy had an effect on infants' cognitive functioning at one year. A more recent study reported that father involvement was related to decreases in infant cognitive delays.[27] Taken together, these studies point to the importance of father involvement during early infancy to enhance cognitive outcomes.

Research indicates that having family leave available can provide working parents more time to bond with their newborns, adjust to new family demands, and improve their overall health and well-being, especially for mothers. Despite these benefits, many parents struggle with balancing work and family time—especially in the earliest months. For a mother, returning to work before she is ready can create additional stress; however, some women do not feel that they have the support from their employers or the financial freedom to take an extended maternity leave.[28, 29] Likewise, fathers may feel stigmatized by supervisors, coworkers, or even their partners and may be pressured not to take paternity leave, especially if that leave is unpaid.

FAMILY LEAVE POLICY

Family leave policies and workplace flexibility may affect parents' employment decisions in the first few months after having a new baby. Studies show that men and women who are offered flexible schedules and/or paid leave plans are more likely to take parental leave, and also to return to work after taking family leave than men and women who work for companies that have few or no leave options.[30, 31, 32] In addition, after the introduction of the 1993 Family and Medical Leave Act (FMLA), which offers unpaid leave and job protection to men and women to care for a sick or injured loved one or new child (see Brown, chapter 12, in this volume), the percentage of mothers who quit their jobs after giving birth declined dramatically.[33, 34, 35] This trend suggests that some mothers may have been exiting the workforce simply because they were not able to take maternity leave without losing their jobs. Providing leave options for new parents can allow them the time they need to bond with their newborns and adjust to being a new parent, while minimizing the cost of turnover and replacement for the company.

FMLA is an excellent initial step in providing family leave options to new parents, but the policy mandates only unpaid leave, and few new parents can afford to take time off of work without pay. In addition, parents must meet certain criteria to use FMLA: they must be employed at a company with more than fifty employees, working for the past twelve months for at least twenty-five hours a week. With these requirements, only about half of men and women in the United States are covered by the policy. To address the needs of working caregivers and parents, some states have implemented their own family leave policies. The California Paid Family Leave (CPFL) program, for example, built upon the foundation set by FMLA, and offers new parents more comprehensive benefits.

California Paid Family Leave

California was the first state in the nation to approve a partially paid family leave policy. Passed in 2002 and fully implemented in 2004, CPFL provides six weeks of leave, accompanied by a stipend of 55 percent of weekly pay (up to a designated limit). The monies are provided through State Disability Insurance (SDI), so men and women must be employed and paying into SDI to qualify for benefits. All workers in California who pay into SDI are eligible to apply for family leave when they are unable to work due to a sick or injured family member in need of care, or to bond with a new child in the family.

The CPFL program allows new parents the opportunity to extend or supplement any paid leave provided by their employer. Using CPFL, mothers are able to take maternity leave without quitting their jobs or exiting the workforce. CPFL increases employee retention rates, which reduces the cost of hiring and training new employees.[36] One study estimated that California businesses could save $89 million with increased employee retention stemming from CPFL.[37]

Caregivers Using California Paid Family Leave

One early study of CPFL examined attitudes toward the policy in a sample of working men and women caring for a sick or injured family member.[38] Participants were recruited from southern California hospitals and centers for specific ailments (e.g., Alzheimer's Disease). Participants were family caregivers age eighteen to seventy. They were mostly women, and were generally caring for a spouse or parent. The data collected on physical, financial, and emotional health showed that caregivers were struggling to meet their multiple responsibilities. Those who were able to take leave from work without fearing job loss reported higher satisfaction with their financial situation, as well as better overall physical and emotional health, than those who were unable to take any time off work. Approximately half of participants reported receiving less than 50 percent of their wages through their employer's paid leave benefits. The caregivers attempting to balance their work and family lives could have benefited from CPFL and felt very positive about the program, but only 1 percent were using the program.

Similar results were found in a study of approximately four hundred working parents of chronically ill children.[39] In this sample, a small percentage of parents (18 percent) were aware of CPFL, and a smaller percentage (5 percent) actually used the program. Among this group of parents, the implementation of CPFL did not increase the amount of leave parents took. In fact, compared to a sample of parents from Illinois, a state with a similar labor market but no paid leave program, parents in California were not more likely to take a longer leave to care for their chronically ill children. The low rates of CPFL usage reported in these studies could be attributed to the timing of the data collections, which were conducted shortly after the introduction of the CPFL policy.

THE CURRENT STUDY

The previous research on family and parent caregivers provides an initial look at CPFL; however, these studies only assessed workers using CPFL benefits due to a sick or injured family member in need of care. CPFL can, however, also be used to bond with a new child in the family. To extend the previous research and provide additional data relevant to the CPFL policy, the current study surveyed new mothers and fathers about their attitudes toward and plans to use CPFL. To better understand parents' perspectives on this family leave policy, this study aimed to answer three primary research questions: (1) How many parents know about CPFL? (2) How do parents feel about the policy? (3) How many working parents plan to use CPFL and why do some parents plan to *not* use CPFL?

RESEARCH METHOD

Participating Parents

A sample of 326 new mothers were recruited through lactation consultants, Mommy and Me classes, hospitals, Women Infants and Children (WIC) centers, and a mailing using California birth record data. These mothers were, on average, thirty years old and ten weeks postpartum. The sample was diverse, with just under half of participants reporting that they are white, and 36 percent reporting that they are Hispanic/Latina. The majority of mothers were married, and almost all who were not married were partnered. Over 75 percent of mothers had at least some college education, with half obtaining a four-year degree or more. Eighty percent of mothers worked while they were pregnant, most of whom were in either entry-level (37 percent) or professional (40 percent) positions, with few mothers who were first-line supervisors or middle managers. With regard to income, 19 percent of mothers reported an annual income of less than $24,999 and

33 percent reported earning more than $95,000. This distribution likely reflects the method of sample recruitment; the WIC centers and hospitals served primarily low-income mothers; lactation consultants and Mommy and Me classes served mothers with higher incomes.

Mothers were asked to provide contact information for the fathers of their newborns. Almost half of mothers provided contact information, and all fathers for whom contact information was provided were sent a request to participate; forty fathers completed surveys, for a response rate of 31 percent. Fathers were thirty-five years old, on average, and their newborns were approximately twenty-seven weeks old, reflecting the fact that the fathers were contacted approximately fifteen weeks after mothers. Just under half of fathers were white, 40 percent were other minorities, and 13 percent were Hispanic/Latino. Fathers were also well educated and reported high family incomes. Almost all fathers worked outside of the home for pay, only three reported that they did not work outside the home.

The Survey

Mothers and fathers were mailed paper-and-pencil surveys asking them questions about their employment decisions, their health and well-being, and the health of their babies. Participants reported their awareness of the CPFL program. Those who were aware of CPFL reported whether or not they planned to use the program's benefits. Those planning to *not* use the program were also asked to explain why. Participants had ample space to respond freely. Parents who had not heard of CPFL were provided with information about the program and its benefits. Then, all participants reported their general attitudes toward the policy on a five-point scale, where 1 indicated very negative attitudes and 5 indicated very positive attitudes.

STUDY RESULTS

Awareness of California Paid Family Leave

Mothers

Of all mothers, 72 percent were aware of the CPFL program. There was a significant difference, however, in the awareness of mothers who worked during their pregnancy and those who did not ($\chi^2 = 45.62$, $p < .001$); mothers who did not work during their pregnancy were less aware of the program than working mothers. For mothers who did not work during their pregnancy, the majority had *not* heard of CPFL, and only 39 percent knew of the program. In contrast, 80 percent of working mothers reported that they knew about the program.

It is likely that mothers who did not work during their pregnancy received less exposure to and information about the CPFL program, and were also less likely to seek out information because the program does not apply to them. If their partners are working, though, it would be beneficial for mothers to be aware of the program and its benefits for their partners. Although a majority of working mothers knew about CPFL, one in five was *not aware* of this potentially advantageous program. These mothers should know about CPFL and its benefits so that they can make informed decisions about their maternity leave plans.

Fathers

Like working mothers, the majority of fathers had heard about CPFL. Only 15 percent of fathers reported that they were not familiar with the program or its benefits. Thus, fathers appear to be knowledgeable about their options and opportunities to supplement their paternity leave. Additionally, if a father's partner is working, he knows about the options available to her.

Attitudes Toward the Policy

Mothers

Mothers had very positive attitudes toward CPFL, with an average score of 4.55 on a scale of 1 (very negative) to 5 (very positive) (SD = .82). Eighty nine percent of mothers reported somewhat or very positive attitudes, and only 5 percent of mothers reported negative attitudes toward the policy (see figure 13.1). An independent sample t-test revealed that there was no difference between the attitudes of working and not-working mothers (t (315) = 1.32, ns). There was also no difference in the attitudes of mothers who had previously heard about CPFL and those who learned about it on the survey (t (317) = 0.88, ns). These findings indicate that mothers are overwhelmingly positive about the program, independent of whether they worked while pregnant, or knew about the program beforehand.

Fathers

Fathers also held generally positive attitudes toward the policy (Mean = 4.21, SD = 1.04), although responses were more mixed than those of mothers (see figure 13.1). Seventy nine percent of fathers reported somewhat or very positive attitudes, and 8 percent reported somewhat or very negative attitudes toward the policy. Mothers' and fathers' attitudes were positively correlated (r = .41, p = .01); there was a trend for fathers to

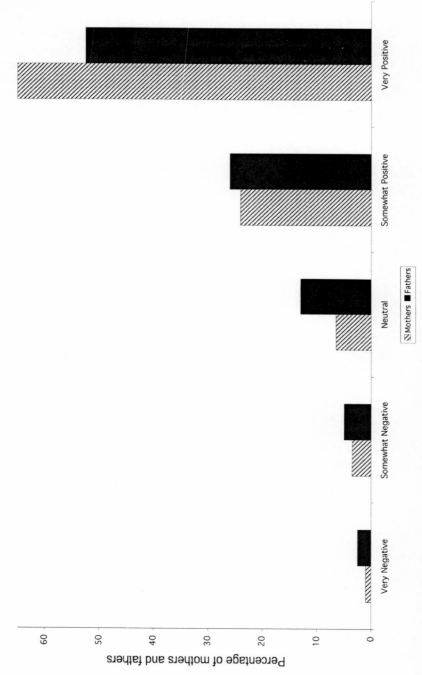

Figure 13.1. Mothers' and Fathers' Attitudes about California Paid Family Leave

report less positive attitudes than mothers (t (36) = 1.92, p = .06). This suggests that when mothers hold more positive attitudes toward CPFL, their partners do also; however, fathers, in general, tend to report less positive attitudes than mothers.

Plans to Use California Paid Family Leave

Mothers

In all, 215 mothers worked while pregnant and planned to return to work, making them potentially eligible for CPFL benefits. Of these, forty-five had not heard of the program (21 percent), 111 planned to use CPFL to supplement their maternity leave (52 percent), and fifty-nine planned *not* to use the program (27 percent). Most of the mothers (90 percent) planning *not* to use CPFL reported the primary reasons for their plans; their responses were reviewed and coded into three primary categories.

First, the majority of mothers planning to *not* use CPFL reported that they were ineligible to receive benefits (77 percent). This indicates that roughly 20 percent of working mothers in this study were ineligible for the benefits of CPFL. Many of the mothers in this sample were teachers or other state employees who do not pay into SDI, and were therefore ineligible. One mother wrote, "I am a teacher and we are not eligible for paid family leave. I am taking family leave time but it is unpaid." Another mother described her situation, saying, "I work for the USPS and do not qualify. I had to use all of my sick and vacation leave." Other mothers were ineligible because their employment status did not require them to pay into SDI. One mother wrote, "I am currently an on-call status employee and therefore do not qualify. I did use the program with my first child however, and was quite happy with it." Considering that one in five working mothers were ineligible for CPFL, the policy may not be reaching a large subset of its intended beneficiaries.

The second most common reason mothers gave for not using CPFL was that the policy did not provide enough money to make it a financially viable option. Sixteen percent of mothers who planned to *not* use CPFL said that 55 percent of their income was not enough money to support their families. Certainly, the addition of a new child can be financially straining, and some families cannot afford to so substantially decrease their income. One mother stated she would not be using CPFL because "I have three kids, [and] the insurance doesn't pay enough money, that is why I [would] rather go back to work." This comment highlights the importance of financial stability in many mothers' employment and leave decisions, and points to a problem in the CPFL policy: the program does not provide enough financial incentive for some mothers.

Finally, a small number of mothers reported needing more information about the program and its requirements. Just under 10 percent of mothers who planned to *not* use CPFL said that they did not know enough about the program to use it. Mothers wrote statements such as, "I don't have enough information about that plan," or "I don't think it applies to me." Even though only a few mothers needed additional information about the policy, this is concerning, as no one can make informed employment decisions without fully understanding the leave options available to them.

Fathers

Unlike mothers, few fathers planned to use CPFL to supplement their paternity leave. Only 17 percent of fathers reported that they planned to use the program. Fathers who planned to *not* use CPFL reported the primary reasons; their responses were categorized into common themes.

Fathers most often reported that the CPFL benefits were not extensive enough to cover their expenses; 32 percent of fathers who planned to *not* use CPFL cited this reason. For example, one father wrote, "My family can't afford for my pay to be reduced to 55 percent for any length of time." Although this was a concern raised by both mothers and fathers, it was far more commonly cited by fathers. This suggests that fathers may bear more of the financial burden during the first few months postpartum. There may be pressure on fathers, not only to provide financially, but also to compensate for the income lost while their partners are on maternity leaves.

The second most common reason fathers gave for not using CPFL was the negative career consequences that could occur from taking paternity leave. Twenty-three percent of fathers stated they could not take time off of work, or were worried about the impact of time away on their career. One father shared that he was "reluctant to put career on hold," and that his "work office also does not cater to new fathers." This was not a reason given by mothers and may be unique to fathers. Fathers typically take shorter leaves and are often not expected to spend the same amount of time with their newborns as mothers.[40, 41, 42] Gender role stereotypes may be to blame for this inequality and for the stigma that fathers face when they want to take extensive paternity leaves.

Other fathers *not* using CPFL reported that they had alternative options to use for their paternity leaves (18 percent). Some fathers had paid leave through their employers; others used their vacation time to take leave. Using alternative leave options was not a reason frequently cited by mothers, perhaps because fathers typically have better leave options through their employers. Alternatively, since mothers typically take longer leaves than fathers, mothers may need to use both CPFL *and* employers' leave to maximize their time at home, rather than using one source.

Finally, 18 percent of fathers not planning to use CPFL reported that they were ineligible for the benefits of CPFL. Many of these fathers were ineligible because they were self-employed or working in a small company not required to pay into SDI. These fathers comprise 10 percent of the total sample of fathers. This is less than the percentage of working mothers who are ineligible (20 percent), but still represents an important subset of working fathers who are unable to access the benefits of this family policy.

IMPLICATIONS OF THE FINDINGS

The national spotlight is on California for information about family leave programs. The research presented here finds that parents generally know about CPFL, have positive attitudes toward the program, and many mothers (52 percent) but few fathers (17 percent) plan to use the program. Results also indicated that mothers and fathers had a number of reasons for *not* using CPFL, including eligibility issues, financial concerns, and, for fathers in particular, worries about negative career consequences. These findings are important for new mothers and fathers as they attempt to negotiate work responsibilities and caring for a newborn. In addition, employer and company policies can also be guided by the findings of this research. Likewise, the results from this study have the potential to shape the CPFL policy as it evolves to meet the needs of caregivers and new parents, and to inform policy-makers throughout the country as they establish paid family leave policies in other states.

Implications for Parents

Individual mothers and fathers should be aware of these findings and the implications for their everyday lives, especially during pregnancy and early in the postpartum period. First and foremost, new and potential parents have to take the time and effort to educate themselves about their employment and leave options, as well as the options available to their partners. In this sample, 20 percent of working mothers and 15 percent of working fathers had not heard of CPFL, and an additional 10 percent of mothers planned to *not* use CPFL because they did not have enough information about the program. Men and women can find information about and resources for CPFL, or similar programs in other states, through state labor departments' websites, within their employer's Human Resources departments, and on family support organization websites. The earlier parents learn about their options, the sooner they can make their employment decisions and leave plans. While situations may change over the course of pregnancy and in the early postpartum period, being prepared and planning ahead can be extremely valuable.

In addition to educating themselves, parents should make their voices heard. Mothers and fathers may choose to *not* use a paid family leave program for a number of reasons. If parents share their needs with their legislators, then states can create policies that more accurately reflect and benefit the people who need the policy most. For example, the 16 percent of mothers and 18 percent of fathers who planned to *not* use CPFL because the income benefits were not enough money could inform their state policy-makers about their concerns. Similarly, the mothers and fathers who are ineligible for the program could also voice their objections to encourage both state and employer leave options that are more sensitive to all parents' needs. Along with this, parents living in states considering paid leave programs, or those with no paid leave policies, should also take action to ensure that policy-makers are aware of their needs for appropriate family leave policy.

Implications for Employers

The findings of this study also hold implications for employers. The concerns shared by new mothers and fathers point to a number of important issues in the workplace. The high number of men and women who chose not to use CPFL because it was not enough income suggests that having a fully paid leave option through employers is incredibly valuable. Although there have been great strides toward family-friendly workplace policies,[43] there is still a need in many organizations for sensitivity to the challenges inherent in being a working parent.

Additionally, fathers' concerns about the negative career consequences associated with taking parental leave point to a serious problem in many workplaces. Gender role stereotypes may create an unrealistic and unhealthy expectation that fathers should not take leave time, yet, given the research tying paternity leave with positive outcomes, fathers should be encouraged to take paternity leave. Considering the worries expressed by fathers in this sample, businesses may need to education themselves about how to develop a more supportive work environment.

Implications for Policy

This study also has implications for work-family policy. First, these findings point to potential improvements that could be made in the policy. For example, 20 percent of working mothers and 10 percent of fathers did not have the option to use CPFL because they were ineligible. There are particular restraints related to the way money is collected and managed (i.e., through SDI), and this leaves many parents without the benefits of partially paid leave. Also, 16 percent of working mothers and 18 percent of fathers elected not to use CPFL because the funding associated with it was too meager. Indeed, many families cannot make ends meet without two full-time incomes, and the financial benefits of CPFL may not be enough to make it a financially viable option. These issues can be addressed through changes to CPFL or the creation of new, more comprehensive programs.

In addition to potential changes to the policy in California, the findings of this study can be considered as legislation is introduced in other states. Many states are initiating or debating family leave policies (see Brown, chapter 10, in this volume), and legislators in these and other states should consider the issues raised in this study as they discuss family leave policies. For example, knowing that distributing funds through SDI limits parents' use of the policy may encourage legislators to use different mechanisms to provide benefits. Similarly, as results show that 55 percent pay is not enough income for many families, policy-makers can change policies and programs to more appropriately meet the needs of their constituents.

CONCLUSION

Paid family leave is an important policy that can be extremely valuable to working parents. Negotiating family and work roles can be highly stressful, and it is clear that taking parental leave can ease the stress associated with the transition into parenthood and improve the health and well-being of parents and their newborns. Social science research needs to continue examining the benefits and usefulness of family policy. Likewise, policy-makers need to continue to turn to social science for evidence about effective policy. With both sides contributing to the discussion about family policy, policies and programs can become more effective and efficient in meeting the needs of families across the country.

NOTES

1. James T. Bond et al., *National study of the changing workforce* (New York: Families and Work Institute, 2003).

2. Elizabeth Warren and Amelia Warren Tyagi, *The two-income trap: Why middle-class mothers and fathers are going broke* (New York: Basic Books, 2003), 255.

3. Sara B. Rayley, Marybeth J. Mattingly, and Suzanne M. Bianchi, "How dual are dual-income couples? Documenting change from 1970 to 2001," *Journal of Marriage and Family* 68 (2006): 11.

4. William J. Wiatrowski, "Documenting benefits coverage for all workers," U. S. Bureau of Labor Statistics, www.bls.gov/opub/cwc/cm20040518ar01p1.htm.

5. U.S. Census Bureau, "Maternity leave and employment patterns: 1961–1995," U.S. Census Bureau, www.census.gov/prod/2001pubs/p70-79.pdf.

6. Roseanne Clark et al., "Length of maternity leave and quality of mother-infant interactions," *Child Development* 68 (1997): 364.

7. Patricia McGovern et al., "Time off work and the postpartum health of employed women," *Medical Care* 35 (1997): 507.

8. U.S. Census Bureau, "Maternity leave and employment patterns: 1961–1995," U.S. Census Bureau, www.census.gov/prod/2001pubs/p70-79.pdf.

9. Ruth Feldman, Amy Sussman, and Edward Zigler, "Parental leave and work adaptation at the transition to parenthood: Individual, marital and social correlates," *Applied Developmental Psychology* 25 (2004): 459.

10. Janet Shibley Hyde et al., "Maternity leave and women's mental health," *Psychology of Women Quarterly* 19 (1995): 257.

11. Dwenda K. Gjerdingen and Kathryn M. Chaloner, "The relationship of women's postpartum mental health to employment, childbirth, and social support," *The Journal of Family Practice* 38 (1994): 465.

12. Pinka Chatterji and Sara Markowitz, "Does the length of maternity leave affect mental health?" (Working Paper 10206, Cambridge, MA: National Bureau of Economic Research).

13. Clark et al., "Length of maternity leave," *Child Development*, 364.

14. Sylvia Guendelam et al., "Juggling work and breastfeeding: Effects of maternity leave and occupational characteristics," *Pediatrics* 123 (2009): e38.

15. Jeanne Raisler, Cheryl Alexander, and Patricia O'Campo, "Breast-feeding and infant illness: A dose-response relationship?" *American Journal of Public Health* 89 (1997): 25.

16. Paula D. Scariati, Laurence M. Grummer-Strawn, and Sara Beck Fein, "A longitudinal analysis of infant morbidity and the extent of breastfeeding in the United States," *Pediatrics* 99 (1997): e5.

17. Sara Beck Fein and Brian Roe, "The effects of work status on initiation and duration of breast-feeding," *Journal of Public Health* 88 (1998): 1042.

18. Feldman, Sussman, and Zigler, "Parental leave," *Applied Developmental Psychology*, 459.

19. Janet Shibley Hyde, Marilyn J. Essex, and Francine Horton, "Fathers and parental leave: Attitudes and experiences," *Journal of Family Issues* 14 (1993): 616.

20. Lenna Nepomnyaschy and Jane Waldfogel, "Paternity leave and fathers' involvement with their young children: Evidence from the American Ecls-B," *Community, Work, and Family* 10 (2007): 427.

21. E. Jeffrey Hill et al., "Studying 'Working Fathers': Comparing Fathers' and Mothers' Work-Family Conflict, Fit, and Adaptive Strategies in a Global High-Tech Company," *Fathering: A Journal of Theory, Research, and Practice about Men as Fathers* 1 (2003): 239.

22. Feldman, Sussman, and Zigler, "Parental leave," *Applied Developmental Psychology*, 459.

23. Martin H. Malin, "Fathers and parental leave revisited," *Northern University Law Review* 19 (1998): 25.

24. Nepomnyaschy and Waldfogel, "Paternity leave," *Community, Work, and Family*, 427.

25. Sakiko Tanaka and Jane Waldfogel, "Effects of parental leave and working hours on fathers' involvement with their babies: Evidence from the UK Millennium Cohort Study," *Community, Work, and Family* 10 (2007): 409.

26. J. Kevin Nugent, "Cultural and psychological influences on the father's role in infant development," *Journal of Marriage and Family* 53 (1991): 475.

27. Jacinta Bronte-Tinkew et al., "Involvement among resident fathers and links to infant cognitive outcomes," *Journal of Family Issues* 29 (2008): 1211.

28. Mary Beth Schirtzinger, W. Lutz, and Ellen Hock, "Timing return of employment, maternal separation anxiety, and depressed mood over the transition to motherhood" (paper presented at the biennial meeting of the Society for Research in Child Development, New Orleans, LA, 1993).

29. Carol Borrill and Jennifer M. Kidd, "New parents at work: Jobs, families and the psychological contract," *British Journal of Guidance and Counseling* 22 (1994): 219.

30. Ruth Milkman and Eileen Applebaum, "Paid family leave in California: New research findings," *The State of California Labor* 4 (2004): 45.

31. Jennifer L. Glass and Lisa Riley, "Family responsive policies and employee retention following childbirth," *Social Forces* 76 (1998): 1401.

32. Jane Waldfogel, "The impact of the Family Medical Leave Act," *Journal of Policy Analysis and Management* 18 (1999): 281.

33. Sandra L. Hofferth and Sally C. Curtin, "Parental leave statutes and maternal return to work after childbirth in the United States," *Work and Occupations* 33 (2006): 73.

34. U.S. Census Bureau, "Maternity leave and employment patterns: 1961–1995," U.S. Census Bureau, www.census.gov/prod/2001pubs/p70-79.pdf.

35. Arindrajit Dube and Ethan Kaplan, "Paid family leave in California: An analysis of costs and benefits," The Institute for International Economics Studies, www-2.iies.su.se/~ekaplan/paidfamilyleave.pdf.

36. Hofferth and Curtin, "Parental leave statutes and maternal return to work after childbirth in the United States," *Work and Occupations*, 73.

37. U.S. Census Bureau, "Maternity leave and employment patterns: 1961–1995," U.S. Census Bureau, www.census.gov/prod/2001pubs/p70-79.pdf.

38. Diane F. Halpern, Sherylle J. Tan, and Melissa Carsten, "California Paid Family Leave: Is it working for caregivers?" in *The Changing Realities of Work and Family: An Interdisciplinary Approach*, ed. Amy Marcus-Newhall, Diane F. Halpern, and Sherylle J. Tan (Oxford: Blackwell Publishing, 2008), 159–74.

39. Mark A. Schuster et al., "Awareness and use of California's paid family leave insurance among parents of chronically ill children," *The Journal of the American Medical Association* 300 (2008): 1047.

40. Feldman, Sussman, and Zigler, "Parental leave," *Applied Developmental Psychology*, 459.

41. Hyde, Essex, and Horton, "Fathers and parental leave," *Journal of Family Issues*, 616.

42. Nepomnyaschy and Waldfogel, "Paternity leave," *Community, Work, and Family*, 427.

43. R. Drago, C. Colbeck, D. Stauffer, A. Varner, K. Burkum, J. Fazioli, et al. (2006). "The avoidance of bias against caregiving." *American Behavioral Scientist, Special Issue: Current Issues at the Intersection of Work and Family*.

14

The Relationship Between Non-Resident Fathers' Social Networks and Social Capital and the Establishment of Child Support Orders

Jason Castillo

Given the profound changes to the American family and household, including an increase in the number of single-parent households and children not living with their fathers, the examination of fathers and their involvement in their children's lives has contributed to a substantial growth in fathering literature and research. One area that has given considerable attention to fathers is the child support enforcement literature and research. Focused primarily on child support collections, the child support enforcement literature has been framed according to the economic contributions non-resident[1] fathers make to the lives of their children.[2, 3, 4] Receiving less attention in this research has been examination of the social context within which non-resident fathers function and the extent to which social relationships and networks contribute and assist non-resident fathers in fulfilling their parental responsibilities of establishing child support orders.[5, 6, 7]

HISTORY OF CHILD SUPPORT POLICY

Since the federal Child Support Enforcement (CSE) inception in 1975, the federal government has instituted several major child support enforcement reforms intended to increase the rates of child support orders, which legally obligates non-resident parents to provide economic support for their children and stipulates the amount of the obligation and the manner in which the obligation is to be paid.[8, 9, 10, 11, 12] Beginning in the early 1980s and continuing through the late 1990s, the federal government required state governments to increase the rates of child support orders by focusing attention on reducing the costs, time, and variability in the establishment of child support orders.[13, 14, 15, 16] State governments responded by establishing an expedited judicial, administrative, or combination of both, process that was intended to reduce the costs, time, and variability in establishing child support orders. In expediting the establishment of child support orders, state governments moved away from a system in which family judges had the authority to take testimony, evaluate and make initial decisions, enter default orders, and approve stipulated agreements[17] to a system in which a surrogate judge assumed the abovementioned responsibilities, which in turn lessened the authority of family judges and the shared decision-making of mothers and fathers in the family court. Collecting aggregate data from each state's Office of Child Support Enforcement (OCSE), the federal OCSE estimates that the percentage of child support orders have increased nationwide.[18] Despite these promising findings, disparities exist among families and households expected to have child support orders established.

ESTABLISHMENT OF CHILD SUPPORT ORDERS

Quantitative studies focusing on diverse subsets of resident and non-resident parents in the establishment of child support orders draw different conclusions with regard to how widespread are the use of child support orders.[19, 20] Between 1979 and 1997, the percentage of resident mothers with established child support orders decreased by 7 percent.[21] Bartfeld and Sandefur[22] found that while 57 percent of resident mothers had child support orders established for at least one of their children, only 24 percent of resident mothers had child support orders established on behalf of all of their children. Several studies report that the establishment of child support orders range from 41 and 60 percent and vary across familial status—divorced, separated, never married.[23, 24, 25, 26, 27, 28] The establishment of child support orders has remained nearly constant at 60 percent since 1978.[29] Sorenson and Zibman[30, 31] found that only 50 percent of children with a non-resident parent had a child support order in 1997. Pirog and Ziol-Guest[32] and Grall[33] found that 41 percent of resident parents did not have a child support order established in 2001.

Other studies that focus on the establishment of child support orders by race, ethnicity, and marital status have found substantial differences in the establishment of child support orders based on such demographic characteristics. Compared to white resident mothers, black and Hispanic resident mothers are less likely to have established child support orders. About 72 percent of white resident mothers had established child support orders whereas 45 percent of black and 47 percent of Hispanic resident mothers had established child support orders.[34, 35] Compared to divorced and separated mothers, never-married mothers were less likely to have established child support orders. Less than 20 percent of never-married mothers had child support orders, whereas 81.8 percent of divorced mothers and 43.1 percent of separated mothers had established child support orders.[36, 37, 38, 39, 40, 41] Finally, when examining barriers to the establishment of child support orders, millions of resident mothers reported they did not feel the need to go to court and establish legal child support orders because they felt non-resident fathers could either not fulfill the obligation or were already providing all of the support they could handle.[42, 43] Although these studies used survey data, several qualitative studies examining unmarried parents' interactions with the child support system report similar findings.

In his study of non-resident fathers, Sullivan[44] found that they knew very little about the processes and components of the child support enforcement system. Most of the fathers were unaware of the requirements and the guidelines used in determining child support orders. Those who did have child support orders resented the process and felt the system was not sensitive to the fathers' relationship with his family or his precarious and shifting circumstances. Furstenberg[45] found that many non-resident fathers were unable to establish a formal child support order if their names were not on the child's birth certificate and the mother of the child had not requested that paternity be established. Other non-resident fathers were confused about the linkage between child support and public welfare and believed that the child support enforcement system was designed to collect on public welfare assistance payments made to non-resident fathers' children and the resident mother. In other words, the fathers saw the public welfare system and child support enforcement systems as being one in the same. Achatz and MacAllum[46] found that the child support enforcement system was adversarial and provided non-resident fathers with little information before their required appearance with a hearing officer or judge.

While these studies contribute to the existing child support enforcement literature and research, they suffer from several limitations. First, few of the quantitative studies use national data in examining the establishment of child support orders focused on the characteristics of non-resident fathers. Second, most of the studies gathered data from resident mothers and administrative sources, while only a few of the studies gathered data from non-resident fathers. Third, the qualitative studies had fairly small samples and used convenience sampling. Finally, few of the studies explicitly examined how, or if, contextual factors, such as non-resident fathers' relationships with former spouses or partners and involvement with family and friends contribute to non-resident fathers fulfilling their child support obligations of establishing child support orders.

CURRENT STUDY

Given the characteristics of non-marital families and the findings of the aforementioned studies, this study moves away from the one-dimensional model employed by the child support enforcement research, which has situated non-resident fathers solely as economic providers. This study emphasizes a multidimensional model situating non-resident fathers within the context of their environment and assuming that these factors contribute to helping non-resident fathers fulfill their parental responsibilities. This paper contributes to the child support literature by addressing each of the limitations previously mentioned. First, this paper examines non-resident fathers' characteristics using a national dataset. Second, this paper uses the self-reports of non-resident fathers. Finally, this paper uses an ecological perspective emphasizing the contextual factors associated with non-resident fathers fulfilling their parental responsibilities toward their children and legal obligation toward the child support enforcement system.

Theoretical and Conceptual Framework

Guided by an ecological perspective and social capital theory as espoused by Bourdieu[47] and Coleman,[48] this study examines non-resident fathers within their larger familial, social, cultural, and environmental contexts. It also explores the power imbalances that exist in the transactions occurring between these fathers and their environment. Social capital theory is particularly salient in the study of men and fathers, including non-resident fathers, because changes in family relationships, households, and networks can lead to changes in social ties.[49, 50] For men and fathers, these changes can have detrimental effects ranging from parental conflict, social isolation, and debilitating emotional and physical health to engagement in risky behaviors, including substance abuse and accidental injuries, all of which may have negative effects on their own well-being, relationship with their children, and fulfillment of their parental responsibilities and obligations.[51, 52]

Because we know little about non-resident fathers' social networks,[53] it is important to see who these fathers turn to for assistance and support. By considering transactions of encouragement, support, information, and opportunities non-resident fathers receive through their relationships and environment, a more balanced picture of non-resident fathers can be achieved. Applied to the study of families and households, the inclusion of social capital theory has primarily focused on the direct and indirect benefits accrued to divorced mothers and children.[54, 55] To a much lesser degree has social capital theory emphasized the benefits accruing to non-resident fathers. Using an ecological perspective and social capital theory defined as linkages between individuals and institutions, the purpose of this study is to examine the intra- and interdependent networks[56] non-resident fathers employ in fulfilling their parental responsibility of establishing child support orders. Such information could suggest directions for improving child support enforcement policy and program service delivery that could ultimately enhance non-resident fathers' engagement with the child support enforcement system and the establishment of child support orders.

Study Hypotheses

The hypotheses for this study are:

- Non-resident fathers with higher ratings of their relationships with their children have higher rates of established child support orders.
- Non-resident fathers with higher ratings of their relationships with their children's mothers have higher rates of established child support orders.
- Non-resident fathers with higher levels of informal network involvement have higher rates of established child support orders.
- Non-resident fathers with higher levels of formal network involvement have higher rates of established child support orders.

METHOD

Data

The data used in this study were taken from the Fragile Families and Child Wellbeing Study (Fragile Families Study hereafter). A national study examining the consequences of non-marital childbearing in low-income families, the Fragile Families Study is a longitudinal study designed to increase the understanding of non-marital childbearing, welfare reform, and the role of fathers.[57, 58] The Fragile Families Study followed a cohort of new parents and their children, approximately 4,700 births (3,600 non-marital, 1,100 marital) in seventy-five hospitals in twenty cities with populations greater than two hundred thousand in the United States. In nearly all of the cities, at least 75 percent of unwed fathers were interviewed. Information gathered from respondents included family characteristics, child wellbeing and fathering, mother-child relationship, father's relationship with mother, current partner, demographics, father's family background and support, environment and programs, employment office, welfare office, fatherhood programs, health and health behavior, religion, education and employment, and income. The final sample of this study included 3,225 non-resident fathers.

Demographic Characteristics of the Sample

Participants of this study included non-resident fathers who reported they do not have custody of their children. The number of respondents decreased when reporting on the independent and social characteristic variables. The age of the respondents ranged from sixteen to eighty years of age with a mean age of 27.96. Two-thirds of the respondents identified as black and Hispanic. Fifty-nine percent of the respondents reported having an education level equivalent to or lower than a high school diploma. Seventy-six percent of the respondents reported being employed. Forty-five percent of the respondents reported having a household income level equivalent to or greater than $25,000 annually.

Measures

Establishment of Child Support Orders

One question was used to measure non-resident fathers' establishment of child support orders: "Do you have a legal agreement or child support order that requires you to provide financial support to your child?" A dichotomous variable was created which measures whether non-resident fathers' report "yes" (=1), child support orders have been established, or "no" (=0), child support orders have not been established. This is the dependent variable in this study.

Non-Resident Fathers' Relationship with Their Children

A father-child relationship index that includes multiple dimensions of non-resident fathers' relationship with their child was employed. The index consists of the summative rating of standardized scores from variables measuring the number of times non-resident fathers engaged and interacted with their children. For example, several questions ask fathers how many days a week do you play peek-a-boo with your child, read stories to your child, and take your child to visit relatives? The father-child relationship includes eight components, and the values range from 0 for none to 7 for seven days a week. The index had a Cronbach's Alpha of .825.

Non-Resident Fathers' Relationship with Former Spouse or Partner

One variable was used to measure non-resident fathers' relationship with a former spouse or partner. One question in the Fragile Families Study asked, "In general, would you say that your relationship with [your child's mother] is excellent, very good, good, fair, or poor?" The original item was reverse coded with 0 representing "poor," and 4 representing "excellent."

Non-Resident Fathers' Involvement with Informal Networks

A father-informal network involvement index that includes multiple dimensions of non-resident fathers' involvement with his parents, extended family, and others was employed. The index consists of the summative rating of standardized scores from variables measuring whether non-resident fathers received support from his mother, father, extended family, former spouses' or partners' family, and others. The father–informal network involvement index includes six components, and the values range from 0, indicating no father–informal network involvement, to 5, indicating high father–informal network involvement. The index had a Cronbach's Alpha of .888.

Non-Resident Fathers' Involvement with Formal Networks

A father–formal network involvement index that includes multiple dimensions of the non-resident fathers' involvement with community institutions and organizations was employed. The index consists of the summative rating of standardized scores from variables measuring whether non-resident fathers received help from the public welfare office, employment office, and any fatherhood programs. The father–informal network involvement index includes three components, with values ranging from 0, indicating no father–formal network involvement, to 2, indicating high father–formal network involvement. The index had a Cronbach's Alpha of .999.

Other Social Characteristics

The social characteristics of non-resident fathers are uniquely related to the establishment of child support orders and are included in this study. The characteristics include age, race/ethnicity, educational attainment, employment, and income.

Jason Castillo

FINDINGS

To determine the odds of establishing child support orders among non-resident fathers, logistic regression was used in this study. Logistic regression is a model of analysis that is used to help predict the probability of an event occurring. For this study, the four key independent variables were entered into three models with the establishment of child support orders as the dependent variable in each model. As presented in table 14.1, the

Table 14.1. Factors Associated with the Establishment of Child Support Orders: Logistic Regression of Coefficients (Three Models)

	Model 1 (n = 1662)		Model 2 (n = 1441)		Model 3 (n = 390)	
	B	*Odds Ratio*	*B*	*Odds Ratio*	*B*	*Odds Ratio*
Race/Ethnicity						
Hispanic/Latino	−0.773	0.462***	−0.920	0.398***	−0.826	0.438**
White/Caucasian	−0.519	0.595**	−0.654	0.520***	−1.050	0.350**
Black/African American						
Education						
Less than high school	−0.098	0.906	0.171	1.186	−0.533	0.587
High school diploma	−0.063	0.939	0.137	1.146	−0.806	0.447
Some College	−0.164	0.849	0.071	1.073	−0.829	0.437
College Graduate						
Employment Income	0.144	1.154	−0.001	0.999	0.016	1.016
< $14,999	−0.080	0.923	−0.071	0.931	0.246	1.279
$15,000–$24,999	0.044	1.045	0.130	1.139	0.198	1.219
$25,000–$49,999	−0.339	0.712*	−0.278	0.758	−0.037	0.963
>$50,000						
Age						
15–22	0.195	1.215	0.053	1.054	−0.778	0.460
23–26	−0.153	0.858	−0.253	0.777	−1.249	0.287**
27–33	0.105	1.110	−0.066	0.936	−0.938	0.391*
>34						
Relationship with child			−0.045	0.956	−0.135	0.874
Relationship with ex-spouses			−0.322	0.724***	−0.273	0.761**
Formal Involvement			0.447	1.564*	−0.966	0.381
Informal Involvement					−0.020	0.980
Chi-Square	34.171		75.608		31.182	
d.f.	12.0		15.0		16.0	
Significance	0.001		0.000		0.013	

*** p ≤ .01; ** p ≤ .05; * p ≤ .10

overall models were significant with several findings demonstrating or approaching statistical significance, one of which was mildly consistent with the hypotheses. As shown in model 2 of table 14.1, non-resident fathers' relationships with their former spouses or partners and involvement with formal networks demonstrated statistical significance. A one-point increase on the father–former spouses or partners relationship scale decreases the odds of establishing child support orders by 28 percent. Contrary to expectations, as non-resident fathers' relationship with their former spouses or partners increased, the odds of establishing child support orders decreased. A one-point increase on the father–formal involvement scale increases the odds of establishing child support orders by 56 percent. The more involved non-resident fathers are with formal networks, the higher the odds of establishing child support orders. However, as shown in model 3 of table 14.1, the introduction of the informal involvement variable mediated the significance and direction of the formal involvement variable in the establishment of child support orders. The absence of a stable pattern in the formal involvement variable across models 2 and 3 undermines the significance the formal involvement variable had in the previous model. The one finding that remained statistically significant between models 2 and 3 was the relationship between non-resident fathers' and their former spouses or partners. Again, as non-resident fathers' relationship with their former spouses or partners increased (stronger = better), the odds of establishing child support orders decreased. Non-resident fathers' relationship with their children and involvement with informal networks were not significant in the models.

DISCUSSION

Given non-resident fathers' vulnerability to high levels of distress following changes in their relationships, family, and household,[59, 60, 61] it is important to understand how non-resident fathers' social relationships and networks may alleviate disengaged parenting and contribute to improved fathering behaviors, which have been shown to have positive effects on child well-being[62] and child support compliance.[63, 64, 65, 66] The two main findings of this study include the relationship between non-resident fathers and their former spouses or partners and their involvement with formal networks in the establishment of child support orders.

Doherty, Kouneski, and Erickson[67] assert that the role of fathers and fathering is contextually situated within both familial and institutional networks of support. Bartfeld and Meyer[68] assert that a strong relationship between non-marital parents will improve child support compliance. The first finding of this study is inconsistent with a majority of the literature that examines the relationship between non-resident fathers' social networks and fulfillment of their child support obligations. In the present study, the finding reveals that a strong relationship between non-resident fathers and resident mothers does not increase the odds of child support orders being established. Instead, the finding suggests that non-marital parents can maintain a favorable relationship and yet this relationship may not yield the intended outcome of establishing child support orders that other entities, including the child support enforcement system and larger society, perceive as fulfillment of parental responsibilities and legal obligations. One explanation for this contrasting finding is the costs associated with fulfilling child support obligations. Although non-resident fathers have maintained a desire and intent to contribute socially and economically to their children,[69, 70, 71, 72] it is possible that the child support enforcement system exacerbates the stress affecting non-resident fathers and precludes non-resident fathers from fulfilling their parental responsibilities and child support obligations.

For example, realizing the child support enforcement system positions non-marital parents against one another in the processes of establishing paternity, establishing child support orders, and collecting child support, non-marital parents may determine that their well-being and the well-being of their children is threatened by involvement with the child support enforcement system. When the child support enforcement system is included in the social and economic affairs of non-marital parents, non-resident fathers may feel undermined by both their former spouses or partners and the child support enforcement system, which may induce many non-resident fathers to retreat from their parental responsibilities and obligations.[73] Recognizing that non-resident fathers may not be able to fulfill their child support obligation, or realizing that non-resident fathers are providing all that they can, non-resident fathers and resident mothers may opt into an informal, covert agreement intended to keep non-resident fathers involved socially with their children and contributing economically to their children in a manner agreed upon by the non-marital parents.[74, 75, 76, 77] Through this agreement, resident mothers and non-resident fathers maintain a relationship that is agreeable to both but does not contribute to the outcome of establishing a legal child support order. Although this finding is not consistent with the hypotheses of the study, it does suggest that future research is needed to better understand the relationship occurring between non-marital parents and the affect their relationship has on intended outcomes: in the case of this study, the legal establishment of child support orders.

The second finding of this study is consistent with literature suggesting that formal networks may help fathers in their day-to-day functioning and fulfillment of their child support obligations. In the present study, the finding reveals that non-resident fathers' involvement with formal networks does increase the odds of child support orders being established. Given the precarious and vulnerable status of non-resident fathers, many of whom have never been married, are non-white, have lower educational status, are employed intermittently or not at all, and are earning a median income of $5,000, it is possible to assume that these fathers may be in need of, and indeed benefit from, organizational and institutional support. Non-resident fathers' involvement with formal networks has only anecdotally been addressed in the child support enforcement literature.[78, 79, 80]

This finding is consistent with the hypothesis of the study; however, it is important to recall that it was significant in model 2 but not in model 3, which may mean that the informal and formal network variables are correlated and share some error variance. The contrasting results between the two models could also be due to several factors including the decrease in the number of cases associated with the informal involvement measure and the operationalization of the formal involvement measure. In model 3, the number of cases decreased by more than 70 percent from model 2, and it is likely that this may have contributed to the nonsignificant finding of non-resident fathers' formal involvement and the establishment of child support orders. Given the challenges associated with the inclusion of divorced, separated, and never married fathers in research studies— underrepresentation—the attrition rate evidenced in this study is consistent with that of previous studies examining this population. After entering the informal involvement measure into model 3, the number of cases decreased by 1,051. An alternative approach, in order to increase the number of cases in the informal involvement variable, may have been to construct the variable from the several waves of research questions asking non-resident fathers about their involvement with their mothers, fathers, relatives, former spouses' or partners' family, or others. Furthermore, the formal involvement measure was constructed according to a limited number of institutional and organizational items. Future research, including other relevant factors such as SSI, Unemployment Insurance, Medicaid, and food stamps, is needed to better understand the role formal networks have in the lives of non-resident fathers.

Other findings of interest in this study occurred along the lines of non-resident fathers' establishment of child support orders by age, race and ethnicity, educational status, and income status. Compared to older non-resident fathers, younger non-resident fathers were less likely to establish child support orders. Compared to black non-resident fathers, white and Hispanic non-resident fathers were less likely to establish child support orders. Compared to non-resident fathers with higher levels of education, non-resident fathers with lower levels of education were less likely to establish child support orders. Compared to non-resident fathers with higher levels of income, non-resident fathers with middle-range levels of income were less likely to establish child support orders. Each of the findings are consistent with the qualitative literature[81, 82] indicating that younger, less educated, and lower-income males are less likely to establish child support orders and engage in the child support enforcement system. Future research examining the establishment of child support orders should examine the effects of non-resident fathers' social networks by considering their age, race and ethnicity, educational status, employment status, and income status. Doing so may lead to further understanding of the arrangements occurring between non-resident fathers and resident mothers in providing for their children.

CONCLUSION

Implications for Policy and Practice

Given Congress's and society's interest in cultivating healthy families and responsible fathering, it seems essential that initiatives be developed and implemented in effecting real change among non-resident fathers who are expected to establish child support orders. To date, few child support enforcement reforms have explicitly included mechanisms assisting and supporting non-resident fathers in fulfilling their child support obligations. While numerous demonstration and pilot projects have occurred across the nation over the last twenty years, these projects have focused exclusively on employment and income, both of which are intricately connected to child support collections. The findings associated with these projects have been mixed, showing few changes in non-resident fathers' employability or income.[83, 84] Additionally, very few of these demonstration and pilot projects have focused on enhancing the capacities of non-resident fathers by including or considering non-resident fathers' intra- and interdependent networks of support.

Based on the findings of this study, federal and state legislatures, governmental organizations, and community-based programs may wish to include and integrate non-resident fathers' intra- and interdependent networks of support in the enactment, enforcement, and implementation of child support policy and programmatic initiatives. By undertaking such endeavors, state legislatures, governmental organizations, and community-based programs may bring together and strengthen a system of care that is fragmented and rarely considers the contextual factors associated with non-resident fathers, which may indeed assist and support non-resident fathers in fulfilling their obligations.

Community-based programs and practitioners working with families involved in the child support enforcement system may wish to reach out to resident mothers and non-resident fathers in a manner that is cognizant of their circumstances. For example, community-based programs and practitioners, recognizing the precarious position of these families in their relationship with one another and the child support enforcement system, may step in to serve as a mediator between resident mothers and non-resident fathers and in non-marital families, especially between non-resident fathers and the child support enforcement system. Serving as a mediator, community-based programs and practitioners can help non-resident fathers: recognize, understand, and cope with their individual, relational, and societal stressors; become more informed and knowledgeable about accessing and navigating opportunities associated with education, employment, health care, and parenting and fathering; become more informed and knowledgeable about the child support enforcement system—establishing child support orders, entering default orders, and modifying child support orders; become more informed, knowledgeable, and skilled in understanding and negotiating within the child support enforcement system. Additionally, by serving as the mediator, community-based programs and practitioners may help and support resident mothers and non-resident fathers in developing and maintaining a co-parental relationship that is responsive to their legal obligations.

The results of this study should be interpreted in the context of several limitations. First, the representativeness of the study is limited only to those families experiencing the birth of a child in one of the twenty cities included in the national sample. This study does not account for families with older children for whom child support orders have not been established or for all cities and communities in the United States. Second, the information on the establishment of child support orders was reported by non-resident fathers and may be subject to reporting bias. For example, studies have found that non-resident fathers tend to report more favorable actions and outcomes than resident mothers.[85, 86, 87] Third, the analyses show associations between non-resident fathers' relationships and involvement with others in the establishment of child support orders, but do not illuminate the mechanisms through which the associations operate. Indeed, the results should not be interpreted as showing causality. Finally, although this study controls for several variables, there may be other unobserved variables, such as non-resident fathers' psychological, emotional, physical, and social well-being, which may not be totally captured and could be driving the associations.

Despite these limitations, the study provides evidence suggesting that the relationship between resident mothers and non-resident fathers affects the establishment of child support orders. Additionally, non-resident fathers' involvement with formal networks appears to have a mild effect on the establishment of child support orders. Consequently, strategies for establishing, maintaining, and strengthening non-resident fathers' relationships with their former spouses or partners and involvement with formal networks of support should be more prominent in policy and programmatic debates. With a broad federal mandate to promote responsible fatherhood, federal, state, and local policy-makers should partner together to expand their efforts in assisting and supporting non-resident fathers in fulfilling their parental responsibilities to their children and their obligations to the child support enforcement system.[88, 89]

NOTES

1. Defined as whom the child lives with, resident parents are those that live with the child all or most of the time. Non-resident parents are those that provide limited care and do not live with the child.

2. Randall D. Day, *Social Fatherhood: Conceptualizations, Compelling Research, and Future Directions* (Philadelphia: Philadelphia National Center on Fathers and Families, 1998).

3. William Marsiglio, "Fatherhood Scholarship: An Overview and Agenda for the Future," in *Fatherhood: Contemporary Theory, Research, and Social Policy*, ed. William Marsiglio (Thousand Oaks, CA: Sage Publications, 1995), 1–20.

4. William Marsiglio, "Father's Diverse Life Course Patterns and Roles: Theory and Social Interventions," in *Fatherhood: Contemporary Theory, Research, and Social Policy*, ed. William Marsiglio (Thousand Oaks, CA: Sage Publications, 1995), 78–101.

5. David S. Degarmo, Joshua Patras, and Sopagna Eap, "Social Support for Divorced Fathers' Parenting: Testing a Stress-Buffering Model," *Family Relations* 57, no. 1 (January 2008): 35–48.

6. Elaine A. Anderson, Julie K. Kohler, and Bethany L. Letiecq, "Predictors of Depression among Low-income, Nonresidential Fathers," *Journal of Family Issues* 26, no. 5 (July 2005): 547–67.

7. Jay J. Belsky, "The Determinants of Parenting: A Process Model," *Child Development* 55, no. 1 (February 1984): 83–96.

8. Elaine Sorenson, Helen Oliver, and the Urban Institute, *Policy Reforms Are Needed to Increase Child Support from Poor Fathers*, 2002, www.urban.org/Elaine Sorensen (10 Nov. 2004).

9. Irwin Garfinkel, Theresa Heintze, and Chien-Chung Huang, *Child Support Enforcement: Incentives and Wellbeing, Working paper 215* (Chicago: Joint Center for Poverty Research, 2001).

10. U. S. Department of Health and Human Services, *State Policies Used to Establish Child Support Orders for Low-income Non-custodial Fathers* (Washington, DC: Office of Inspector General, 2000).

11. U. S. Department of Health and Human Services, *The Establishment of Child Support Orders for Low-income Non-custodial Parents* (Washington, DC: Office of Inspector General, 2000).

12. Irwin Garfinkel, Sara McLanahan, Daniel Meyer, and J. A. Seltzer, *Fathers under Fire: The Revolution in Child Support Enforcement* (New York: Russell Sage Foundation, 1998).

13. Sorenson, Oliver, and the Urban Institute, *Policy Reforms*.

14. Garfinkel, Heintze, and Huang, *Child Support Enforcement*.

15. U.S. Department of Health and Human Services, *Non-custodial Fathers.*

16. U.S. Department of Health and Human Services, *Non-custodial Parents.*

17. U.S. Department of Health and Human Services, Office of Child Support Enforcement, *Administrative and Judicial Processes for Establishing Child Support Orders: Final Report,* by Karen N. Gardiner, John Tapogna, and Michael F. Fishman (Washington, DC: Government Printing Office, 2002).

18. U. S. Department of Health and Human Services, *Child Support Enforcement, FY 2006 Preliminary Report* (Washington DC: Office of Child Support Enforcement, 2006).

19. Timothy Grall, "Custodial Mothers and Fathers and Their Child Support," *Current Population Reports No. P60-217* (Washington, DC: U.S. Census Bureau, 2002).

20. Judi Bartfeld and Gary Sandefur, "Paternity Establishment and Child Support Orders among W-2 Participants," in *W-2 Child Support Evaluation Phase I: Final Report, Volume II* (Madison: Institute for Research on Poverty, University of Wisconsin–Madison, 2001): 1–41.

21. U. S. House of Representatives, Committee on Ways and Means, *2000 Green Book* (Washington, DC: Government Printing Office, 2000).

22. Bartfeld and Sandefur, "Paternity Establishment," 1.

23. Maureen A. Pirog and Kathleen M. Ziol-Guest, "Child Support Enforcement: Programs and Policies, Impacts and Questions," *Journal of Policy Analysis and Management* 25, no. 4 (October 2006): 943–90.

24. Timothy Grall, *Child Support Receipt* (Washington, DC: Child Trends Databank, 2003).

25. Elaine Sorensen and Chava Zibman, "Getting to Know Poor Fathers Who Do not Pay Child Support." *Social Service Review* 75, no. 3 (September 2001): 420–34.

26. Elaine Sorensen, Chava Zibman, and the Urban Institute, *To What Extent Do Children Benefit from Child Support? Assessing the New Federalism Discussion Papers 99-19* (Washington, DC: The Urban Institute, 2000).

27. U. S. House of Representatives, *2000 Green Book.*

28. Laura Wheaton and Elaine Sorenson, "Reducing Welfare Costs and Dependency: How Much Bang for the Child Support Buck," *Georgetown Public Policy Review* 4, no. 1 (1998): 23–37.

29. U. S. House of Representatives, *2000 Green Book.*

30. Sorenson and Zibman, "Know Poor Fathers," 420.

31. Sorenson, Zibman, and the Urban Institute, *Do Children Benefit?*

32. Pirog and Ziol-Guest, "Enforcement Programs and Policies," 943.

33. Grall, *Child Support Receipt.*

34. U.S. Department of Health and Human Services, *Non-custodial Fathers.*

35. U.S. Department of Health and Human Services, *Non-custodial Parents.*

36. Timothy Grall, "Child Support for Custodial Mothers and Fathers," *Current Population Reports No. P60-212* (Washington, DC: U.S. Census Bureau, 2000).

37. Bartfeld and Sandefur, "Paternity Establishment," 1.

38. U.S. Department of Health and Human Services, *Non-custodial Fathers.*

39. U.S. Department of Health and Human Services, *Non-custodial Parents.*

40. U.S. House of Representatives, *2000 Green Book.*

41. Robert I. Lerman and Theodora J. Ooms, *Young Unwed Fathers: Changing Roles and Emerging Policies* (Philadelphia: Temple University Press, 1993).

42. Grall, "Child Support for Custodial Mothers and Fathers."

43. Timothy J. Nelson, "Low-income Fathers," *Annual Review of Sociology* 30, no. 1 (August 2004): 427–51.

44. Mercer L. Sullivan, "Noncustodial Fathers' Attitudes and Behaviors," in *Caring and Paying: What Fathers and Mothers Say about Child Support*, ed. Frank Furstenberg Jr. (New York: Manpower Demonstration Research Corporation, 1992), 6–33.

45. Frank Furstenberg, "Daddies and Fathers: Men Who Do for Their Children and Men Who Do Not," in *Caring and Paying: What Fathers and Mothers Say about Child Support*, ed. Frank Furstenberg Jr. (New York: Manpower Demonstration Research Corporation, 1992): 39–64.

46. Mary Achatz and Crystal A. MacAllum, *Young Unwed Fathers: Report from the Field* (Philadelphia: Public/Private Ventures, 1994).

47. Pierre Bourdieu, "The Forms of Capital," in *Handbook of Theory and Research in the Sociology of Education*, ed. John G. Richards (New York: Greenwald Press, 1986), 183–98.

48. James S. Coleman, *Foundations of Social Theory* (Cambridge, MA: Belknap Press, 1990).

49. William J. Doherty, Edward F. Kouneski, and Martha F. Erickson, "Responsible Fathering: An Overview and Conceptual Framework," *Journal of Marriage and the Family* 60, no. 2 (1998): 277–92.

50. Belsky, "Determinants of Parenting," 83.

51. Degarmo, Patras, and Eap, "Support for Divorced Fathers," 35.

52. Anderson, Kohler, and Letiecq, "Predictors of Depression," 547.

53. The terms "social networks" and "social supports" have been used interchangeably as social capital. This study employs the term "social networks" to imply non-resident fathers' social capital (i.e., intra- and interdependent networks).

54. Rosalind Edwards, Jane Franklin, and Janet Holland, *Families and Social Capital: Exploring the Issues* (London: Families and Social Capital ESRC Research Group, 2003).

55. Alejandro Portes, "Social Capital: Its Origins and Applications in Modern Sociology," *Annual Review of Sociology* 24, no. 1 (August 1998): 1–24.

56. This study employs the term "intra- and interdependent networks" to imply non-resident fathers' relationships with their children, former spouses or partners, and involvement with informal and formal networks.

57. Nancy E. Reichman, Julian O. Teitler, Irwin Garfinkel, and Sara S. McLanahan, "Fragile Families: Sample and Design," *Children and Youth Services Review* 23, no. 4/5 (April-May 2001): 303–26.

58. Irwin Garfinkel, Sara S. McLanahan, Marta Tienda, and Jeanne Brooks-Gunn, "Fragile Families and Welfare Reform," *Children and Youth Services Review* 23, no. 4–5 (April-May 2001): 277–301.

59. Doherty, Kouneski, and Erickson, "Responsible Fathering," 277.

60. S. L. Braver et al., "A Longitudinal Study of Nonresidential Parents: Parents without Children," *Journal of Family Psychology* 7, no. 1 (1993): 9–23.

61. Belsky, "Determinants of Parenting," 83.

62. Valerie King and Juliana M. Sobolewski, "Nonresident Fathers' Contributions to Adolescent Well-being," *Journal of Marriage and Family* 68, no. 3 (August 2006): 537–57.

63. Judi Bartfeld and Daniel R. Meyer, "Child Support Compliance among Discretionary and Nondiscretionary Obligors," *Social Service Review* 77, no. 3 (September 2003): 347–72.

64. Judi Bartfeld and Daniel R. Meyer, "Are there Really Deadbeat Dads? The Relationship between Ability to Pay, Enforcement, and Compliance in Non-marital Child Support Cases," *Social Service Review* 68, no. 2 (June 1994): 220–35.

65. Elizabeth Peters et al., "Enforcing Divorce Settlements: Evidence for Child Support Compliance and Award Modifications," *Demography* 30, no. 4 (1993): 719–35.

66. Jay D. Teachman, "Who Pays? Receipt of Child Support in the United States," *Journal of Marriage and the Family* 53, no. 3 (August 1991): 759–72.

67. Doherty, Kouneski, and Erickson, "Responsible Fathering," 277.

68. Bartfeld and Meyer, "Child Support Compliance," 347.

69. Achatz and MacAllum, *Young Unwed Fathers*.

70. Furstenberg, "Daddies and Fathers," 39.

71. Kay E. Sherwood, "Child Support Obligations: What Fathers Say about Paying," in *Caring and Paying: What Fathers and Mothers Say about Child Support*, ed. Frank Furstenberg Jr. (New York: Manpower Demonstration Research Corporation, 1992): 57–76.

72. Sullivan, "Noncustodial Fathers," 6.

73. Doherty, Kouneski, and Erickson, "Responsible Fathering," 277.

74. Achatz and MacAllum, *Young Unwed Fathers*.

75. Furstenberg, "Daddies and Fathers," 39.

76. Sherwood, "Child Support Obligations," 57.

77. Sullivan, "Noncustodial Fathers," 6.

78. Elaine Sorenson and the Urban Institute, *Child Support Gains Some Ground: Snapshots of America's Families III, no. 11* (Washington, DC: The Urban Institute, 2003).

79. Sorenson and Zibman, "Know Poor Fathers," 420.

80. Cynthia Miller and Virginia Knox, *The Challenge of Helping Low-income Fathers Support Their Children: Final Lessons from Parents' Fair Share* (New York: Manpower Demonstration Research Corp, 2001): 1–43.

81. Sullivan, "Noncustodial Fathers," 6.

82. Esther Wattenberg, Robert Brewer, and Michael Resnick, *A Study of Paternity Decisions: Perspectives from Young Mothers and Young Fathers* (Minneapolis, MN: Center for Urban and Regional Affairs, 1991).

83. Miller and Knox, *Helping Low-income Fathers*, 1.

84. Fred Doolittle and Suzanne Lynn, *Working with Low-income Cases: Lessons for the Child Support Enforcement System for Parents' Fair Share* (New York: Manpower Demonstration Research Corporation, 1998): 1–69.

85. Maureen Waller and Robert Plotnick, "Effective Child Support Policy for Low-income Families: Evidence from Street Level Research," *Journal of Policy Analysis and Management* 20, no. 1 (Winter 2001): 89–110.

86. Furstenberg, "Daddies and Fathers," 39.

87. Sherwood, "Child Support Obligations," 57.

88. Kirk E. Harris, "Crafting Cooperative Agreements: Community-based Organizations and Child Support Enforcement," *Collaborator* 4, no. 1 (1998): 3–4.

89. James A. Levine and Edward W. Pitt, *New Expectations, Community Strategies for Responsible Fatherhood* (New York: Families and Work Institute, 1995).

15

Integrating Mothers' Views of Resources That Foster Growth for Children with Autism Spectrum Disorders into Policy

Judy Doktor, Laura Dreuth Zeman, and Jayme Swanke

Parents raising children with autism spectrum disorder often spend a lifetime serving as their children's voice. This chapter examines the perspectives of an informal virtual social network of these mothers. Their voices were captured as they posted journals about their everyday lives on their own public blogs. These mothers' views provide insight into their desires for their children and the successes they experience as they maneuver social and academic systems as their children's advocates. The themes from their journals were sorted into categories reflecting resources attributes that foster adequacy, accommodations, accessibility, and availability. As systems adapt to incorporate the needs of this growing group of children, it is beneficial to also incorporate their parents' understanding of resource successes into policy and program planning.

The Center's for Disease Control classifies autism spectrum disorder (ASD) as a cluster of conditions that encompass a wide range of social, communication, and behavioral impairments.[1] The National Institute of Mental Health[2] classification of ASD includes five pervasive developmental disorders. The two most common conditions are autism and Asperger's syndrome. Also included in the spectrum are two less frequently identified conditions of Rett syndrome and childhood disintegrative disorder, where the child develops typically until around the age of two before ASD symptoms emerge. The final condition included in the autism spectrum is a broader classification labeled pervasive developmental disorder, not otherwise specified.[3] These disorders are referred to as conditions first identified in early childhood by the American Psychiatric Association as they are typically identified before the child enters preschool.[4]

Social ASD symptoms broadly include disturbances that interfere with the child's ability to interact with peers, caregivers, and family. Some of these symptoms include a lack of interest in social activities, problems in expression or engaging with others emotionally, and an inability to respond to requests or to determine socially appropriate behaviors. Communication symptoms vary as some individuals have only slight language impairments while others are not able to speak. Some persons with ASD may have communication problems that include not understanding gestures or facial expressions or they may have problems engaging in verbal exchange to the extent that they may adapt speech patterns that mimic others, or they deliver monologues. Symptoms also include odd or repetitious behaviors. These behaviors may include rocking, spinning, flapping their arms, or other actions considered self-stimulated. Individuals with ASD may perform rituals that may appear irrational or obsessive. They may also throw tantrums when they are disrupted, agitated, or in strange surroundings.[5]

There has been a drastic increase in the incidence of persons diagnosed with an ASD. This increase can be partially attributed to changes in the way these symptom clusters are diagnosed. For instance, in 1994 the American Psychiatric Association included Asperger's syndrome as a formal diagnosis, including symptom clusters that were not previously diagnosable, thus expanding the dimension of ASD.[6] Advocates who work with and on behalf of persons with ASD, such as Autism Speaks, suggest that the increase is at least partially due to environmental factors and may be related to childhood vaccinations; governmental and scientific sources dispute the latter claim.[7]

ASDs are now the second most common childhood developmental disorder.[8] In 2007, the CDC reported that 1 in 150 (0.6 percent) children in the United States are diagnosed with an ASD.[9] This rate is up from 1999 when roughly twelve out of every ten thousand (0.12 percent) children lived with an ASD.[10]

It logically follows that this increase in incidence accompanies an increase in the cost of care. Conservative estimates suggest that the educational costs associated with educating children with ASD are roughly $15,000 a year when adjusted for inflation, while additional therapies may cost families on average $22,000 annually.[11] With an estimated annual cost of total care for each child with ASD at roughly $37,000, the school and family may be faced with an estimated $660,000 cost of care over the first eighteen years. Further, if 1 in 150 (0.6 percent) children live with an ASD, with 77.5 million children enrolled in school from nursery school to college,[12] then families, school districts, and universities in the United States face an estimated $1.7 trillion in annual costs of support for 46.5 million children with ASDs.

POLICY BACKGROUND: SPECIAL EDUCATION
AND PARENT INVOLVEMENT

The early history of special education had been one of segregating special needs children from general education students. Initially, special education was based on a medical model that framed disabilities as pathologies. Children were "prescribed" educational activities based on their pathology. Children with disabilities were selectively allowed to attend schools, based on local school district practices. The passage of the Education for all Handicapped Children Act of 1975 (P.L. 94-142)[13] established the right of all children with disabilities to a Free Appropriate Public Education (FAPE).[14] There are many instances where segregated settings enhance the academic and social skills of a child with disabilities; yet the consensus of most parents and educators is that the detrimental effects of segregated settings far outweigh any specialized instruction.

Recently the policy discourse related to special education has focused on educating children with disabilities in general education settings, a practice called "inclusion." Supporters of inclusion believe that all learners have the right to be educated in the general education classroom and children with disabilities benefit most when they are fully engaged with the curriculum and social activities of general education classrooms. In inclusion models, general education and special education services are merged into a unified service delivery system, which some believe helps with the socio-emotional growth of children with disabilities and promotes a broader acceptance of persons with disabilities by society in general.[15]

Autism is one of the thirteen disabilities recognized by the federal government under the Individuals with Disabilities Education Act (IDEA) of 2004 (PL 108-446).[16] This act provides a free appropriate public education including related services, in the least restrictive environment, and documented within an individualized learning plan (DOE 34 CFR Parts 300 and 301). Many parents feel, however, that the educational and related services offered by school systems are inadequate for their child. Even though the specific term "inclusion" was not directly written into the IDEA, proponents of inclusion claim that the least restrictive environment (LRE) principle clearly means that children with disabilities should receive their instruction in a general education classroom with same age peers. Rud Turnbull and his colleagues[17] note the following,

> IDEA defines the term *general curriculum* as consisting of three components, so it accordingly requires integration/inclusion in each of the three: (1) The general (academic) curriculum; (2) Extracurricular activities (school-sponsored clubs and sports); and (3) Other nonacademic activities (such as recess, mealtimes, transportation, dances and the like) (20 U.S.C. Sec. 141(d)(I)(A)(i)(IV).

Thus, a student's IEP (Individualized Educational Plan) must include an explanation of the extent, if any, to which the student will not participate (with students who do not have disabilities) in the general class and its extracurricular and other non academic activities.

The burden is on the IEP team to explain why a student's program and placement will not be within each of these three components of the general education environment. Some parents feel that additional training for teachers in positive behavioral supports or other specialized methods of teaching children with ASD must be incorporated into the IEP. Other parents insist that the child has the right under "related services" to be afforded alternative therapies.[18]

However, as decided in 1982 by the legal case *Board of Education v Rowley* (458 U.S. 176.1025. ct. 3034),[19] IDEA only requires that the student receive a level of benefit such that her access to educational services is meaningful. Therefore, IDEA does not require schools to provide maximum benefit. The *Rowley* ruling specifically declined to create a single test for determining whether a student has benefited from her IEP that the student has received an appropriate education. Instead, the court adopted a case-by-case approach, stating that the standard for benefit in any IEP be "reasonably calculated to enable the child to receive educational benefits."

Parents, who are financially capable, privately secure additional therapies, such as speech and occupational therapies, behavioral training, and nutritional interventions. These therapies come with a great financial and time burden on parents, usually mothers.[20] Coordinating these therapies and becoming active participants in their child's individualized educational plan (IEP) have given rise to another role, which we characterize as the "*über* case managers."

Furthermore, under IDEA parents are afforded the right to be an integral part of the educational planning for their child (Sec. 300.501 (b-c); Sec. 672 (a-b) (2)). Some parents interpret this right as license to demand more services than the school system has the capacity to provide.[21] This tension between what parents desire and what school systems provide causes parents to question the adequacy of the system and to expect costly services. This tension is at the heart of the study that is examined in this chapter.

RESOURCE FRAMEWORK

This chapter integrates mothers' views into a framework for understanding resources. Richard Rapp[22] previously forwarded the framework used here. The term resource refers to services or modifications that when added to typical settings enhance the functioning of persons with disabilities and help people function at higher levels with the goal of improving their ability to live independently. The resource categories in this analysis integrate the policy components of adequacy, accommodation, availability, and accessibility.

Adequacy

The issue of what constitutes adequacy from the perspective of parents and/or school districts continues to be a source of disagreement. Directions from the court systems are ambiguous at best. For most parents, the core of their child's education is the academic curriculum. For example, some parents of children with ASD feel that behavioral or social therapies are more important than a standard educational curriculum. Without incorporating these therapies into the school day, parents argue that their child's educational services are inadequate. Parents feel that they have a right to request these therapies under the "related services" clause of IDEA. Both schools and insurance companies typically argue that these therapies are not scientifically validated and do not benefit the child's ability to benefit from an educational program, as all related or covered services must.

Accommodation

Legally, accommodation refers to modifications to physical space, teaching strategies, and employment so that persons with a disability can fully participate.[23] Section 504 of the Rehabilitation Act of 1973 (Title 29, 1614.203)[24] specifies reasonable accommodations for persons with disabilities. Federal law requires that employers, schools, and programs receiving federal support make accommodations for persons with known conditions unless making the accommodation disrupts program operations. In general, accommodations move beyond altering the physical space to modifying work schedules and providing devices or translators that assist communication and reading. In schools, accommodations often include modified assignments and tests, including reduced time or frequent breaks, aids or counseling for classroom functioning and study skills, small classrooms. The National Autism Society and other advocates[25] suggest that students with ASD may also benefit from specialized accommodations designed to reduce tantrums and help students stay on task[26] such as seat plans, social stories, assisted transitions, quiet times and quiet spaces, earplugs, minimal exposure to crowds, and picture schedules.

Availability

Availability is one of the cornerstones of service policy analysis and program evaluation. Simply put, availability is the examination of whether persons who need services can access them.[27] In policy analysis, discussions of availability often examine insurance coverage for care, provider distributions across geographic areas, and the match between patient need and provider specialty. These are similar themes among parents raising children with disabilities, yet the themes are expanded to incorporate the application of funding, provider, and specialty concerns in school and community contexts. As in general medical policy analysis, providing services for disability-related conditions often requires unique specialization. It is common for parents to report that their child's provider is unskilled. For example, their child has a special education teacher who lacks training in autism-related conditions. Parents also face challenges of availability related to open spots for coveted positions on provider caseloads, independent of location. The result may be overcrowded classrooms or therapy groups, long waiting lists, poor matches between child and services, and problems coordinating services among highly demanded providers.

Accessibility

Accessibility relates to access to the environment, information, and communication mechanisms that include the design of services. This includes the physical structure and routines that shape environments so that the person with disabilities does not need further modifications in order to perform at or near their highest level of functioning. Ideally, we assume that when resources are accessible, people can easily maneuver through the environment. For persons with social and communication disorders, accessibility incorporates environmental alterations that manage sound, stimulation, and allow interaction with peers while managing crowds. Some of these environmental modifications include private areas for small group interactions, room-quieting insulation, quiet spaces, or soothing background sounds.[28]

This study intended to examine the inner worlds of mothers who raised children diagnosed with ASD, as written in their virtual journals. The intention was to use their collective voice to shape policy related to children diagnosed with ASD. Capturing parents' unique perspectives may forge family-oriented policies and by implementing policies that incorporate their unique view, resources may be available that help foster growth among children living with ASDs.

METHOD

Weblogs, or blogs, provided a source of rich authentic data. We established criteria to shape the data file development. First, we wanted to assure that the bloggers intended to create a public voice by including only blogs that were available on public blog search engines. In this study, we used live-journals and Google's blog search. We secured approval to conduct research involving existing data with human subjects from the university institutional review board. We altered the identities of the bloggers in the findings to protect their privacy. Second, we wanted to assure that the expressions represented an ongoing view rather than a snapshot in time. Therefore, we included only blogs that had one entry a month for the eighteen-month period between January 2006 and July 2007. Since the focus of the study was parents' expressions of their inner world, we eliminated blogs that were public information resources or that were dedicated primarily to track the experiences of a child. We reduced the blog count to twenty-six blogs that met the preliminary criteria, then further reduced the data file by eliminating the blogs authored outside the United States to foster sample heterogeneity. We also removed the only two blogs authored by fathers because we assumed readers could trace the quotes to the authors and we sought to protect author privacy. We then reduced the data to create an analysis data file by removing newspaper articles, discussions of politics, religion, and events unrelated to parenting.

The analysis data file consisted of a sample of twenty-one blogs. Almost all of the mothers were between the ages of thirty-two and forty-three. More than 70 percent (nine) of the mothers identified themselves as college educated. Two mothers indicated that they were single. Over one-half worked at least part-time. Six of the fourteen mothers included statements about their faith and religious celebrations. Of those with religious statements, four mothers indicated they were "very religious" practicing Christians and two mothers described celebrating Jewish holidays. These mothers were raising fifteen children with ASD, as one of the mothers had twins. Most of the children were in elementary school (seven) or kindergarten (four). Over one-third of the children attended a private religious school. One mother reported that she combined homeschool with an IEP at the local school to provide social and communication services for her child with ASD.

The data analysis for this chapter included a three-stage deductive process. First, we created a subset of the main data file that included only statements discussing resources. The second phase included systematically categorizing statements into predetermined categories consistent with the policy framework. These categories included adequacy, accommodation, availability, and accessibility. In the third phase we sorted the data into classifications of resources that foster growth and resources that inhibit growth. We read and discussed the results of this deductive analysis and made changes in classification based on the results of this verification process. We selected quotes that represented the collective voice of the mothers and focused this discussion only on resources that parents identified as fostering their child's growth.

RESULTS: VIEWS OF RESOURCES THAT FOSTER GROWTH

Adequacy

The definition of adequacy depends on the focus of the family. Most typically, we found that parents of children with ASD who were nonverbal and judged to be developmentally delayed were most satisfied with a segregated setting that devoted a great deal of time to speech therapy and learning appropriate social skills. For those mothers whose children demonstrated milder symptoms, specifically those with age-typical communication abilities, this was not usually the case. They preferred their children to be educated in inclusive settings.

Mothers expressed that for an educational program to be considered adequate, the IEP must address social and behavioral skills while engaging the child with other children and adults in a school setting. Because of the wide variety of abilities displayed across the spectrum, the determination of whether a school program is adequate is a highly individualized decision. One mother reflected:

> I believe in individualized education. For *everyone*. And I believe that education occurs 24 hours a day, seven days a week, so most parents need to remember to be vigilant about educating their child. . . . Most of the parents who communicate with me through this blog seem to be doing a *very* fine job with this. Some folks send their kids to residential schools. Some keep them home. Most mix the school—public or private—and home schooling, with a generous peppering of therapies and activities. We've become experts at individualized education. After all, the laws for our kids require it. We know they have a right to it, and it is our responsibility to preserve their rights.

The mothers seemed to be aware of their ability to influence the type of educational program offered to their children. In general, parents of children with severe ASD were most satisfied with a segregated setting that devoted a great deal of time to speech therapy and learning appropriate social skills. For example, one mother wrote that her child's current school felt "institutional," yet "beyond the dreariness and rigidity, are many young lovely teachers who think [MY CHILD] is a star."

For those children who were higher functioning academically, the focus of adequacy usually involves "acceptance by others" associated with inclusive educational settings. The following mother's definition of adequacy is heavily weighted towards social acceptance by neurotypical children. This mother shared her experience at an IEP meeting where she was asked about her most important goals for her child. Her answer provides insight into her belief in peer acceptance as the major indicator of a successful school intervention. She wrote, "I just don't want the other kids to hate him or ostracize him or throw food at him or make fun of him."

Accommodation

These mothers identified resources that facilitated inclusion in school, community, and home settings related to communication, behavioral, and social symptoms. The themes that emerged included supplemental home-to-school communication, supports to assist emotional regulation such as schedules, behavioral interventions, incorporating ritual behaviors into daily routines, and creating modifications that attempt to facilitate peer interaction.

Communication tools, such as notebooks, that facilitate parent-teacher communication emerged as a theme. One mother described their notebook as a tool used to "keep track of [child's] comings and goings, send suggestions back to teachers" and other therapists. Another mother shared this reaction to the notebook when she wrote, "that notebook is the only way I know whether he ate his lunch, played nicely, wet his pants, stole his friend's cracker, [and] went to the library." To this mother, reading the notebook allowed her an opportunity to "talk to [my child] about his day and fill in both sides, so we are having a conversation." Parents also understood that the communication notebook enhanced the teacher's understanding of the child.

Other school-based accommodations included adjustments to support emotional regulation and to support sensory processing, such as schedules, support during transitions, and adjustments to prevent overstimulation. One mother's reflection expressed this theme regarding adjusting to a new school. The staff allowed the mother and child to make "dry runs" of the daily schedule to promote familiarity with the new school routine. In another case, a teacher visited the home before the school year: "[The teacher] took time out of her day to come to our house, with her three year old in tow, to get to know [my child] a little bit before school starts; to help [my child] feel more comfortable." Another mother shared accommodations with a new school year as a process of "easing [child] into the transition." She wrote, "[The teacher] created opportunities for [the child] to visit his [new] classroom . . . [and to] interact with him."

Accommodations addressing changes in schedule also occurred. One mother reported that a teacher phoned the family to prepare their child for adjusting to a substitute special education teacher. The mother wrote that the teacher emphasized the need to "minimize . . . potential problems" related to changes in the school day. Other accommodations to support emotional regulation included incorporating ritual behaviors, or obsessions, so that the child could be functional, such as wearing special hats, carrying dog tags, or rubbing together special objects. Teachers worked with parents to incorporate rituals into the school routine in order for the child to feel safe and to help the child function to his/her best ability while in school. Behavioral support accommodations included assuring continuity in positive behavioral reinforcements or therapies coordinated with home and other professionals involved in the child's life.

Accommodations aimed at improving peer interaction tended to prepare children in general educational settings to accept persons with odd or eccentric behaviors. One mother wrote: "Children are smart. There is not a single child in [my child's] class who didn't recognize that [my child] was different." Accommodations for peer interaction included preparing children to understand that "different is not 'better than' or 'worse than'; different is just different." Another mother wrote about a teacher who successfully integrated nonverbal children in her grade school classroom: "She teaches the other children that being 'different' can be an asset . . . not a detriment."

Social stories and songs were also incorporated to prepare children with skills for responding to social situations. Examples of accommodations for overstimulation included home-based activities that transitioned to group activities, such as private music lessons until the child adjusted to the teacher and the new skill before the classes were introduced.

The mothers expected accommodations to follow from structured activities designed for persons with disabilities to the community at-large. Whether it was the hairdresser, dentist, or a restaurant, mothers expected resources to alter their delivery style to accommodate their child's functioning needs. One mother described a restaurant encounter. The waitress helped the family by interacting with the child by "corralling him whilst bribing him with dinosaur coloring sheets and red crayons." She wrote that her child engaged with the server, a rare occurrence for a child who struggles with social interactions. In her reflection, this mother wrote of the server's reaction to her child: "I think the waitress felt honored to have been graced with [my child's] attention, which continued in starts and stops for the rest of the meal."

Availability

The mothers identified resources that increased the availability of accommodations for their child. The availability of resources such as choice, support, and services affected both the mother and child. Availability of choice refers to the instances where either the child or the mother has the opportunity to take control of the situation and make a choice based on their own preferences. Availability of support refers to the supportive peer or professional relationships. Availability of services refers to the financial, geographical, and community services that are available to these mothers and their children to help meet their needs.

Within the setting of the school system, mothers wanted to be sure that their children were having their learning, emotional, and social needs met. One theme identified in the context of availability is choice. Mothers wanted to be sure that they and their children had a say in what programs and services their children were receiving. One mother described an instance of her child working with an aide in his classroom. When it was time for her son to complete a math lesson, he communicated to his aide that he wanted to do it on his own. The aide allowed the child the independence to attempt the assignment on his own, and the result was the child succeeding not only in completing the assignment but also interacting appropriately with his peers. Another mother described an IEP meeting that she attended for her son. She wrote that the IEP committee consulted with her about the programs that she thought would be best for her son. The mother responded with her first choice, and the committee backed her up.

Availability of support is another theme that emerged within the context of the school setting. One mother described the language that she and her son's teacher use to discuss his behavior. Rather than identifying the child as being "aggressive" the mother and teacher referred to it as "emotional dysregulation." The mother described this as being a better approach to solving her son's problems, being more supportive of him, and also being more "respectful." Another mother noted the support that her son received from his peers at school. She described an instance after a school program in which the environment became overly stimulating for her son to handle. After removing her son from the noisy room, another student in the class came and offered her son his sound-blocking headphones so that he could be more comfortable in the classroom. These mothers also wrote about the support that has been offered to their children by their teachers. One mother wrote that her son's kindergarten teacher had been working with the first grade teacher to make the transition smoother for her son and ways to include in him in various classroom activities in the first grade. Another mother wrote that her son was lucky to have teachers that would "stick by him and help him remember how to act."

Availability of services also emerged as a theme within the context of the school setting. Many of the mothers described the process of attending IEP meetings for their children, and having the support services of advocates, therapists, and psychologists to help them in their plight to gain the proper services for their children. One mother described an IEP meeting that occurred at the end of the school year and how the school was going to work to find a suitable summer camp for her son, and that his future teacher seemed "so sweet and always smiling."

Two of the three themes, availability of support and availability of services, emerged within the context of the community. Two mothers blogged about the support they received from other parents of children with ASD. One mother wrote about joining a twelve-week class to learn effective communication strategies to use with her sons. The mother wrote that she was "just happy to meet and know other parents with children like ours." A second mother wrote that of all the resources she had, "fellow parents were still the best resource and support" and that they were free. Another mother blogged about her son's plans to attend a summer camp. She wrote about the aide that would be attending with him. She reported that the aide was a former teacher of her son's, and that this aide would provide a familiar support within this new environment.

Availability of service is a theme that strongly emerged in the context of the community. Two mothers wrote about the services provided by emergency response personnel. One mother wrote about contacting the 911 dispatch to let them know that in case of an emergency that there was a four-year-old autistic child in their home. She closed by saying that the emergency response personnel were trained to deal with these types of children. Another mother blogged about her son being picked up and returned by a police officer after he had wondered out of a birthday party. She wrote about how kind the officer had been to her and her son during the ordeal. Several mothers wrote about the cost and availability of services in their regions. One mother wrote that their insurance would cover "12 neuropath visits per year" and that there was an approved provider within their community. Another mother wrote about her son attending auditory integration therapy. She reported that she was not sure how it worked, or what it was supposed to accomplish, but it was covered by their insurance and it couldn't do any harm to try.

The final setting was the home environment, and all three themes emerged within this setting: availability of choice, support, and services. One mother wrote about the lack of control her son had in many aspects of his life. She wrote that between the changes in his therapists and toilet training, there was little over which he had control. She blogged about giving her son more control to make choices regarding the types of food he ate and other things that would allow him more freedom: "I figure he needs to also feel in control of his Personhood." Another mother wrote about an appointment with her son's psychiatrist. The psychiatrist gave the mother a choice regarding whether or not she wanted to start her son on medication or take a "wait and see approach." This ultimately gave the mother more control over her son's treatment.

The availability of support is another theme that emerged within the context of the home setting. One mother blogged about her son attending a birthday party and that her son found a way to comfortably engage in the activities and that the other children included him. She talked about what a success the event was. Another mother wrote about supporting her son by meeting him at his level. She wrote about laughing and being silly with her son as opposed to scolding him for laughing inappropriately. She ultimately decided that she needed to be "looking beneath the surface" in order to support her child. One mother wrote about her own support system. She talked about her friends, and how they had always accepted her son for who he was. She wrote that they were not embarrassed to go out for dinner with her and her child. Another mother wrote about the support that she received from an autism consultant. She reported that she was always learning something new from this woman, and that she was always supportive of her child.

The final theme was the availability of services within the home setting. One mother talked about insurance coverage of her son's medication. One mother wrote about teaching her son at home. She wrote about a tutor that came to their house during the week, and how this woman worked with her son and undid any "mistakes" that she may have made with her teachings.

Accessibility

Resources identified as accessible were marked by environmental and information characteristics that fostered successful functioning. These characteristics were consistent with accessible resources as identified in the prior literature examined on disability. The mothers whose stories were included in this data file identified an emerging theme of tolerance for outbursts and ritual behavior that was unique to the symptoms of children with ASDs.

The statements that addressed accessible resources tended to describe environments that afforded inclusion by incorporating routine and small areas, which are accessible features for many disabilities yet adjusted for ASD symptoms. Resources identified as environmentally accessible included larger spaces arranged with small areas for private play or small group interaction. Public parks, beaches, and family centers identified as accessible included play areas that allowed interacting or private play. Sometimes mothers described parks or centers with mazes where children with ASD wandered along with same-age peers. The maze appeared to foster independence within a group setting. One mother described her child's behavior in the maze as "running around in circles," and another mother wrote a reflection about her child who engaged in a rare social interaction on a day her child followed another child through a maze at a local park. Other space features included what one mother described as "a private room to de-escalate," which allowed the child an opportunity to adjust his/her behavior and emotionally regulate him/herself without disrupting the setting and drawing attention to his/her outburst.

Knowledge and information sharing were additional features of accessible resources. Mothers repeatedly identified providers who incorporated knowledge of care that supported children with ASD as fostering their children's functioning in school, community, and society. For example, one mother described a preschool's policy of incorporating children's differences into the curriculum. One mother wrote that a teacher said: "We believe it's a teachable moment. Consideration for others, you know. It's a good opportunity to learn about compassion."

Tolerance for public outbursts or ritualistic behaviors emerged as a unique accessibility theme. One mother voiced a shared sentiment about tolerant settings when she described a classroom as "magical." She wrote: "The other children were big fans of [my child] and he returned their affection wholeheartedly." Community tolerance was also identified; one mother described the tolerant reaction her child experienced following an episode she called a "meltdown" that she understood was marked by acceptance. She wrote:

> Nobody looked at us like we were freaks, or bad parents, or anything. Everybody was SO nice, and SO sympathetic. I'm not just talking about people who worked there—the visitors, even older people who were taking a stroll, were all smiling and trying to be polite and nice. I was grateful.

The data we classified as accessible statements reflected the mothers' perspective of the child's ability to function, independently or appropriately for their age, in either the school or community. As themes typical of other disability accessibility literature emerged, such as environmental and information accessibility, the theme of tolerance for behaviors associated with either rituals or challenges to emotional regulation emerged as a dominant theme.

CONCLUSIONS

Blogging allowed these mothers an opportunity to discuss various aspects of the social, medical, and educational resources available to their children. We have noticed that most mothers felt these systems are not responsive to the total needs of the family. Mothers expressed their exasperation with the scarcity of quality services for their children. Besides seeking other therapists and physicians, there are not many remedies for inadequate social and medical services. Mothers expressed disgust with the lack of comprehensive insurance coverage and shared letters of appeal to insurance companies and their experiences lobbying legislators and insurance companies to provide more inclusive coverage. Some families moved to a different location in order to be near resources, a form of ASD migration.

As IDEA encourages accountability, parent participation, and choice, parents play an influential role in crafting their child's educational experience. Based on these findings, there appear to be ongoing disagreements between schools and parents regarding identification, evaluation, programming, placement, and formal and informal conferences. Yet, there are areas in school and communities that mothers consider to foster their children's growth. For instance, these mothers considered their child's educational services to be adequate when they believed their child's setting, be it inclusive or secluded, was the best match for their child. Accommodations that personalized their child's social and behavioral symptoms were highly valued. Also, support for supplemental therapies either through payment or by integrating the recommendations into school IEPs was considered fostering growth.

A change in insurance coverage is critical to families faced with ASD, as currently many treatments are not covered. If the rules and regulations for Medicaid policies become more lenient toward treatment for ASD, this will be a great public victory for targeted families. School districts also would benefit from less stringent Medicaid policies and would be allowed to charge more related services to Medicaid (as opposed to paying for these services from the school district budget).

As parents move from schools to community with their expectations on accommodations, our attention turns to work being attempted in local communities by examining the concept of local capacity. Adequate local capacity to meet the challenges for our targeted families consists of two distinct parts: individual and organizational. For instance, individual or personal capacity can be defined as skills or understanding belonging to an individual; individual capacity allows the person to "get the job done." Mothers in this study often praise the individual efforts of a teacher or a therapist. Clearly for mothers in this study both individual and organizational capacities in the school and community must be at high levels. However, the adequacy, accessibility, accommodations, and availability vary greatly based on the geographic location of the family residence.

To summarize, these mothers believe that there will be substantial progress made towards preparing the medical, social, and educational systems when providers are prepared to serve families such as their own. While these findings provide insight into the needs and perceptions of a group of mothers raising children with ASDs, it does not reflect the experience of all mothers. The views of this limited subset of active blogging mothers are rather informative but may reflect a highly motivated and capable set of parents. Therefore, their voices may be best considered a view of the possibilities of parents, in order to be effective, policy-makers and program planners would benefit from using these themes as a starting point from which they begin conversations with parents most affected by their services.

NOTES

1. CDC. "About Autism." Autism Information Center. www.cdc.gov/ncbddd/autism.

2. National Institute of Mental Health. *Autism Spectrum Disorders: Pervasive Developmental Disorders.* www.nimh.nih.gov/

3. National Institute of Mental Health.

4. American Psychiatric Association. *Diagnostic and Statistical Manual of Mental Disorders (fourth ed.).*

5. American Psychiatric Association.

6. American Psychiatric Association.

7. Autism Speaks. *Prevalence of Autism Now 1 in 150.* www.autsmspeals.org.

8. CDC, 2009.

9. CDC, 2009.

10. U.S. Department of Health and Human Services. *Mental Health: A Report of the Surgeon General* (Rockville, MD: Author, 1999).

11. Chasson, G., Harris, G., and Neely, W. "Cost comparison of early intensive behavioral intervention and special education for children with autism." *Journal of Child and Family Studies* 16 (2007): 401–13.

12. U.S. Census Bureau. *Back to School 2006-2007. Facts for Features.* CB06-FF, 11-2, Reissued August 16, 2006. www.census.gov.

13. Education for all Handicapped Children Act of 1975. P.L. 94-142.

14. Free Appropriate Public Education for Students With Disabilities. P.L. 102-119.

15. Price, B., Mayfield, P., McFadden, A., and Marsh, G. *Collaborative Teaching: Special Education for Inclusive Classrooms.* Kansas City: Parrot Publishing, www.parrotpublishing.com/ (2001).

16. Individuals with Disabilities Education Act of 2004. P.L. 108-446.

17. Turnbull, R., Stowe, M., and Huerta, N. *What Every Teacher Should Know about the IDEA as Amended in 2004, second edition* (Merril, WI: Merrill, 2007).

18. Fish, W. "Perceptions of parents of students with autism towards the IEP meeting: A case study of one family support group charter." *Education* 127, no. 1 (2006): 56–68.

19. *Board of Education v Rowley.* 458 U.S. 176.1025. ct. 3034.

20. Boyd, B. "Examining the relationship between stress and lack of social support in mothers of children with Autism." *Focus on Autism and Other Developmental Disabilities* 17, no. 4 (2002): 208–15.

21. Fish, 2006.

22. Rapp, C., and Goscha, R. *The Strengths Model: Case Management with People with Psychiatric Disabilities* (New York: Oxford University Press, 2006).

23. Turnbull, Stowe, and Huerta, 2007.

24. The Rehabilitation Act of 1973 (Title 29, 1614.203).

25. Stahmer, A., Colling, N., and Palinkas, L. "Early intervention practices for children with autism: Descriptions from community providers." *Focus on Autism and Other Developmental Disabilities* 20, no. 2 (2005): 66–79.

26. Dymond, S., Gilson, C., and Myran, S. "Services for children with autism spectrum disorders." *Journal of Disability Policy Studies* 18, no. 3 (2007): 133–47.

27. Rapp and Goscha, 2006.

28. Dymond, Gilson, and Myran, 2007.

Index

Arizona, 196, 197
autism spectrum disorders, 245-59

California, 83-84, 194, 195-96, 211-23
child and family policy. *See* family policy
child and family programs, 5
child care: child care policy, 50-51; collaborations and, 59-60; consequences for not having, 55-56; income level and, 51; nontraditional hours and, 50; rely on social networks for, 51-52; short-term child care, 49-60; short-term child care—models for, 57-59. *See also* education
child development, 173-86
child support: employment training programs and, 238; Federal Child Support Enforcement, 227, 236; mother-father relationships and, 222, 233, 235-40; orders and, 227-40; social capital and, 227-40

child well-being, 173-86. *See also* domestic violence; domestic violence shelters
child welfare system, 83-94, 97-113, 135-50; adoption and 84, 85, 86, 87-89, 91, 92-93; Adoption and Safe Families Act of 1997, 84; African Americans and, 85, 87, 88-91, 92-93, 135-50; age of child and, 84-94; age of care provider and, 135-50; California Assembly Bill 1524 and, 83, 84-94; Child Welfare Act of 1980, 83-84; child well-being and, 135-50; family reunification, 84; foster care, 83-84, 135-50; kinship care, 135-50; guardian ad litems, 103, 105, 109-10; Latinos and 86, 89, 90, 91, 92; multidisciplinary teams and, 97-113; reasonable efforts, 84; reunification time frames, 83-94; social support and, 135-50; substance abuse and, 85, 86, 87, 88, 89-90, 91, 92-93. *See*

also domestic violence; domestic violence shelters
children's motivation. *See* education
Colorado, 84
Connecticut, 84, 194, 196

daycare. *See* child care
domestic violence, and children, 117–32
domestic violence shelters: collaboration with community agencies, 128, 130, 131; screening for children's mental health and, 117–32

early childhood, 63–76, 83–94
Early Childhood Longitudinal Study (ECLS), 29–45
econometric analyses, 179–81
education, 11–24, 29–45; children's motivation toward, 29–45; classroom characteristics, 43; cultural differences, 11–24; daycare use and, 43; family characteristics and, 43, 45; home environment and effect on learning and, 33–34; No Child Left Behind, 30; parental involvement in, 29–45; parental involvement in extracurricular activities and, 31, 38, 42, 44; primary school, 29–45; school characteristics, 43; student gender and, 42, 45; student race and, 42–43, 45. *See also* special needs children
Education for All Handicapped Children Act, 247
emerging adulthood, 153–68; educational achievement and, 164, 165–68; employment and, 164, 165–68; social support and, 164–68; substance use and, 157–58, 162–64, 165–68

family leave policy, 191–208, 211–23; benefits of, 211–13; California Paid Family Leave, 195–96, 211,

214–23; failure to use, 215, 216, 219–23; Family and Medical Leave Act, 191–95, 196, 197, 213; fathers, 217–23; gender stereotyping and, 222; knowledge of, 215–23; limitations and, 193–94; mothers, 216–23; paid leave and, 197–208; reasons to use, 215–23; state policy and, 194–208
family policy, 1–5; definition, 1–2; family perspective in, 2; history, 1, 3–4; professional associations and, 4; social science and, 4
family violence, 117–32
fathers, 173–86, 227–40; incarceration and, 173–86
foster care, 135–50
Fragile Families and Child Wellbeing Study (FFCWS), 175–76, 178

Hawaii, 194
Hispanic families, 11–24
home visiting services, 14–15, 16, 17–18, 20, 22,–23, 24, 63–80; Healthy Families America (HFA), 63–64, 65–66, 73, 75–76; Healthy Start, 14, 15; literacy skills and, 11–24; Parent-Child Home Program (PCHP), 14, 16, 17, 20, 22, 24; parent-provider relationship, 64–65, 70–76

Illinois, 136–37, 196, 197
immigrants, 11–24
Individuals with Disabilities Education Act (IDEA), 247, 248, 259

justice system, 153–68, 173–86

life course theory, 155–58
literacy skills, and Spanish language speakers, 11–27
Louisiana, 84

Maine, 194
Massachusetts, 16, 22, 194, 196, 197
Minnesota, 84, 194, 196
Missouri, 155, 160

New Hampshire, 53, 57–58
New Jersey, 194, 196, 197
New York, 84, 196, 197
North Carolina, 58–59, 117–18

Oklahoma, 84
Oregon, 194, 196, 197
Ottawa, Canada, 58

Pennsylvania, 84, 196
partner violence, 117–32
Personal Responsibility and Work
    Opportunities Reconciliation Act, 50

respite care, 52–53
Rhode Island, 194

social controls, 158–60
social policy development theory:
    compromise, 206–7; existing
    frameworks, 202–3; familiarity
    with legislation, 205–6; political

institutions, 192–93, 203–4;
    special interest groups, 193, 201–2;
    structural changes, 192; timing,
    204–5
social science. *See* family policy
special needs children, 245–59;
    accessibility as resource and, 250,
    257–58; accommodation as resource
    and, 249, 253–54; adequacy
    as resource and, 249, 252–53;
    availability as resource and, 249–50,
    254–57; families and, 245–59;
    mothers and, 245, 248–49, 250,
    251–59

use-inspired research, 7

Vermont, 194

Washington, 194, 196, 197
West Virginia, 97–113
Wisconsin, 194

About the Editor

Emily Douglas, Ph.D., is an assistant professor of social work at Bridgewater State College in Massachusetts. Her scholarship focuses on child and family well-being, the connection between social science and policy, and how programming and policy action can affect overall family functioning. Specifically, her expertise is in the child welfare system; children who die as a result of maltreatment, partner violence, corporal punishment; families of divorce; and how to facilitate the flow of evidence-based information from researchers to policy- and decision-makers. Dr. Douglas's doctorate is in public policy from the University of Massachusetts-Boston; she completed an NIMH-funded postdoctoral research fellowship at the Family Research Laboratory at the University of New Hampshire, under the mentorship of Dr. Murray Straus. Dr. Douglas is the founder and chair of the National Research Conference on Child and Family Programs and Policy; she has presented her own research numerous times at national and international academic and professional conferences, is the author of multiple articles and chapters in peer-reviewed sources, and is the author of a book on social policies for divorced families, *Mending Broken Families: Social Policies for Divorced Families—How Effective Are They?* (2006). The chapters that she presents in this book come from the first National Research Conference on Child and Family Programs and Policy held in July 2008.

About the Contributors

Loretta L. C. Brady, Ph.D., is an assistant professor of psychology at Saint Anselm College where she teaches personality, health, organizational, and cross-cultural psychology courses. She received her doctoral degree from Fordham University in the Bronx, New York, and completed her postdoctoral fellowship with Families In Transition, a homeless housing service agency, in Manchester, New Hampshire. In the community she works as a clinical psychologist, specializing in treating trauma, addiction, and interventions to promote resiliency. She also continues her work with Families In Transition, where she has helped to design interventions to strengthen disadvantaged and multiply vulnerable families. Her research emphasizes trauma, resiliency, and the unique interconnections between poverty, violence, and addiction. She has expanded her research to examine the ways individual and community interventions to promote positive family interactions serve to protect children and families. The chapter included in this book represents recent community-based research conducted to support these efforts. She lives and works in Manchester, New Hampshire, with her husband and two children.

Melissa Brown, M.S.W., is pursuing her doctoral degree in social work at Boston College, where she is now pursuing her doctoral degree in social work. In her doctoral dissertation, she is focusing on evaluating the efficacy of workplace resources in supporting employed caregivers of older adults.

Ms. Brown is also a research associate at the Sloan Center on Aging and Work at Boston College, where she is involved in numerous research projects related to work-family issues and productive aging. Her research interests include the state and federal policy responses to changing workforce demographics and their role in promoting individual and family well-being.

Esther F. S. Carvalhaes is a Ph.D. student in the educational psychology department at the Graduate Center at the City University of New York. She specializes in education policy analysis. She is interested in the application of statistical methods to the study of policy-related issues as well as program evaluation. Research interests include the impact of parental involvement in children's academic development, large-scale educational assessment, educational resources allocation, and educational access and quality in developing countries.

Jason Castillo, Ph.D., is an assistant professor of social work at the University of Utah. His scholarship focuses on child and family well-being with an emphasis on fathers, notably low-income, non-resident fathers. Dr. Castillo's doctorate is in social work from Arizona State University. Dr. Castillo has presented his own research at numerous national and international professional conferences and has published several articles in peer reviewed sources. His chapter in this book reflects his interest in examining the relationship between non-resident fathers' social networks and the establishment of child support orders.

Corey J. Colyer, Ph.D., is an assistant professor in the Division of Sociology and Anthropology, located in the School of Applied Social Sciences at West Virginia University. Dr. Colyer's area of specialty focuses on linkages between the criminal justice system and human services. His current research program examines interdisciplinary dynamics in child welfare proceedings. Through this project, he works closely with West Virginia state government. Dr. Colyer's work has appeared in several peer-reviewed journals including *Children and Youth Services Review* and *Criminal Justice Policy Review*. He has made presentations at national conferences including the American Sociological Association and the National Research Conference on Child and Family Programs. Dr. Colyer holds a Ph.D. in sociology from the Maxwell School of Citizenship and Public Affairs at Syracuse University. Prior to joining the faculty at West Virginia University, he was a research associate at the University of Michigan's Institute for Social Research.

Terry-Ann L. Craigie, Ph.D., received her doctorate in economics from Michigan State University in August 2009. She is now a postdoctoral research associate at the Center for Research on Child Well-being at Princeton

University and is under the mentorship of Dr. Sara McLanahan. Her scholarship focuses on the relationship between paternal presence in the home and child well-being. In particular, her dissertation distinguished between family structure and stability effects of paternal presence on early child development. Her contribution to this book examines the issue in more specificity, by estimating the effect of paternal incarceration on early child cognitive and behavioral outcomes.

Amy D'Andrade, Ph.D., received an M.S.W. and Ph.D. from the School of Social Welfare at University of California–Berkeley. She is currently an assistant professor in the School of Social Work at San Jose State University, where her research interests focus on the public child welfare system, particularly policy and practice issues affecting parental reunification with children removed for maltreatment. She has conducted research studies on reunification services, concurrent planning, reunification bypass, reunification for incarcerated parents, and California's reduction of reunification time frames for parents of children under three. She has presented her work at academic and professional conferences, and published numerous peer-reviewed articles and book chapters on child welfare issues. Prior to her academic career, Dr. D'Andrade was a child welfare services social worker in California for over six years, working in a variety of programs with children and families.

Judy Doktor, Ph.D., has been actively engaged both professionally and personally as a parent advocate and trainer for over thirty years. Through her career as a teacher, school administrator, and a director she has pioneered programs for special learners that enhance their learning opportunities and that focus on inclusion. She has served as a fair hearing officer, and an evaluation specialist for family resource center programs in Hawaii, Florida, Kentucky, and Indiana. She has served as an expert witness in numerous special education meetings and mediations as a strident advocate. Her master's degree in public administration from the University of Hawaii combined with her Ph.D. in educational policy from Vanderbilt University affords her the ability to understand the complex social systems that families with children must navigate. Judy is currently busy writing implementation grants for charter schools, with particular emphasis on programs for children with exceptional needs. Her teaching and scholarship examines ways to enhance inclusion and participation among students and their parents as well as enhancing opportunities to improve training for teachers of special learners in professional development schools and in university-based teacher training programs. Judy is currently the director of school policy with the Resource Center for Research on Parenting as well as a university faculty member in education. Her scholarship has been presented and published in national and international contexts.

Audrey Foster, B.S., is a data technician at the Center for Child and Family Policy, Duke University.

James P. Gleeson, Ph.D., A.C.S.W., is an associate professor at the Jane Addams College of Social Work, University of Illinois at Chicago. He has extensive experience as a child welfare practitioner, administrator, consultant, and researcher. He has been principal investigator for a number of federal- and state-funded child welfare research, curriculum development, and training projects. Dr. Gleeson's research and publications focus on kinship care policy and practice, child welfare training, how child welfare workers learn, and evaluation of child welfare programs and practice. He is coeditor (with Dr. Creasie Finney Hairston) of *Kinship Care: Improving Practice Through Research* (1999) and is coauthor (with Faith Johnson Bonecutter) of *Achieving Permanency for Children in Kinship Foster Care: Training Manual and Videotapes*, which is a product of a U.S. Children's Bureau grant. Dr. Gleeson is a member of the review board for the *Child Welfare* journal and is a member of the editorial board for the *Journal of Public Child Welfare*. He serves on the Child Welfare League of America's National Kinship Care Advisory Committee and the League's National Advisory Committee on Research to Practice.

Diane F. Halpern, Ph.D., is a past president of the American Psychological Association, is the trustee professor of psychology, and is the founding director of the Berger Institute for Work, Family, and Children at Claremont McKenna College. Dr. Halpern has published many books, including *Thought and Knowledge: An Introduction to Critical Thinking* (fourth ed.), *Sex Differences in Cognitive Abilities* (fourth ed.)—a two-volume edited issue of the *American Behavioral Scientist*—*Changes at the Intersection of Work and Family* (with Heidi R. Riggio, 2006), *From Work-Family Balance to Work-Family Interaction: Changing the Metaphor* (with Susan Murphy, 2005), and *Women at the Top* (with Fanny Cheung, 2008). Her most recent books are *Undergraduate Education in Psychology: A Blueprint for the Future of the Disciplines* (edited, 2009) and the textbook *Psychological Science, third edition* (with Michael Gazzaniga and Todd Heatherton). Dr. Halpern was president of the Western Psychological Association, the Society for the Teaching of Psychology, and the Division of General Psychology of the American Psychological Association and has won many awards for her teaching and research. Most recently, Dr. Halpern participated in the National Academy of Sciences convocation on Women in Academe and *Science Friday* on National Public Radio. Her recent work includes studies on the effects of California's paid leave insurance, how flexible work policies affect stress and health, and a school-to-work project for low-performing high school students.

Arden Handler, Dr.P.H., is a professor of community health sciences and
maternal and child health at the University of Illinois School of Public
Health. She is PI and codirector of the UIC Maternal and Child Health
Training Grant and director of the MCH epidemiology program at UIC.
Her research focuses on approaches to improving pregnancy outcomes in
high-risk communities; women's access to, use of, and satisfaction with
prenatal care; and the effect of a variety of exposures on reproductive and
perinatal health. Dr. Handler teaches courses in reproductive and perinatal
epidemiology, as well as maternal and child health policy and advocacy.
She is actively involved in a number of local, state, and national task forces
and advisory committees including the Illinois Maternal and Child Health
Coalition, the Illinois PRAMS Advisory Committee, the National Awards
for Excellence in MCH Epidemiology, and the Workforce Committee of the
Association of Maternal and Child Health Programs.

Stacy Ann Hawkins, M.A., is a doctoral candidate in applied social psychology at Claremont Graduate University, where she received her master's
degree in psychology. Her research interests focus on partner and parent-child relationships, especially within nontraditional families, such as
military families, families affected by divorce, and families headed by gay
or lesbian parents. Ms. Hawkins has received the Grace Berry Award for
Women in Graduate Studies (2006–2007), a student research grant from
the Claremont Graduate University School of Behavioral and Organizational Sciences (2008–2009) and a Claremont Graduate University Dissertation Award (2009–2010). While pursuing her doctoral degree, Stacy has
worked as a project coordinator at the Berger Institute for Work, Family,
and Children at Claremont McKenna College, and has twice been a summer associate with RAND Corporation. At Claremont Graduate University,
Ms. Hawkins created and co-chaired a committee that organizes lectures
and discussions on social psychological research and current social issues.
For her dissertation research, Stacy is examining interparental relationships, parent-adolescent relationships, and adolescent behavior in families
headed by heterosexual, gay, and lesbian couples. This project, supported
in part by the Roy Scrivner Memorial Research Grant, will provide evidence
to help frame the ongoing political and social debate about family and
child functioning in diverse families.

Anne Dannerbeck Janku, Ph.D., is the manager of a thirteen-person research unit in the Missouri Office of State Courts Administrator. Prior to
assuming this position, she was a research assistant professor in the School
of Social Work at the University of Missouri–Columbia. She has conducted
numerous research projects integrating human development with juvenile
and criminal justice issues including parental incarceration and its impact

on children; the intersection of gender, race, and drug courts; and female delinquency viewed with a relational lens. While at the university, she also taught a class on human development and the social environment. She has worked and studied in a variety of countries in Europe, Africa, and the Americas. She holds graduate degrees in international relations (University of South Carolina) and agricultural economics (Purdue University). Her doctorate is in consumer and family economics (University of Missouri).

Karen McCurdy, Ph.D., is an associate professor of human development and family studies at the University of Rhode Island. Her research examines the types of supports and obstacles that impact parenting among vulnerable populations. She has focused her recent work on multilevel predictors of parental engagement and retention in home visiting programs, and on the impact of family food behaviors on child overweight and food security. Dr. McCurdy received her doctorate in human development and social policy from Northwestern University. Prior to her current position, she served as deputy director of research for Prevent Child Abuse—America, in Chicago, Illinois. She has over fifteen years experience evaluating child abuse prevention programs and has presented and published her research widely, most recently at the 2008 International Congress on Child Abuse and Neglect in Hong Kong. She authored *Supporting Families: Lessons from the Field* with Elizabeth Jones.

Robert A. Murphy, Ph.D., serves as executive director for the Center for Child and Family Health, a consortium of Duke University, the University of North Carolina, and North Carolina Central University focused on child traumatic stress. Dr. Murphy is an associate professor in the Department of Psychiatry at Duke University Medical Center and adjunct associate professor in the Department of Maternal and Child Health at the University of North Carolina School of Public Health. Dr. Murphy has a background in services evaluation and intervention for traumatized and violence-exposed youth.

L. Christopher Plein, Ph.D., is an Eberly Professor of Outstanding Public Service at West Virginia University and serves as assistant dean for the West Virginia University School of Applied Social Sciences. Christopher Plein's area of specialty is public policy formation and implementation. Recently, his research has concentrated on the study of social programs, with a special emphasis on the effects of welfare reform and state health policy. Professor Plein's research has reached national audiences through numerous publications and presentations. He is coauthor of the book *Welfare Reform in West Virginia* (2004) and of the recently published *West Virginia Politics and Government* (2008). As author or coauthor, his work has appeared in various journals, including *Journal of Health and Human Services Administration* and *Health Affairs*. He has made presentations at numerous conferences, including events sponsored by the Brookings Institution and the National Association of Welfare Research and Statistics. In 2004, he was appointed by the governor of West Virginia to serve on the board of directors for the newly established AccessWV state health insurance program, which provides health coverage to those with high-risk health conditions. L. Christopher Plein holds a Ph.D. in political science from the University of Missouri–Columbia.

Donna Potter, L.C.S.W., is a clinician with the Center for Child and Family Health of Duke University. She has worked with evidence-based trauma treatment models for over seven years, and provided training across the nation related to the use of implementation science in fostering the use of evidence-based mental health practices.

Margaret Samuels, L.C.S.W., is executive director of Orange County Partnership for Young Children. Ms. Samuels has extensive experience in intervention and program development for children and families affected by domestic, community, and ethnic violence. She has worked domestically and internationally to develop and implement protocols for postterrorism and postdisaster response to traumatized children and families.

Lorrie Schmid, M.A., is a graduate student in the Department of Educational Psychology, Evaluation, and Measurement at the University of North Carolina–Chapel Hill. She previously served as a data manager/analyst at the Center for Child and Family Policy, Duke University.

Terry A. Solomon, Ph.D., M.P.H., M.S.W., is an advocate for social justice on behalf of African American children, families, and communities. Solomon is the founding executive director of the Illinois African American Family Commission. Dedicated to improving the quality of life of communities through family-centered public policy and culturally sensitive programs, Solomon is recognized as an authority in her field and is often called upon to speak on issues related to health, infant mortality, child abuse prevention, kinship foster care, and other issues affecting African American communities and families in general. Solomon is past president of the Chicago Chapter of the National Association of Black Social Workers; the School of Public Health, Alumni Association at the University of Illinois at Chicago; and the Illinois Maternal and Child Health Coalition. She received her Ph.D., master's of public health, and master's of social work from the University of Illinois at Chicago.

Leslie Starsoneck, M.S.W., is a consultant to the Center for Child and Family Health. She previously served as project director for the Child Well-Being and Domestic Violence project housed at Prevent Child Abuse (North Carolina) and as the former director of the Domestic Violence Commission in the North Carolina Department of Administration.

Jayme Swanke, M.S.W., Ph.D., completed her doctoral studies in rehabilitation at Southern Illinois University in Carbondale. Jayme has coauthored several articles and has presented nationally and internationally on scholarly topics ranging from policy analysis, care management, technology enhanced teaching, teaching method evaluation, and parenting persons with disabilities. Jayme has also taught classes in substance abuse, case management, human behavior, practice, and research and statistics. Jayme's dissertation was an analysis of employment patterns among persons who report methamphetamine use. A certified alcohol and drug counselor, Jayme has specialized her clinical practice in the community-based treatment of persons with methamphetamine abuse and dependence disorders.

Sherylle J. Tan, Ph.D., is a developmental psychologist and the associate director of research and internships at the Kravis Leadership Institute at Claremont McKenna College. Much of Dr. Tan's research and publications focus on applying developmental theory and methods to understanding the issues of child development, parenting, and work and family. Recently, Dr. Tan coedited a book with Amy Marcus-Newhall and Diane Halpern, *The Changing Realties of Work and Family: A Multidisciplinary Approach* (2008). Prior to her current position, Dr. Tan spent five years with the Berger Institute for Work, Family, and Children at Claremont McKenna College as the associate director, where she managed and coordinated the institute's research projects, including the California Paid Family Leave Studies, which examined the impact of paid family leave on health outcomes of caregivers and new parents, and assessed whether it can help to alleviate the stresses and demands of combining work and family care responsibilities. Dr. Tan has also worked with various community agencies as an evaluator and consultant. She was the primary evaluator at the Los Angeles Child Guidance Clinic for two early intervention, preschool-based mental health programs funded by First 5 Los Angeles (Proposition 10 Commission): the award-winning Building Block program and the Stepping Up to School Readiness program.

Michelle P. Taylor, M.S., is the director of evaluation and performance improvement at NRI Community Services, a behavioral healthcare organization that serves children, adults, and the elderly with mental health and substance abuse issues. For the last eleven years, Ms. Taylor has chaired the

North Smithfield Special Education Local Advisory Committee, which pro-vides support, advocacy, and education for parents of children with special needs. An important emphasis of this committee is to advise administrators and the school committee regarding gaps in services, as well as to recom-mend changes to existing services. Her chapter in this book documents her master's thesis work and reflects her interest in both the welfare of children and families, as well as the factors that contribute to long-term retention in services aimed at promoting long-term well-being for individuals and their families. Through consecutive grants from the Center of Substance Abuse Treatment, Network for Improvement of Addiction Treatment, and the Robert Wood Johnson Foundation, Ms. Taylor served as the principal investigator on agency- and state-wide projects that promoted the imple-mentation of evidence-based practices through the use of performance improvement strategies.

Yvonne Wasilewski, Ph.D., M.P.H., is a research scientist at the Center for Child and Family Policy and adjunct assistant professor in the Department of Health Behavior and Health Education at the University of North Carolina School of Public Health. Dr. Wasilewski has extensive experience designing, evaluating, and disseminating community- and evidence-based interventions for children and families in school, clinic, and worksite settings.

Patricia Hrusa Williams, Ph.D., is an assistant professor of family studies and community development at Towson University in Baltimore, Mary-land. She is also graduate program codirector for the master's in child life, administration, and family collaboration. Her scholarship focuses on children's socio-emotional well-being, factors impacting family literacy development and parent-child interaction, and educational and home-based interventions to support families with young children. Dr. Williams received her Ph.D. in applied child development from Tufts University and taught at Tufts University and Providence College prior to coming to Tow-son. She served as principal investigator for the Massachusetts Department of Education/Early Education and Care's Indicators and Assessment Project from 2001 to 2007. The project examined the progress of Parent-Child Home Programs (PCHP) across the state. Her scholarly publications in-clude articles on court-based child care, family preservation efforts, family development, home visiting, and service learning.

Laura Dreuth Zeman, L.C.S.W., Ph.D., is professor of social work and women's studies at Southern Illinois University in Carbondale. As an un-dergraduate she studied family sociology and women studies at Indiana University. She earned a master's degree from Jane Addams College of Social Work at the University of Illinois at Chicago and a doctorate which concentrated on policy development and program evaluation in education and human services from the Peabody College of Education at Vanderbilt University. She is a clinical social worker specializing in mental illness, addiction, and family care. Her understanding of families and trauma was developed through years of extensive research and enhanced by her experiences working as a therapist in psychiatric hospitals and in private practice. She established the Resource Center for Research on Parenting in 2005. The center seeks to advance the understanding of the experiences and needs of parents as they manage the delicate balance between raising children and interacting with social support systems, such as schools, child protective services, and health and mental health care providers. Her research findings have been published in over thirty papers, and she has presented her findings nationally and internationally.

Breinigsville, PA USA
14 December 2010
251411BV00002B/6/P